DIVORCE AMICABLY

DIVORCE AMICABLY
YOUR ROADMAP TO RESOLUTION

TRACY ANN MOORE-GRANT

Founder of The Amicable Divorce Network

NAPLES, FL

Copyright © 2025 by Tracy Ann Moore-Grant
All rights reserved

Published in the United States by O'Leary Publishing
www.olearypublishing.com

The views, information, or opinions expressed in this book are solely those of the authors involved, and do not necessarily represent those of O'Leary Publishing, LLC.

The author has made every effort possible to ensure the accuracy of the information presented in this book. However, the information herein is sold without warranty, either expressed or implied. Neither the author, publisher, nor any dealer or distributor of this book will be held liable for any damages caused either directly or indirectly by the instructions or information contained in this book. You are encouraged to seek professional advice before taking any action mentioned herein.

All rights reserved. No part of this book may be reproduced or transmitted in any form by any means: electronic, mechanical, photocopy, recording, or other, without the prior and express written permission of the author, except for brief cited quotes. For information on getting permission for reprints and excerpts, contact: O'Leary Publishing.

ISBN: (paperback) 9781952491900
ISBN: (ebook) 9781952491917
ISBN: (hardcover) 9781952491931
Cataloging-in-Publication Data is on file with the Library of Congress.

Developmental Editing by Heather Davis Desrocher
Line Editing by Kat Langenheim and Boris Boland
Proofreading by David Aretha
Cover and Interior Design by Jessica Angerstein

Printed in the United States of America

To my husband for everything and all of the wishes granted.

To my parents for never dulling my sparkle.

To Patterson Moore Butler for allowing me
to take the amicable path.

To the members of the Amicable Divorce Network,
who put clients first.

Scan to Connect with Us Online

CONTENTS

Preface Why the Amicable Divorce Network? *by Tracy Ann Moore-Grant* 1

PART 1 Are You Ready for a Divorce?

Chapter 1 The Amicable Divorce Mindset: Your Guide to Taking the First Steps *by Storey Jones* 9

Chapter 2 To Divorce or Not? *by Kathleen Shack* 12

Chapter 3 Legal Separation vs. Divorce *by Kathryn Harry* 16

PART 2 What Is a Divorce Really Like?

Chapter 4 Myths About Divorce *by Jeanette L. Soltys* 25

Chapter 5 The Cost of Divorce Isn't Just Financial *by Jeanette Soltys* 28

Chapter 6 Fault: Do You Bring It Up? *by Tracy Ann Moore-Grant* 32

PART 3 What Type of Divorce Do You Want?

Chapter 7 The Three Ways to Divorce *by Tracy Ann Moore-Grant* 37

Chapter 8 The Three Steps to Take *by Tracy Ann Moore-Grant* 41

Chapter 9 The Amicable Divorce Process *by Tracy Ann Moore-Grant* 45

Chapter 10 Comparing the Different Lanes of the Divorce Highway *by Tracy Ann Moore-Grant* 53

PART 4 Who Benefits from an Amicable Divorce?

Chapter 11 Gray Divorce *by Andrew Hatherley* 61

Chapter 12 LGBTQIA+ Divorce *by Dennis G. Collard* 66

Chapter 13 Cultural Diversity in Divorce *by Neena Saxena* 70

Chapter 14 Who Can Benefit from the Amicable Divorce Process? *by Tracy Ann Moore-Grant* 73

PART 5 How Do You Prioritize Mental Health in a Divorce?

Chapter 15 Preparing Emotionally *by Katheen Shack* 77

Chapter 16 The Psychological Stages of Divorce *by Stephanie Robins* 82

Chapter 17 The Role of Mental Health Professionals *by Stephanie Robins* 86

Chapter 18 Tips for Managing Stress *by Ashley Pepitone* 91

Part 6 How Do You Prepare for a Divorce?

Chapter 19 Hiring a Divorce Attorney *by Tracy Ann Moore-Grant*............................101
Chapter 20 Using Divorce Technology *by Storey Jones*.......................................111
Chapter 21 How to Talk to Your Spouse About Divorce *by Alexandra Geczi*............112
Chapter 22 How Lawyers Bill Their Time *by Tracy Ann Moore-Grant*.....................118
Chapter 23 Building a Solid Divorce Team *by Nanette Murphy*.............................124

Part 7 How Do I Have a Child-Centered Divorce?

Chapter 24 Creating a Child-Centered Divorce *by Traci A. Weiss*...........................133
Chapter 25 Types of Co-Parenting *by Michael Cohen*...135
Chapter 27 How to Have a Child-Centered Divorce *by Kathleen Shack*..................140
Chapter 27 Your To-Do List for a Child-Centered Divorce *by J. Ashley Heredia*......144
Chapter 28 Children's Developmental Stages and Divorce *by Kathleen Shack*.........149
Chapter 29 The Child's Perspective *by J. Ashley Heredia*....................................155

Part 8 How Do I Handle Difficult Issues Amicably?

Chapter 30 Complex Issues *by Tracy Ann Moore-Grant*......................................161
Chapter 31 Intimate Partner Violence *by Tori E. Owens*......................................163
Chapter 32 Personality Disorders *by Tori E. Owens*...167
Chapter 33 Handling Addiction in Amicable Cases *by Tracy Ann Moore-Grant*........173
Chapter 34 Pet Custody *by Karis Nafte*...178
Chapter 35 Going Public with Your Divorce *by Stephanie Robins*.........................179

Part 9 How Do I Avoid Roadblocks on the Road to Resolution?

Chapter 36 Staying Clearheaded *by Stephanie Robins*..187
Chapter 37 Avoid These Common Mistakes *by Stephanie Robins*........................191
Chapter 38 To Date or Not to Date? *by Stephanie Robins*...................................196
Chapter 39 Communicating Effectively with Your Spouse *by Holly Schymik*...........199

Part 10 How Can Technology Help in a Divorce?

Chapter 40 Technology in Family Law *by Steven Bradley*....................................207
Chapter 41 Using dtour.life in a Divorce *by Storey Jones*....................................209
Chapter 42 OurFamilyWizard *by Steven Bradley*...211
Chapter 43 Using AI Tools *by Susan Guthrie*..214
Chapter 44 Protecting Your Digital Privacy *by Holly Schymik*...............................216

Part 11 What Do I Need to Know About Alimony and Child Support?

Chapter 45 Understanding Alimony: Spousal Support *by Holly Schymik* 225

Chapter 46 Understanding Child Support *by Holly Schymik* 230

Part 12 How Do We Divide Our Finances?

Chapter 47 Overview of Financial Divisions *by Tracy Ann Moore-Grant* 237

Chapter 48 Create a Values-Based Divorce Strategy *by Hirsch A. Serman* 242

Chapter 49 Achieve the Best Financial Results *by Andrew Hatherley* 247

Chapter 50 The Marital Balance Sheet *by Traci A. Weiss* 253

Chapter 51 Valuing a Small Business *by Dan Branch* 256

Chapter 52 Complex Asset Valuation *by Laurie Dyke* 262

Part 13 What Do We Do with the Marital Home?

Chapter 53 Selling the Marital Home *by Lauren Loper* 269

Chapter 54 Appraising the Marital Home *by Mike Congemi* 272

Chapter 55 Post-Divorce Housing *by Tami Wollensak and Jennifer Brown* 276

Chapter 56 Real Estate Collaboration Specialists *by Lauren Loper* 283

Part 14 How Is Our Case Resolved?

Chapter 57 Overview of Settlement Options *by Tracy Ann Moore-Grant* 291

Chapter 58 Alternative Dispute Resolution *by Kathy J. Bloom* 292

Chapter 59 The Mediation Mindset *by Chloe Ouditz* 303

Chapter 60 Types of Divorce Mediation *by Tracy Ann Moore-Grant* 308

Chapter 61 Resolving Impasses in Negotiation *by Dara L. Marias* 313

Part 15 What Makes a Good Settlement Agreement?

Chapter 62 Components of a Good Settlement Agreement *by Kathryn Harry* 323

Chapter 63 Qualified Domestic Relations Orders *by Kathryn Harry* 329

Chapter 64 The Tax Consequences of Divorce *by Jason Wiggam* 335

Part 16 How Do We Make a Good Parenting Plan?

Chapter 65 Legal vs. Physical Custody *by Neena Saxena* 341

Chapter 66 Create a Parenting Plan *by Neena Saxena* 345

Chapter 67 Holiday Schedules by Morgan Given..349

Chapter 68 Long-Distance Parenting *by Chloe Ouditz* 354

Chapter 69 Keeping Schools in the Loop *by Stephanie Robins* 360

Part 17 How Do We Go from Partners to Co-Parents?

Chapter 70 Co-Parenting 101: Nurturing Children Through Divorce *by Dara L. Marias* 369

Chapter 71 Relationship Between Children and Parents *by Kathryn Harry* 374

Chapter 72 Dealing with a Challenging Co-Parent *by Dara L. Marias* 378

Part 18 How Do I Move Forward After Divorce?

Chapter 73 The Post-Divorce Checklist *by Tracy Ann Moore-Grant* 387

Chapter 74 Finding Yourself Again *by Stephanie Robins* 388

Chapter 75 Estate Planning After Divorce *by Misty Ralston* 392

Chapter 76 Rebuilding Financially *by Andrew Hatherley* 398

Chapter 77 Prenuptial Agreements for Remarriage *by Alexandra Geczi* 403

Chapter 78 Cultivating Mindfulness *by Dara L. Marias* 408

Chapter 79 Moving Forward *by Stephanie Robins* 413

Chapter 80 Closure and Healing *by Suzanne Winlove-Smith* 418

About the Author 423

Preface
Why the Amicable Divorce Network?
by Tracy Ann Moore-Grant

Divorce is stressful. Whether you are the person going through divorce or a professional who is helping with the process, divorce is full of emotions, high stakes, and time deadlines. Attorneys deal with complex issues and see clients at their most vulnerable and most distressed – and often, at their lowest point.

Divorces deal with every aspect of a client's life, including their home, their children, their finances, and their future. There are hundreds of different areas of law that a lawyer can specialize in. The attorneys that chose family law did so because they wanted to help clients navigate difficult times. They wanted to have a positive impact on their clients and their future.

However, many professionals leave the practice of family law when they realize that the system does not support peaceful, meaningful, and efficient resolutions. In addition, many lawyers themselves encourage conflict and drawn-out divorce battles.

I became frustrated with seeing well-meaning clients waste their hard-earned money, simply because the other spouse unknowingly hired a high-conflict attorney. As a mediator, I saw couples initially say that their matter was uncontested – but after they hired attorneys, somehow things spiraled out of control. On the other hand, I have seen parties – with complex issues – who were so fearful of hiring attorneys that they did the paperwork themselves. But it was done so poorly that it left one party financially devastated, and the errors were unfixable.

As a professional in the field, I was sick of getting vile emails from other lawyers at 10 p.m. about various cases, unnecessarily spewing hate and inflaming problems. They could have spent the same amount of time solving a problem. Family law and divorce are inherently emotional, stressful, and never free. But there are professionals who intentionally make the case worse for everyone involved, and frankly, I was tired of dealing with them.

I understand that a client will be emotionally charged and upset, but attorneys take an oath to protect their client's best interest. Increasing conflict in cases, simply to get more in fees, does not protect clients – or their children. Making the divorce more difficult is only in the best interest of the high-conflict lawyer. Because so many people only go through one divorce, they have nothing to compare it to. They are vulnerable and they believe that lawyer is fighting for them.

The Amicable Divorce Network was founded to vet professionals and educate the public on the inner workings of family law cases. The network was designed to empower couples to make the best decisions for themselves.

To understand the inner workings of family law, it is important to understand the system. Specifically, the United States, United Kingdom, Canada, and Australia have adversarial court systems. Other countries have such systems as well. An adversarial system is a legal framework in which two opposing parties present their cases to an impartial judge or jury. The adversarial system is primarily used in countries that have followed common law traditions, where litigation involves dispute resolution after evidence and arguments are presented by both sides. This system is used for cases involving anything from car accidents to murder cases.

It is also used in family law in the aforementioned countries; a separate system does not exist for the dissolution of families. So, due to its very nature in the court system, family law in the United States is structured to be adversarial. In contrast, countries like France, Germany, and Japan operate on an inquisitorial legal system, where judges play an active role in investigating the facts. In an inquisitorial system, the judge will guide the case to a conclusion, rather than relying solely on the arguments of opposing parties. An adversarial system is designed to determine a winner; an inquisitorial system is designed to find the truth.

At its heart, an adversarial process means that each person must present their best facts, witnesses, evidence, and circumstances to a court, and then must try to cast the other side and their witnesses in a bad light. At the end, the judge or jury picks a winner. In an adversarial system, there is no situation where two really great parents can approach the judge and say, "We both really love our kids; we just have different ideas about what our parenting plan should look like – can you help?"

Instead, spouses who once loved each other enough to marry – and who are expected to be terrific co-parents and rear emotionally healthy children after the divorce – are virtually required by the system to sling mud at each other to advance their position. It is understandable that the adversarial system might be ideal for a murder case or contract dispute, but it is not conducive to the delicate nature of a family dissolution. Nor is it emotionally healthy or financially reasonable for the parties and their children.

The reality is that about 90 percent of family law cases in the United States settle outside of court. Some studies have that statistic as high as 95 percent. Yet, many divorce attorneys are preparing cases from their very inception to go to trial – a trial that they know probably will never happen. And all along the way, it is those same family law professionals who will profit from preparing for a trial that will not happen. And it is those family law professionals who have the ability to stoke the flames of conflict – and increase the fees and the length of a case. Or they can decide to take a different path by managing expectations and conflict and guiding the case to a resolution.

Not all lawyers intentionally increase costs for financial gain. As mentioned earlier, many family law professionals choose their line of work so they can help people. But others are financially motivated, and when they are involved in a case, the cost, conflict, and duration can shoot through the roof. In my many years of practice as a family lawyer, mediator, arbitrator, parent coordinator, and guardian ad litem (GAL), I have encountered both kinds of professionals – the helpers, and those who escalate conflict.

The Amicable Divorce Network was founded to identify the helpers for the public and put them in one centralized database. All members are vetted, including lawyers, mediators, Realtors, financial professionals, mental health professionals, coaches, and more. Amicable Divorce Network members' backgrounds are reviewed by colleagues to consider experience, their focus on resolution over conflict, and their use of fair billing practices. Those three criteria are essential for determining if the professional is motivated by doing what is in the client's best interest, and not their own. It is actually the professional members, and not the divorcing parties, who are the "amicable" part of the Amicable Divorce Network. To clarify the criteria:

Experience: We ask that our members have a minimum of five years of experience in each category of membership. Amicable cases are not always easy cases. They can still involve high emotion, complex assets, addiction issues, and more of the same challenges you might see in any other family law matter. Experience enables the professional to guide difficult situations to a resolution.

Resolution focus: Colleagues and mediators know which professionals dig in to look for solutions and provide realistic advice. They also know which professionals give poor advice, do not communicate, stonewall settlement negotiations, and promote litigation. We vet our members to make sure they have a resolution focus.

Fair billing practices: In the family law field, professionals get to see the billing statements from other professionals in negotiations or in a hearing. There is often the ability to review bills of others and see what led to increased costs. Certain family law professionals use tactics to charge as much as four times more than other comparable attorneys. For that reason, we vet our members for fair billing practices.

As noted, the out-of-court settlement rate is at least 90 percent or higher in family law cases; yet, lawyers are still providing litigation-oriented services. The high rate of settlement in family law cases stems from the desires of the parties to minimize legal fees, maintain privacy, and have a child-focused process. Couples want to expedite resolutions and do not want to expend unnecessary funds.

> **Rates vary by region.** It is important to know that professionals charge different rates in different jurisdictional areas. What may be a fair rate in New York City will be different than a fair rate in rural North Carolina. We look at geographic norms and a member's colleagues to determine industry fairness and professional reputation when it comes to billing. The Amicable Divorce Network does not govern the individual members' rates or overall process costs, because forms, procedure, and steps vary by jurisdiction.

The Amicable Divorce Network wants to pair family law clients with the qualified and vetted professionals to guide them efficiently and arrive at a resolution. The goal is to take the adversarial tone out of a family dissolution. Although both parties may still negotiate and argue for their desired result, the process:

- Keys on the best interests of the children.
- Considers the most likely result in a contested proceeding when applying the law.
- Moves toward the quickest and most financially efficient outcome.

The Amicable Divorce Network is the only organization in the world taking this particular approach to family law. It is the only organization that vets attorneys and other professionals regarding the essential criteria that apply to divorce cases. The network is actively working to make divorce more efficient, child-focused, and healthier for all involved. If you are facing divorce, we are glad that you are exploring this option. We hope you find helpful information in this book to guide you into your future.

Tracy Ann Moore-Grant
Founder, Amicable Divorce Network
Attorney, Mediator, Arbitrator with Patterson Moore Butler
Certified Amicable Divorce Professional
Georgia

PART 1

Are You Ready For a Divorce?

Chapter 1
The Amicable Divorce Mindset:
Your Guide to Taking the First Steps
9

Chapter 2
To Divorce or Not?
12

Chapter 3
Legal Separation vs Divorce
16

Chapter 1

The Amicable Divorce Mindset: Your Guide to Taking the First Steps

by Storey Jones

Divorce is one of the most significant life transitions many of us will face – a transition that will challenge every aspect of our social, emotional, and financial lives. So, where do we start? We must begin with the right *mindset* and dispel the myths you may have absorbed from endless online searches or conversations with friends.

While it might not sound particularly romantic, when you said, "I do," you effectively started a business with your spouse. From a legal perspective, your romantic partner became your business partner. Now, five, 10, perhaps even 25 years later, you are selling the business. It might surprise you to hear, but the divorce process is an analysis of how the company performed. What assets and debt did it acquire? What revenue was generated? What expenses did it incur? And equally, if not more important, how can both partners move forward independently?

What Is a Divorce, Really?

Everyone has a story – a narrative of how you got here – and it is crucial to work with a therapist to address your role in that partnership so that you do not repeat unhealthy relationship patterns and learn how to co-exist in the future. Perhaps you are dealing with changing the structure of your relationship, addiction, personality disorders, special needs children, infidelity, or any number of other relationship challenges. While some of the nuances of your story might be relevant, the divorce process is not an autopsy of the past. Instead, it is a review of the current facts and the development of a settlement agreement that allows you to move forward independently.

Our goal, with the development of user-friendly technology and the innovative Amicable Divorce Process, is to dramatically transform the divorce experience so it no longer emotionally and financially bankrupts families. By starting with the right mindset and approaching the process holistically – considering the family and financial aspects – you can significantly reduce anxiety, save a tremendous amount of money, and feel more in control.

When we think about the divorce transaction – the process to reach a Marital Settlement Agreement – we think about it in three macro buckets, four if you have children:

1. **Biographical information:** Names, ages, dates, and other relevant family information.
2. **Assets and Debts:** Characterization of ownership, equity, debt, and carrying costs that will result in property distribution.
3. **Income and Expenses:** Identification of all sources of revenue and family expenses for applicable support/maintenance calculations, and how to build a settlement that will meet both spouses' needs and child-related needs going forward.
4. **Parenting Plan:** For families with children, a Parenting Plan details co-parenting agreements and a parenting schedule.

Getting Started

Now that we have deconstructed the components of divorce, I cannot overemphasize the value of a step-by-step sequential approach to start. *Before* you start calling lawyers, begin with organizing your family's financial information. Remember, the divorce process is an analysis of how your business partnership fared. Legal advice is most effective when you have at least a basic financial roadmap as well as a rational and organized outline of the qualitative issues that are relevant to the legal process.

When you seek legal advice, you will want to know things like: Will you be okay financially? How much support will you have to pay or receive? Can you keep your retirement savings? Should you refinance the house now or later? These questions are best answered if you have a preliminary net worth and cash flow report. Without clear financial facts, a legal consultation will likely result in confusion and higher costs.

If you are in a relationship where you don't know much about the finances, don't worry. Start by gathering tax returns, bank statements, and any financial documents you can access. Use *dtour.life* to begin building a clear picture of your situation. If your situation is complex – such as having executive compensation, various business holdings, or income-producing properties – consider hiring a Certified Divorce Financial Analyst (CDFA). Invite them to *dtour.life* and they will work with you to develop a comprehensive financial profile, which will save you time and money and provide your attorney with a solid foundation for giving you actionable and substantive advice from day one.

Quarterback the Process

Divorce is a full-time job and a complex life transition, but this is *your* divorce, *your* future. The best outcome is a settlement that you help create, reflecting a clear path forward. We know the emotional complexity of navigating your new day-to-day reality, handling new family dynamics, and a myriad of other challenges. That is why the visual design of *dtour.life* is customized for your active participation in the process. Each component is designed to allow you to continually update relevant information and, more importantly, to ensure that your holistic family and financial picture is clear, without having to have extensive knowledge about spreadsheets! This empowers you to work collaboratively with your team, and to actively participate and more easily make informed decisions throughout the process.

Historically, we believed that all we needed for a successful divorce was a good, a.k.a., *expensive*, lawyer and they would handle everything. In the modern age with technology and with Amicable Divorce Network professionals, we are fundamentally changing the experience for everyone.

Note: While the emphasis in this chapter is on the financial organization, we know that if you have children, *that* is more important and more concerning than any other aspect of the process. However, the exact same principles apply. Beginning with the right *mindset* and organization, you will critically align all of your efforts and energy toward designing a schedule and co-parenting agreement that supports your family in the short and long term.

Storey Jones
Founder, dtour.life (divorce management platform)
New York, NY

Chapter 2
To Divorce or Not?
by Kathleen Shack

Sometimes the decision to divorce is clear-cut, but many people struggle with making the decision for a long time, often remaining in limbo for months or years. You may be worried that you won't make the "correct" decision. You may be experiencing anger, fear, confusion, sadness, or denial. You have probably tried talking with friends or family; you've read books or material on the Internet, and you have spent countless hours reflecting on the state of your relationship. Through a process called *discernment counseling*, a therapist can give you an objective perspective to help you make the best decision about your marriage's future.

Surveys find that up to 40 percent of divorced people have regrets about their divorce decision, often because they feel they (and their partner) may have not tried hard enough to make the marriage work. After discernment counseling, people usually feel more settled and confident about their next steps (whether they decide to work on the marriage in counseling or to move toward divorce).

The work done in discernment counseling helps couples stay more calm through the divorce process, which helps the process go smoother. If you choose to work on the marriage instead of pursuing a divorce, discernment counseling includes writing clear individual and couples goals. That focus can give you the best chance of being successful.

Discernment Counseling: What Is It?

It is a brief counseling program (a maximum of five sessions; often less) in which you will gain clarity and confidence about the direction of your marriage. You will move forward with a deeper understanding of what's happened to the marriage and how each person contributed to the problems. The sessions are designed to meet each partner where they are, with an emphasis on individual conversations and carefully structured couple-sharing. The sessions do not look like traditional couples therapy. There is an emphasis on what each partner can learn about themselves by looking at the contributions of each partner within the problems of the marriage.

A therapist will help you decide whether to try to restore your marriage to health or move toward divorce – or to just take a timeout and decide later. The goal is for you to gain clarity and confidence about your direction, based on a deeper understanding of your relationship and its future possibilities. During the counseling process, you are not working to solve your marital problems – you are trying to figure out if they are solvable. Nevertheless, you will each be treated with compassion and respect, no matter how you feel about the state of your marriage. No bad guys or good guys.

You will come into counseling as a couple, but the most important work occurs in the one-to-one conversations with the therapist. Why? Because you are starting out in different places. The therapist respects your reasons for divorce while trying to open up the possibility of restoring the marriage to health. It is important that each of you sees your own contributions to the problems – and possible solutions. What each person discovers during counseling will be useful in future relationships, even if this one ends.

Discernment Counseling: Who Is It For?

The unique process of discernment counseling is for couples on the brink of divorce. You should participate in it when you or your spouse are considering divorce but are not completely sure that is the best path. It's a chance to slow down, take a breath, and look at all options for your marriage. Often, one spouse is "leaning out" of the relationship – and is not sure that regular marriage counseling would help. The other may be "leaning in" – that is, interested in rebuilding the marriage. Occasionally, both partners may be leaning out, but each wants more clarity so they can decide whether the marriage can be worked on.

If you are the partner who is leaning out, the therapist will seek to understand your pain, hear your story, process path choices, and discuss your contributions to the status of the marriage. The therapist will also help you communicate your concerns and feelings to your spouse.

You may have already been to multiple couples counselors, and are wary or exhausted about the thought of more counseling! However, discernment counseling is an opportunity to explore the status of the relationship and communicate your concerns to your spouse without having to do more traditional couples counseling. The majority of the time in the sessions is spent one-on-one with the counselor – with only brief, structured time with your spouse.

If you are the leaning-in partner, the therapist will help you bring your best self to the marriage crisis and to understand the pain and complaints of your spouse. You will work on processing path choices, and you'll discuss your contributions to the status of the marriage. You can't immediately change your spouse's mind about working on the marriage, but you can ask your spouse if they will consider doing discernment counseling with you. The purpose of the counseling is not to fix the marriage but to see if it is fixable.

Discernment counseling is designed for couples who are genuinely unsure about the future of their relationship. It is not for couples in which there is a clear power imbalance or a lack of ambiguity about the desired outcome of the relationship. To give some examples, counseling would not be recommended when: one spouse has already decided to divorce and wants to use counseling to pressure the other partner to accept that decision; when one spouse is coercing the other to participate; or when there is danger of domestic violence.

Discernment counseling focuses on three potential paths: ending the relationship via separation or divorce; carving out a six-month period of time for an all-out effort in couples counseling (and sometimes other services) to preserve the marriage; and staying the course and deciding later. The counselor can help you transition into whichever path you choose. You can usually segue into couples counseling with the same counselor. Or, they can recommend another counselor for you to work with. Recommendations for amicable divorce professionals can also be provided by the counselor if divorce is the path that is chosen.

Path 1 is deciding to maintain the status quo of the relationship, neither moving toward divorce nor reconciliation. The 19 percent of clients who choose this path often want to take more time to process their choices. Or, they may have life circumstances that they want to get through before making a clear-cut decision, such as family time during the holidays, children graduating from school, or going into retirement.

Path 2 is deciding to begin the process of separation or divorce. Thirty percent of clients choose this path. The work done in discernment counseling helps the divorce process go more smoothly. Each person has had the opportunity to explore their own contributions to the relationship, to understand how the couple got to the point of divorce. That knowledge helps each person process their feelings and also understand their spouse's reasons and feelings. Often, discernment counseling helps each person soften toward their partner. The couple can then go through the divorce process in a calmer, more productive way instead of getting into blame games, causing hurt feelings, and being reactive.

Path 3 is deciding to do couples counseling for six months, with divorce off the table. Prior to starting this path, agenda items for each individual and the couple are clearly defined and written down. With that agenda spelled out, couples counseling has the best chance of being successful. Typically, the 51 percent of clients who choose this path are more confident going into new sessions of couples counseling than they were in previous sessions. This time, each partner has taken the time to clearly define what he or she is going to work on. Clearly defined goals help eliminate finger-pointing, and will help couples get to work quickly. They will feel more confident about the decision they have made about their marriage.

Kathleen Shack, M.S., LMFT
Family Solutions Counseling
Certified Gottman Couples Therapist
Certified Discernment Counselor
Certified Amicable Divorce Professional
Divorce Coach and Mediator
Alpharetta, Georgia

Chapter 3
Legal Separation vs. Divorce
by Kathryn Harry

If you're at the beginning of your legal journey, you may feel unprepared to make such a life-changing decision as divorce and may want to consider legal separation. This chapter will guide you through the distinctions between legal separation and divorce, the situations in which each might be beneficial, and factors to consider before choosing your path. By the end of this chapter, you'll have the knowledge to confidently take the next steps in your legal journey. With the information provided here you will be equipped to make decisions that align with your personal and financial goals, and you'll be ready to seek the professional legal advice necessary to move forward with confidence.

What Is Legal Separation?

Legal separation is a court-recognized arrangement in which a married couple decides to live apart while maintaining their marital status. Unlike simply moving out or informally splitting up, legal separation involves a formal, legal process that is different from a divorce process. It results in a binding agreement or court order that must be followed by the parties. This document typically addresses issues like division of property, child custody and support, and alimony.

Importantly, while legal separation allows couples to live apart and resolve major issues, it does not dissolve the marriage and the parties are not legally divorced; they are legally separated. This distinction carries significant implications for your legal and financial situation, as well as for your personal life and ability to move on.

What Is Divorce?

Divorce, also known as the dissolution of marriage, is the legal process that ends a marriage. Once a divorce is finalized, the marital relationship is permanently severed, and both individuals are free to remarry. Like legal separation, divorce requires a final resolution for critical issues such as property division, custody, and support.

The key difference is finality. Divorce legally and emotionally closes the chapter of marriage, severing financial ties and eliminating most legal obligations between former spouses. Once divorced, neither party can claim rights or responsibilities associated with the marital relationship, except those specifically outlined in the divorce decree, such as ongoing alimony or child support.

Differences Between Legal Separation and Divorce

Understanding the distinctions between legal separation and divorce can clarify your options:

1. **Marital status**
   - **Legal separation:** You remain legally married. This means you cannot remarry unless you later obtain a divorce.
   - **Divorce:** Your marriage is officially terminated and you are free to remarry after any specified waiting period dictated by your state law.

2. **Religious or cultural considerations**
   - **Legal separation:** For individuals whose religious or cultural beliefs discourage or prohibit divorce, legal separation provides an alternative that allows for physical and financial independence without breaking the marital bond.
   - **Divorce:** While divorce may conflict with certain beliefs, it provides a clean break for those ready to move forward without the benefits of marriage, such as health insurance provided by a spouse's employer.

3. **Financial benefits**
   - **Legal separation:** Couples can retain certain benefits, such as shared health insurance plans, tax advantages, or military spouse benefits, which might otherwise be lost in divorce.
   - **Divorce:** These benefits typically end with divorce. However, spousal support (also referred to as alimony) or other financial arrangements may mitigate the loss of such advantages. Accounts like 401k and IRA accounts can be divided upon divorce.

4. **Reconciliation**
   - **Legal separation:** This offers a structured period for living apart while leaving the door open for reconciliation. Should the couple reconcile, they remain married without the need to remarry.
   - **Divorce:** This represents a permanent legal end to the marriage, making reconciliation more complicated and less likely.

5. **Jurisdiction recognition**
   - **Legal separation:** Not all states recognize legal separation as a formal process. As of December 2024, the following states do not offer legal separation: Delaware, Florida, Georgia, Mississippi, Pennsylvania, and Texas. In these states, couples seeking to formalize the aspects of their living separate and apart must explore alternative legal arrangements. For instance, in Georgia, while legal separation isn't recognized, couples may pursue an action for "separate maintenance" under O.C.G.A. § 19-6-10, which allows them to live apart while resolving issues like alimony and child support without divorcing – which is essentially the same thing as a legal separation. Other issues like the allocation of property or debt between the parties would have to be set out in a postnuptial agreement.

     In states where it is available, the procedures and outcomes may vary. For example, in Illinois, Legal Separation is recognized as a marital status, and issues of child support, child custody, alimony, and allocation of assets and debts between the parties may be addressed in a formal agreement or Judgment for Legal Separation.
   - **Divorce:** Divorce is universally recognized across the United States and is governed by well-established legal frameworks in each state, although outcomes vary significantly from state to state. They may even vary from venue to venue within a state. Much is left to judicial discretion in divorce, as well, which may result in differing outcomes depending on the judge you have.

> Note that when a divorce is initiated, amicable or not, the parties have the ability to enter into a "Temporary Agreement." This is an agreement that the parties operate under until the divorce is finalized. It can address how financial, parenting schedule, payment of debts, possession of the home, and support issues are handled.

When Might Legal Separation Be Right?

Legal separation over a divorce may be preferable in specific circumstances. The decision should be made on a case-by-case basis. What are your future goals? What is important to you? Are you ready to live separately from your spouse? Consider legal separation if:

1. Religious or moral beliefs prevent divorce
2. You need to retain shared benefits
3. You are not emotionally ready for divorce
4. You want to maintain stability for your children
5. You are considering reconciliation

When Is Divorce the Better Option?

Sometimes divorce may be the clearer and more practical choice, especially when:

1. The marriage is over
2. You wish to remarry
3. You want to eliminate financial entanglements
4. There is conflict or abuse

What Factors Should You Consider?

Changing your marital status isn't something to be taken lightly. Making the right choice between legal separation and divorce requires careful consideration of several issues such as:

1. **Emotional readiness:** Are you prepared to permanently end your marriage, or do you need more time to process this major life change?
2. **Financial security:** How will each option affect your financial stability, including access to benefits, division of property, and support obligations?
3. **Children's best interests:** How will your decision impact your children's emotional and practical needs? Will a change in your marital status require them to move to a different location or change schools?

Do you have a support system in place for the children to help them deal with major changes like these?
4. **State laws:** Does your state recognize legal separation? If not, you may have no choice but to proceed with divorce.
5. **Future goals:** Are you seeking closure, or do you want to leave room for reconciliation?
6. **Cost:** Do you have enough money to fund your pursuit of a divorce if you decide legal separation is not for you? It is also very important to note that parties may go through a negotiated legal separation, which is finalized with legal documents, but if one or both parties wants to move forward with a divorce in the future, they may need to go through all of these steps all over again. For many, doing the same process twice is cost-prohibitive.

Decision Time

The decision between legal separation and divorce is deeply personal and depends on your unique circumstances, beliefs, and goals. Legal separation can be a great option for those seeking financial or emotional stability without permanently ending the marriage. However, divorce is often the better choice, providing clarity, independence, and closure.

No matter which path feels right to you, the key to navigating this phase of your life is to learn as much about the subject as possible, and to avail yourself of professionals. Consulting an attorney ensures you fully understand your options and are equipped to make decisions that reflect the way you want to live in the future.

Taking the first step toward resolution may feel daunting, but with the right information and guidance, you can move forward with confidence toward the future you want.

Kathryn Harry
Family Law Attorney
Georgia and Illinois

PART 2

What is Divorce Really Like?

Chapter 4
Myths About Divorce
25

Chapter 5
The Cost of Divorce Isn't Just Financial
28

Chapter 6
Fault: Do You Bring It Up?
32

Chapter 4
Myths About Divorce
by Jeanette L. Soltys

Divorce is often portrayed as a harrowing experience, filled with emotional battles, financial devastation, and prolonged legal proceedings. While it's true that divorce is rarely easy, much of the dread surrounding it stems from myths that create unnecessary fear and misunderstanding. In this chapter, we'll explore the most pervasive myths about divorce – and reveal the truth behind them. By dispelling the misconceptions, you will be empowered to make informed, constructive decisions that lead to a smoother, more amicable process.

Divorce Myth No. 1: It's best to hire an aggressive lawyer

Many people believe that if they have children, significant assets, or disagreements with their spouse, high-conflict litigation is inevitable. They believe that they will need a "bulldog" or "shark" divorce lawyer. The reality, however, is quite different. While litigation might be necessary in extreme cases, most divorces can be resolved without entering a courtroom.

Reality check: The Amicable Divorce Process offers a viable path to avoid the traditional litigation process, and provides structured frameworks for negotiation while minimizing conflict. For example, in an amicable divorce, each spouse retains their own attorney, but the attorneys specialize in low-conflict resolutions, ensuring expert advice without unnecessary aggression. An amicable approach can save time, money, and emotional energy, making it possible to reach a fair resolution without prolonged battles.

In contrast, a lawyer who takes an aggressive stance in every situation unnecessarily drives up legal fees – without getting a better result. In fact, the result achieved by using the Amicable Divorce Process is often superior to what one would receive in litigation. Negotiations between the parties can lead to a customized settlement that a judge would not have the time to create.

Divorce Myth No. 2: My spouse is a narcissist

A common narrative in divorce is labeling one's spouse as a narcissist. While it's true that some individuals exhibit toxic behaviors, labeling your spouse as a narcissist can exacerbate conflict and derail productive communication.

Reality check: Most difficult spouses are not clinically narcissistic. They may be acting out due to stress, fear, or unresolved grievances – or maybe they are simply a jerk or a toxic person.

Rather than focusing on labels, it's better to prioritize solutions. Skilled mediators and attorneys can help navigate personality clashes and difficult personalities while keeping discussions centered on practical outcomes.

Don't fall for the attorneys who use narcissism heavily in their marketing. If you are divorcing an actual narcissist, the professional who can help the most is a therapist. The therapist will give you support to stay mentally healthy while you are divorcing a narcissist and will help you work on effective communication skills if you must co-parent. Additionally, an excellent resource is the High Conflict Institute: www.highconflictinstitute.com.

Divorce Myth No. 3: Fault matters significantly in divorce

Another persistent myth is the idea that fault will significantly affect the outcome of a divorce. Many people believe that proving their spouse's wrongdoing – whether it was infidelity, irresponsibility, or neglecting the marriage – will sway key decisions in their favor.

Clients typically believe the myth about fault when it comes to property division; they will argue that they should keep a much larger portion of the assets, because their spouse refused to work and financially contribute, or because the spouse mismanaged finances.

Reality check: In many jurisdictions, fault plays a minimal role in divorce outcomes. For example, in Georgia – even though there are 13 grounds for divorce, including cruel treatment and adultery – most courts rarely focus on punitive measures. Lawyers who encourage you to focus on fault often accomplish nothing but higher legal fees.

The extent to which fault matters varies by jurisdiction and even by judge, so discuss your specific facts with your Amicable Divorce Network attorney. However, when you recognize that assigning blame probably has limited practical benefits, you can focus on trusting your lawyer to achieve forward-looking solutions. That's more productive than rehashing past grievances.

Divorce Myth No. 4: It doesn't matter who files first

With a traditional divorce that is filed with the court before negotiations begin, it often does not matter who files first. However, making the first move in the divorce process does matter with an amicable divorce.

Reality check: Being the party to initiate an amicable divorce allows you to set the tone for the entire process and guide it down the right path. If you wait for your spouse to make the first move, they may hire an unnecessarily aggressive lawyer. Once aggressive litigation has begun, it is very difficult to correct that misstep and change the course toward a more amicable solution. Making the first move and hiring an attorney from the Amicable Divorce Network makes it more likely that your divorce will be handled in a way that minimizes time, stress, and attorney fees.

Separating Fact from Fiction

In navigating the complexities of divorce, separating fact from fiction is crucial. Established facts simply dismantle some of the most persistent myths surrounding divorce, from the belief that aggressive lawyers are essential to misconceptions about fault and personality labels. We can instead focus on amicable resolutions, forward-looking strategies, and personalized legal guidance. Divorce does not have to be an emotionally and financially draining ordeal. You can chart a path that prioritizes clarity, respect, and a healthier future.

Jeanette Soltys
Founding Attorney, Atlanta Holistic Family Law
Marietta, Georgia

Chapter 5
The Cost of Divorce Isn't Just Financial
by Jeanette Soltys

Divorce is rarely easy, even under the best circumstances. When most people consider the costs of divorce, their minds jump to the obvious: attorney fees, court costs, and the division of assets. But while the financial toll can be significant, the emotional and relational costs often weigh just as heavily – and, in many cases, even more so. For those contemplating such a life-changing decision, understanding divorce's non-financial costs is crucial to making informed, thoughtful choices.

There are many hidden costs of divorce, ranging from the emotional toll it takes on individuals and families to the public exposure of private matters. Nevertheless, the Amicable Divorce Process is a solution designed to minimize such costs and guide you toward a smoother, less adversarial experience.

Emotional Cost: A Roller Coaster of Stress and Grief

The end of a marriage is inherently emotional. It represents the unraveling of shared dreams, routines, and futures. Even if the decision to divorce is mutual, the process often triggers intense feelings of loss, anger, and fear. For many, the emotions can manifest as:

- **Grief and mourning:** Even if the marriage wasn't working, the loss of a partnership and shared history can feel like a death.

- **Stress and anxiety:** Facing an uncertain future – financially, emotionally, and socially – can be overwhelming.
- **Mental health struggles:** Depression, insomnia, and feelings of failure are common when people navigate upheaval in their lives.

The feelings that surface during and after a divorce often don't just affect the couple, but also ripple outward to their children, families, and friends. The emotions can add layers of complexity and guilt.

Relational Cost: Strained or Broken Bonds

Divorce doesn't happen in a vacuum. It touches every relationship in a person's life. Children, in particular, often bear the brunt of the conflict and the changes that come with divorce. While parents may try to shield their children from harm, litigation and high-conflict separation can lead to:

- **Strained parental relationships:** Children may feel torn between their parents or manipulated into taking sides.
- **Disrupted stability:** Moves, school changes, and altered routines can create stress and insecurity.
- **Long-term emotional impact:** Studies have shown that children in high-conflict divorces are more likely to struggle with relationships and mental health issues as they grow.

Beyond the parent-child dynamic, extended families and friend groups may also suffer. Divorces that play out in courtrooms often force others within the couple's circle to take sides, creating rifts that may never fully heal.

Public Cost: Loss of Privacy

Few people consider how much personal information becomes public in a litigated divorce. Court filings often reveal deeply personal details about both parties. Such information – ranging from mental health diagnoses to financial history – becomes part of the public record. It becomes accessible to employers, acquaintances, and even future romantic partners. And frequently, allegations in court records are embellished or hold no truth. The collateral damage of airing dirty laundry can lead to:

- **Professional repercussions:** Employers may view private struggles as a liability.
- **Social stigma:** Friends and community members may judge the spouses, or gossip about the details revealed in court.
- **Inhibited healing:** Knowing your private life is now public can make it harder to move forward.

Time and Energy Cost: Years of Fighting

Traditional divorce litigation is rarely swift. Cases often drag on for 12 to 14 months – or longer – with only a few court appearances during that time. The rest of the process consists of endless delays, negotiations, and formal discovery – an exhaustive effort to dig up evidence on both sides. During that time, individuals may experience:

- **Lost time at work:** Court dates and attorney meetings can require significant time off, affecting income and career progression.
- **Emotional exhaustion:** The constant state of conflict can drain even the most resilient individuals.
- **Inability to move on:** As long as the divorce is unresolved, life feels like it's on hold.

Solution: The Amicable Divorce Process

Fortunately, divorce doesn't have to come with all those hidden costs. The Amicable Divorce Process offers an alternative that minimizes conflict, preserves relationships, and protects your privacy. It is an out-of-court approach, designed for couples who are willing to negotiate and prioritize their family's well-being over "winning."

Key Features of the Process

Confidentiality: Unlike what happens as a result of courtroom litigation, the amicable process keeps your private life private.

Collaborative focus: Each party works with their own attorney (trained in amicable practices), ensuring that everyone's voice is heard without fostering conflict.

Neutral experts: Financial advisors, child specialists, and other professionals provide guidance to help craft solutions tailored to your family's unique needs.

Efficiency: Without delays due to court dates and judges, the process moves at your pace, allowing you to reach a resolution faster.

Forward-looking solutions: The focus is on creating agreements that support your future, rather than rehashing past grievances.

Divorce as a New Beginning

Divorce marks the end of one chapter in your life, but it doesn't have to define your story. By choosing an amicable approach, you can minimize the non-financial costs of divorce – preserving your relationships, protecting your mental health, and moving forward with dignity.

The path to starting over doesn't have to be paved with pain and conflict. The Amicable Divorce Process offers an opportunity to rewrite the narrative, focusing on collaboration and respect rather than division. By making informed decisions, you can close one chapter of your life with grace and begin building the best possible future.

Jeanette Soltys
Founding Attorney, Atlanta Holistic Family Law
Marietta, Georgia

Chapter 6
Fault: Do You Bring It Up?
by Tracy Ann Moore-Grant

When approaching divorce, usually one spouse believes – and may even have significant evidence – that the other spouse is "at fault" for the end of the marriage. The aggrieved spouse often wants the other to "pay" for their behavior – either financially or through the custodial schedule. That means they will want to pursue fault grounds.

When deciding the direction of your divorce, it is important for you to understand the difference between fault and no-fault divorce.

No-Fault Divorce History

The history of no-fault divorce in the United States (and around the world) reflects a significant cultural and legal shift in the approach to marriage dissolution. In the United States prior to 1969, a person could only get a divorce from their spouse if they could prove the other had, in fact, committed an act of fault. They would need to prove that fault to the court with proper evidence to get the divorce granted. Common fault grounds were (and continue to be) adultery, abuse, and habitual drunkenness. It is similar to proving someone guilty of a crime in a criminal case but with a lower burden of proof.

The process was (and continues to be) adversarial, and it required private misconduct to be aired publicly in court. In some cases, couples would fabricate evidence of fault because they mutually wanted a divorce but couldn't meet the legal requirements. In the circumstance of one party wanting a divorce and the other wanting to stay married, the second spouse could fight the evidence and contest the divorce. If the judge didn't find that there was enough evidence to find one party at fault, they would have to stay married.

It became evident that there had to be a better way. The concept of no-fault divorce originated from criticisms of the fault-based system. Reformers argued that the system then in place increased conflict, encouraged dishonesty, didn't protect victims of domestic violence, and created expensive and time-consuming litigation, causing a waste of taxpayer resources.

In 1969, California became the first state in the United States to allow no-fault divorce. Instead of proving fault, couples could claim "irreconcilable differences," meaning that the marriage just wasn't working out. Parties no longer had to go through a trial with a judge to get a divorce. They could agree that the marriage wasn't working, reach a settlement themselves, and efficiently dissolve their marriage. Many states followed quickly, but it was only in 2010 that the last state, New York, adopted no-fault divorce. Canada adopted no-fault divorce in 1985. In the United Kingdom, it was not until 2020 that Parliament passed the Divorce, Dissolution, and Separation Act, introducing no-fault divorce in England and Wales.

Although the no-fault solution was added as a way to get a divorce, that does not mean that fault grounds have gone away (except in California, where laws do not provide for fault grounds). So, when pursuing divorce, parties usually still have the option to proceed with the route of getting a judge to declare the other at fault. But is it even worth it?

Most Cases Settle out of Court

However, as mentioned elsewhere in this book, over 90 percent of divorce cases settle outside of court, which means they are making use of a no-fault basis. Although some may still add a reason – like adultery, for example – to their paperwork, statistics show that most people rarely pursue the grounds. It is also unlikely that the remaining 10 percent of divorces – the litigated cases – all involve fault grounds. Sometimes people just can't reach a resolution, or a case could involve mental health challenges or scheduling issues.

Those who do list fault grounds for divorce are using the actions of the other party as leverage to get their desired result. And you know what? That is perfectly fine. In an amicable case, the negative actions or behavior of one of the spouses is not simply ignored. They may be used as part of the negotiation, just as they are in every other divorce case.

But in an amicable divorce, the focus is on being efficient and transparent, and on helping clients look to the future – not back on the past. The professionals in an Amicable Divorce Process give realistic advice on what the evidence could actually accomplish in negotiations. They guide clients to a result, even with difficult circumstances and strong emotions involved.

When initiating a divorce and deciding to pursue fault grounds, it is vital to understand the substantial cost of gathering the proper evidence. That cost should be weighed against any likely financial result. In short: Is the juice worth the squeeze? Amicable divorces and mediation rely upon no-fault divorce and vesting parties – not courts – to determine outcomes for families.

Key Features of No-Fault Divorce

Irreconcilable differences: Most laws allow couples to cite a breakdown of the marriage with no hope of repair as a reason for divorce instead of a fault ground.

Simplified process: Couples can jointly petition for divorce, or one spouse can unilaterally seek it without needing evidence of the other's fault. Parties have the flexibility to use an out-of-court process, like amicable divorce, to resolve their case.

The Current Landscape

The transition to no-fault divorce revolutionized the legal landscape for marriage and family in the US. It reflected broad societal changes regarding individual autonomy, gender equality, and attitudes toward marriage and family life. While still debated in some circles, no-fault divorce is the standard framework nationwide. Removing the legal requirement of proving in a court of law that one party is at fault in order to obtain the divorce is the threshold of everyone's ability to safely, economically, and peacefully exit a marriage.

PART 3

What Type of Divorce Do You Want?

Chapter 7
The Three Ways to Divorce
37

Chapter 8
The Three Steps to Take
41

Chapter 9
The Amicable Divorce Process
45

Chapter 10
Comparing the Different Lanes of the Divorce Highway
53

Chapter 7
The Three Ways to Divorce
by Tracy Ann Moore-Grant

In order to understand the different ways to get a divorce, it is important to understand the legal system itself. In the United States, Canada, and the United Kingdom, the legal system is an adversarial system. An adversarial court system is a legal system where two opposing parties present their evidence and arguments to an impartial judge or jury, who then decides the outcome. The same adversarial system is used in murder trials and determining the parenting plan for a special needs child. The Amicable Process allows parties to step out of the adversarial process and engage in an organized and lower-conflict parallel process. In family law cases, most states do not allow juries – and so, most cases that go to court are heard by a single judge.

The Adversarial System

Here are some characteristics of the adversarial court system in family law:

Each party presents their own case. The spouses are responsible for their own investigations and arguments. They often hire lawyers and experts to help present and prove their case.

The court is supposed to be impartial. The court does not conduct its own investigation, nor does it create its own version of events. It can only consider evidence and testimony that are properly put into evidence. Although a judge is ideally impartial, they are human too, and they bring their own experiences and judgment to the decision.

The court's decision is based on the evidence presented. The court only makes decisions on the issues presented by the parties.

The judge is the sole decision-maker. When you hand your case to a judge, they will make decisions about your children, your home, your money, and any other marital issue that you and your spouse could not work out on your own.

The adversarial system is based on the idea that the best way to get to the truth of a matter is through a competitive process. Due to the way the court system is set up, each party must put forth negative information about the other; they will argue their version of the facts to persuade the judge to decide in their favor. In the adversarial system, there is no option for a spouse to affirm that the other spouse is a good person and that they just need help on how to sort things out.

In contrast to an adversarial system, some countries have an inquisitorial system. The inquisitorial process can be described as an official inquiry to ascertain the truth. In this type of system, there may be one or more judges. They may actively engage in asking questions and sometimes may call their own witnesses. The goal in the inquisitorial system is to ascertain the truth; in the adversarial system, the goal is to select the winner.

Many have found the very nature of the adversarial process to be a bad fit for family law. The system, by its design, forces spouses and co-parents to say bad things about the other to try to achieve their preferred outcome. The adversarial process of divorce runs contrary to the post-divorce ideal of two people co-parenting and moving on with their lives in a healthy way. In fact, if the ex-spouses don't co-parent well, they can be subject to contempt-of-court or modification actions.

> It is important to know that only around 5 to 8 percent of divorce cases ultimately go in front of a judge for a final hearing. The vast majority of cases are now resolved outside of court. When a case does need a final hearing with a judge, the average time frame to reach that final hearing in the US is 19 months and about 24 months in the United Kingdom.)

Three Types of Divorce

Often, people facing divorce do not understand that they can choose the way they approach their divorce. There is not just one way to divorce. Most people have the impression that the only way to obtain a divorce is to "lawyer up" and "duke it out" in court – and truthfully, in some circumstances, the involvement of the court is absolutely necessary. However, in the majority of cases, spouses engage in the traditional approach with attorneys, take months doing extensive discovery, are pitted against one another to fight for what they want, and spend hard-earned money on exhaustive attorney fees – and then end up settling their case anyway.

With the Amicable Divorce Process, parties take control of their case themselves. The Amicable Divorce Network provides a professionally guided, out-of-court process that is low-conflict and efficient. The Amicable Divorce Network (ADN) focuses on resolution, not court.

Couples facing divorce should first decide how they wish to approach their divorce, then find an attorney who aligns with their perspective. Clients should never be afraid to question any attorney under consideration about that attorney's attitude regarding the divorce process, and about whether he or she will honor the client's choices and goals. The ways to divorce differ in three main areas: cost, time, and level of conflict. So, in general, a divorce will fall into one of three categories:

Uncontested divorce: Often called a "kitchen table agreement," the parties already have all of their issues worked out. They only need a lawyer to assist with the preparation and filing of the paperwork. The Amicable Divorce Network can be used to find attorneys who believe in a low-conflict approach and who will assist with the process. It is always a good idea – even if a divorce is uncontested – that both parties have access to legal advice, and have the documents reviewed and prepared by an attorney. Using the ADN will assure that both parties get advice from a professional who will honor their wishes to keep the matter uncontested, while giving each party the advice and guidance they need. Using online forms and trying to navigate the system without an attorney is never advised.

Amicable divorce: The process is centered around the attitude of the spouses and their desire to resolve their family law matter efficiently and with low conflict. The parties both agree to utilize the process and professionals in the Amicable Divorce Network, because they share their mindset and will work to keep the matter on track to resolution. The parties may or may not have their issues worked out at the outset, but if there are disagreements, they will agree to use alternate ways of dispute resolution (such as mediation) to resolve differences instead of the court system. The discovery process is streamlined; the focus is on each spouse being able to obtain the information they need to make informed decisions. Settlements are worked out before anything is filed with the court. And, all documents are filed with the court at the same time, so that the court knows that the case is fully settled. The amicable process can also be used for other case aspects, such as child support modification or visitation modification.

Traditional or contested divorce: In contrast to an amicable divorce, which *ends* with filing a divorce with the court, a traditional/contested divorce *begins* with the filing of the divorce paperwork by one party and the other party being served (depending on jurisdictional rules) – sometimes by law enforcement. The case is placed on a timeline dictated by their particular jurisdiction, and the couple may or may not use alternate methods to resolve disputes. The selection of attorneys is entirely up to the parties, and the attorneys may be resolution or litigation-oriented. Litigated divorces are more expensive, take much longer, and have higher conflict between the parties. However, in some situations, it is appropriate to use the traditional court process.

Keep in mind that Amicable Divorce Network attorneys are experienced in all forms of family law cases, and can help you weigh your options and arrive at a decision. Once the decision is made on the type of divorce desired, the next step is to find an attorney who will assist you with meeting your goals. If an uncontested or amicable divorce is chosen, the Amicable Divorce Network can identify all of the professionals who can assist you with the process – from start to finish. The ADN has vetted members to confirm that they are resolution-focused, that they have the appropriate experience in family law, and that they hold professional licenses in their respective professions.

Note also that the ADN professionals also handle traditional/contested divorce. They can continue to assist if you choose a contested divorce from the outset – or if the divorce that you initially hoped would be amicable does not continue that way.

Chapter 8
The Three Steps to Take
by Tracy Ann Moore-Grant

Regardless of what type of divorce the parties select from the three types that were previously noted, each and every divorce case – no matter how complicated or how easy – has the same three stages or steps.

Step 1: information gathering.

What are the issues that require resolution? What are the assets and debts? What is the income of the couple? What are the needs of the children? What issues do we need to identify and which ones do we need to resolve? Without correct and complete information, the parties will find it difficult to move forward.

A couple who has not been married too long and does not have a home or children may glide through this first stage quite easily. They may have nothing or little to address. However, in a long-term marriage – where a couple has children, stock options, retirement accounts, a small business, and more – it may take some time to develop a list. They will also want to make sure that each party is working with the same list.

In a traditional, contested divorce, information gathering can be a very time-consuming and expensive process called *formal discovery*. In formal discovery, each party serves written questions upon the other, asking for information (such as a list of bank accounts). Each side's attorney also asks for documents under oath and takes depositions from the parties (and perhaps other witnesses). Subpoenas may be served upon third parties, such as banks or schools, to get records and other information directly from the source.

Sometimes, a request can reach back 10 years or more. Collecting the information is not only a process that takes time; attorneys and their staffs must review the documentation gathered, so they can pull out the data that's needed.

> If you feel that the only way to get the necessary and accurate information in your case is by issuing a subpoena, please speak with your lawyer. As the Amicable Divorce Process is out of court, it does not have the ability for parties to issue subpoenas. Subpoenas require an active case in the court system.

In most divorce and family law cases, full formal discovery (going back years) and depositions are unnecessary. In an amicable divorce, the spouses can serve questions upon the other and ask for documents; however, such requests are streamlined to get to the heart of what's needed.

Also, using dtour.life, a digital divorce management platform, can cut down on much of the information gathering. Moreover, dtour.life can provide more reliable gathering, by using the Income & Expense Sync and Report feature. With this tool, a party can log into dtour.life and sync, for example, their checking account. The dtour.life system will pull not just a daily, updated balance of the account – which considerably cuts down on time – but also pull account data to populate the expenses tab. Want to see how much was spent at McDonald's? You can search using "McDonalds," by date range or location. By using that feature, the data is pulled directly from the institution, which means it is accurate. It is not passing through human hands, which could lead to errors or miscalculations. The dtour.life system then organizes it, leading to fewer billable hours from your legal team (which would have had to pull data from antiquated records).

The goal of stage one is that each spouse has the same list of marital assets, debts, and issues (such as custody, child support, and spousal support), and the couple can move on to step two.

> For those of you using dtour.life, you will find this list under assets & debts-Net Worth Report).

Step 2: information assessment.

Stage one will deliver a complete list of all marital assets, debts, and issues. However, a dispute may still exist as to the value of an item or how to handle it, like what to do with custody. The goal of step two is to sort through the differences and gather information.

For example, one of the most common issues is the value of the marital home. To settle the dispute, one or both parties may get an appraisal, which is a good example of a task that's done during stage two. Some other tasks that may occur are:

- Pension valuation
- Small business valuation
- Determining if any part of an asset or debt is "premarital," or not to be considered a marital item
- Calculation of child support
- Assessment of potential spousal support payments
- Budgets for the parties post-divorce
- Alcohol or drug assessments
- Vocational assessments
- Determining the needs of the children regarding their mental health, physical health, and other issues impacting their care and custody

It is during this second stage that other professionals may be enlisted to help you assess and clarify information. If, after stage one, you and your spouse have a different list of items (for example, one party is seeking spousal support but the other says it's not an issue), you will want to develop your position on the dispute in stage two.

On most issues, however, both parties desire a resolution. When that occurs, the Amicable Divorce Process encourages the couple to mutually hire one expert. Let's say that the parties have a small business at issue in the case. The financial experts in the Amicable Divorce Network have been vetted for their experience and fair billing practices, and can assist. To develop a sound business valuation, all experts collect the same information and use the same methodology whether the case is uncontested, amicable, or the War of the Roses. There is little to no value in hiring two experts to do the same work twice, so the parties can use one expert to save time and money if they choose. What if you get the expert's results and you don't like them? If that should happen, then you would be able to use the expert's work to have a separate expert provide a second opinion, instead of starting from scratch.

During the information assessment stage, your team will calculate support and budgets, develop proposed parenting plans, calculate the value of any businesses and complicated assets, and explore options with real estate. No matter how complicated the issues may seem, our experienced professionals can assist you. They will help obtain the proper information and assessment on your issues, so that you have the facts you need to make decisions.

At the end of step two, the parties should have the same list of assets, debts, and issues. Hopefully, they will have resolved most disputes about the value of possessions, real estate, marital components, and other items. The issues that remain will be those that require negotiation.

Step 3: Resolution.

Every case reaches a conclusion. Every case is like a lock and every lock has a key – a solution. Whether the parties figure out the solution themselves, or with a mediator, or with a judge who hands them their key, the divorce case will end. Who is controlling what happens is the important part.

The Amicable Divorce Network focuses on negotiation, mediation, and other dispute-resolution tools to bring a case to an efficient conclusion. Control of the case remains solely with the couple. Many surveys and studies have been conducted, and it's been determined that only 5 percent of divorces end up having a final court trial. That means that as many as 95 percent of cases are settled outside the court system. The Amicable Divorce Network focuses on getting your case concluded by resolving issues, not on preparing you for trial.

Chapter 9
The Amicable Divorce Process
by Tracy Ann Moore-Grant

The Amicable Divorce Process was designed to assist parties and their chosen professionals to resolve their family law matters in a low-conflict and efficient manner. The process can be used to assist parties in all types of family law matters, as well as cases with complex issues or those with relatively few issues. The process allows parties to seek independent legal counsel in their case, exchange information and negotiate, and use experts to help them make decisions. Even with all these resources, the process remains streamlined and low-conflict. When disputes arise, parties agree to use alternate dispute resolution techniques to resolve issues outside the courtroom such as mediation, parent coordination, and arbitration. Members of the Amicable Divorce Network are invited to join based on their requisite education and experience combined with their reputation among their colleagues. They must focus on resolution instead of engaging in unnecessary litigation or over billing practices that can be an issue in the divorce industry.

The Amicable Divorce Network is comprised of many different professionals who are involved in the divorce process before, during, or after divorce. Members include: attorneys, mental health professionals, financial professionals, mediators, arbitrators, insurance agents, real estate agents, appraisers, coaches, wellness professionals, certified divorce financial analysts, certified divorce lending professionals, mortgage brokers, parent coordinators, business evaluators, and more who are available to assist you throughout this process, and after.

A current list of member professionals is on our website at **www.AmicableDivorceNetwork.com**, then Membership Directory.

The Amicable Divorce Process: Initial Case Forms

A traditional divorce begins with one party filing an action for divorce against the other with the court, and the other party served with that action, sometimes by law enforcement. With an Amicable Divorce the first forms executed are the retainer agreement with your attorney (or other professional as you may start an Amicable Divorce with any number of professionals), the *Acknowledgement of the Amicable Divorce Process*, and the *Agreement to Maintain Status Quo*.

The **Acknowledgement of the Amicable Divorce Process** details the process for the divorce and how it is different from a traditional divorce so that you understand everything about the Amicable Divorce Process. It is important to understand that an amicable divorce is a streamlined process. It is not an active court case, and the professionals do not have the ability to subpoena documents from a party or a third party (like directly from a bank). Please make sure you understand this document and ask your attorney if you have any questions.

The **Agreement to Maintain Status Quo** means that you will agree to keep certain things in place while the divorce is pending and follow certain agreed-upon rules. Often jurisdictions have a similar court order that is issued upon the filing of a divorce. Some are called *Standing Orders*. For example, in Georgia, each county has a different *Standing Order* and each jurisdiction has different rules for maintaining status quo, deadlines, mediation, and rules about children and finances. To make sure that everyone who uses the Amicable Divorce Process follows the same rules, the parties execute this form in which they agree to not cancel insurance, not cancel utilities, and not make any major financial changes and certain rules regarding children and parenting.

The two attorneys involved in your case will discuss all of the factors for your case and put into your **Case Planning Form** the following:

- Timeline to exchange financial and other needed information.
- Timeline to exchange other case documents and the deadlines.
- When mediation will occur and who are their selected mediators.
- If other professionals are used to assist in settlement (business valuation experts, CPAs, Parent Coordinators...), they are also identified in the document as well as any deadlines that they may have provided.
- The attorneys also decide when arbitration would occur if the case is not settled in mediation, and who are the selected arbitrators so that the case continues to move forward to a conclusion. Often this last piece is not done until after a failed mediation.

You should make sure that you communicate with your lawyer about all of the topics listed, and any other questions you may have, so that he or she knows how to structure your Case Planning Form to meet your needs. In litigation cases in the court system, parties are allowed up to six months, or longer, to engage in the exchange of documents, take depositions, and complete discovery. This extended and fixed timeline promotes protracted divorce cases and increased costs and attorney's fees, and in many cases that much time is completely unnecessary. However, your case timeline can be accelerated with the Amicable Divorce Process, or even slowed down in the event that is more appropriate for your situation. Once the Case Planning Form is complete, you will get a copy so you also are aware of all of the details and deadlines in your case. Don't worry, if deadlines need to be changed they can be. The Amicable Divorce Process is flexible to fit your needs.

Document and information exchange: If the parties need to exchange documents with one another, or get answers to any questions, these items are detailed on a Document and Information Exchange Form. Common documents that are exchanged are tax records such as W2 forms, 1099 forms, pay records, values of accounts and retirement accounts, and statements regarding debts. The deadlines for sending the requests, and providing responses, is detailed in the Case Planning Form. Parties can also upload documents into the secure document portal on dtour.life or share their transaction history in the program to avoid downloading or scanning multiple documents.

The Amicable Divorce Network has partnered with the technology company dtour.life as the host of the Amicable Divorce Network Technology Platform. Your lawyer will provide you with a login to dtour.life and specific information on how to use the program. Using dtour.life allows efficient gathering of financial information. You will sync your bank accounts, investments, and credit card accounts with the program. When you do this, the program will pull out budgeting information and organize spending into categories. You can also manually add items that are not "syncable," such as a home, cars, and other property. When using the program to the fullest, it will provide a Marital Balance Worksheet, which is constantly revised so that budgets, assets, and debts are updated every day.

When not using the program, professionals are required to constantly ask for updates from their client, and use that information to adjust Excel spreadsheets manually. This old-fashioned manner of data collection increased the time and expense of professionals and was prone to human error. Streamlining the data collection process significantly cuts down on time, cost, and errors. You will also be able to add any additional professionals to view this information such as financial analysts, mediators, or mortgage specialists to prevent providing the same information time and time again. The use of dtour.life is not required as some professionals and clients have different comfort levels with technology; but its use is intended to reduce time, human error, and cost, and increase transparency and efficiency.

Building Your Team

During this time when information is being gathered, it may be a good idea to seek advice and support from other members of the Amicable Divorce Network. The Amicable Divorce Network members are all vetted for their experience in family law, having a focus on resolution and engaging in fair billing practices. Often people going through the life change of a divorce have the need for many to assist them before, during, and after the process. The Amicable Divorce Network is made up of members of the following broad categories: Attorneys, Mental Health Professionals, Wellness Professionals, Coaches, and Financial, Mortgage and Real Estate Professionals. Whether you need a business valued, someone to assist you emotionally during this time, a coach to keep you on track and assist you, or a person to advise you on your mortgage options post-divorce, our network is designed to easily connect you to the best professionals in order to assist you.

Many are unaware that there are special certifications attributable to the divorce professions. A Certified Divorce Lending Professional can assist with evaluating your options about refinancing your home; a Certified Divorce Financial Analyst can assist with advising on how to divide marital assets and debts; and a Parent Coordinator can help with developing a Parenting Plan if you have minor children. There are many other members of the network who can assist you with any other needs you may have, including a home appraisal, obtaining a new health insurance policy, establishing new retirement accounts, or listing your home for sale. Mental health professionals can assist if you or your children need extra support during this time. Refer to the Amicable Divorce website to review the professionals available to you.

Negotiation and Settlement

Once parties have the information they need to engage in informed negotiations, they can begin working on an agreement. The parties may try to negotiate directly, but many feel unable to handle the emotions and complexities of their case, and that is entirely fine. The attorneys can exchange settlement proposals with one another to settle the case and try for an early agreement. Their professionals will work to capture the issues on which the clients do agree in an effort to only focus on contested issues. Mediation, however, is a common way to resolve any disputes. In a mediation, the parties meet with a mediator (often in separate rooms), a neutral professional who is trained to find common ground and assist in guiding the case to a settlement. Mediation can be done in person; but post-COVID-19, mediations have become conducted more frequently on Zoom, or a similar online format. Many have found great convenience in resolving their matter from the comfort of their own home. Mediations are a highly successful way to resolve issues, settle your case, and reach a binding agreement.

Sometimes parties want to take the time to specifically focus on their visitation and custody regarding their minor children. If this is the case, parties are encouraged to work with a Parent Coordinator. This professional can work with the parties to develop a full Parenting Plan. This plan details their year-round schedule of time with the child(ren), rights and obligations, and any special circumstances that need to be addressed. The Parenting Coordinator works with the parties to finalize the parenting issues between them and keep conversations and decisions focused on the best interest of the child.

If mediation is not successful, the Amicable Divorce Process is designed to have all issues resolved without involving the court system. Therefore, the parties are encouraged to hold an arbitration to resolve their remaining issues. An arbitration is also held with a neutral person; however, an arbitrator is vested with the authority to make a binding decision for the issues presented. Unlike a court hearing, an arbitration can be scheduled at a specific time agreeable to the parties with a result that is rendered quickly.

Like a court hearing, each party, through their attorney, can present documents, witnesses, and argument to an arbitrator to show their side of the issue in dispute. The efficiency and convenience of using arbitration is ideal for amicable divorce cases.

Exiting

It is important to know that you can exit the Amicable Divorce Process if you feel this is not the right process for you or you reconcile your marriage. However, it is very common at one point in every case that a client says, "This isn't amicable anymore." Divorce is highs and lows, compromise, and sometimes a harsh dose of reality. Although the Amicable Divorce Network strives to make divorce easier, quicker, and child-focused, we cannot make it stress- or challenge-free. Make sure you discuss exiting with your legal professional and team. They can help you walk through your options. If you do decide to choose traditional litigation, you can keep your team members and use the information you have already gathered in the new case. If you do exit, you will need to fill out a form to notify everyone that the Amicable Process has ended.

Finalization

Once a settlement is reached, or an arbitration order issued, the attorneys will prepare not only the settlement documents but also all documents needed to both file and finalize a divorce. Typically, all documents are filed on the same day so that the court knows that the matter is completely uncontested. Each county and jurisdiction has different procedures for how it finalizes a divorce. Some will require a short court appearance while others will finalize the matter completely without anyone ever entering the courthouse. In some states, from the day a divorce is filed, a divorce can be finalized 31 days later. In some states, a six-month waiting period, or longer, begins. Your chosen legal professional can guide you on the particular procedure for your jurisdiction, which may include filing before settlement. Often judges are not sitting around waiting on your particular deadline. Your attorney can assist with getting the divorce finalized when the deadline is reached. During this waiting period, some jurisdictions require parties with children to attend a Seminar for Divorcing Parents or a similar requirement for a divorce to be finalized. Your lawyer can give you further information on what is required in your area. The divorce is finalized with a document called a Final Judgment and Decree or Final Dissolution or similar that is executed by the judge assigned to your case.

The Amicable Divorce Process: Post-Finalization

Often once the divorce is finalized, more work needs to be done. Your attorney and other selected professionals can guide you on the next steps of getting a Qualified Domestic Relations Order, refinancing a mortgage, getting new health insurance, or establishing your own financial planning. We are here to assist you to properly transition to this new phase of your life.

The Amicable Divorce Process is designed to directly address the issues in your case and to partner you with resolution-minded and experienced professionals. If at any time you feel that this process is not for you and you want to either not pursue a divorce at all or instead file a divorce with the court, you have that option at all times. Should that occur, please discuss next steps with your attorney. The goal of the Amicable Divorce Network is to help individuals divorce respectfully and efficiently and move forward in their lives without the cost and conflict of traditional litigation.

Chapter 10
Comparing the Different Lanes of the Divorce Highway
by Tracy Ann Moore-Grant

When thinking of the "road" of divorce, imagine that this road has three lanes. On the left, you have the fastest lane – uncontested divorce. In the middle lane, you have amicable divorce. On the right, you have the slowest lane, which is traditional or contested divorce (for our friends in the United Kingdom, just reverse the lane order!). As described in the prior chapter, these are the three main ways to obtain a divorce.

It is important to note that for an uncontested or amicable divorce, or for any method other than the slow lane, both parties must agree to an alternative process – not traditional divorce. When one of the spouses will not agree to do something different – when he or she will not cooperate in the process, or cannot be located – then only the traditional (contested) route will be available.

In comparing divorce processes, it is true that amicable divorce is actually not the only process to operate in the middle lane. In some areas, groups of professionals have developed local processes and groups to help people through divorce; that type of assistance would fall into the middle lane. On a broader scale, another middle-lane process is called "collaborative divorce." Because that is also an out-of-court process, you may see many Amicable Divorce Network (ADN) processionals offer both amicable divorce and collaborative divorce.

Divorce Type	Uncontested	Amicable	Collaborative	Contested
Overall Cost	$0 – $7,500 (low-cost option, depending on lawyer use or DIY feasibility)	$2,500 – $8,000 (less costly, due to reduced conflict and use of technology)	$15,000 – $30,000+ (varies, based on complexity)	$15,000 – $100,000+ (can be very expensive)
Duration	1 to 3 months	1 to 4 months	3 to 6 months	1 to 3 years (varies by case complexity and court backlog)
Key Characteristics	Both parties agree on all terms (assets, custody, etc.). Simplified process; often involves only filing paperwork. Requires little to no court involvement or negotiation. Parties could only pay a filing fee or more for different DIY services.	Parties must hire lawyers in the Amicable Divorce Network. May or may not involve other professionals. Requires mutual cooperation and communication.	Both parties hire attorneys and a team of professionals (mental health, coaching, and financial professionals are required) and agree to work together respectfully. Negotiations are conducted outside court. Focuses on finding mutually agreeable solutions.	Parties cannot agree on terms, requiring court intervention. Involves attorneys, litigation, and often a trial. Can be emotionally and financially draining.

The statistics for the above were gathered from many sources, including Legal Zoom, the American Bar Association, the US Census Bureau, and an article in *Kiplinger Personal Finance* magazine by Amicable Divorce Network member Andrew Hatherley. The time frames and costs are averages collected from multiple sources. Both cost and length will depend on jurisdiction rules, waiting periods, the complexity of the case, and the degree that additional professionals are needed.

When comparing the two processes in the middle lane, it is useful to clarify the differences between amicable and collaborative divorce.

Amicable	Collaborative
Organized out-of-court process. Negotiations are conducted outside of court.	Organized out-of-court process.
Members are vetted first, then invited to join the Amicable Divorce Network. Training on the Amicable Divorce Process is free to all members.	Practitioners take the required collaborative law training first and can then offer collaborative divorce as a service.
Members include any professionals that help people before, during, and after divorce. All are vetted.	Collaborative professionals are lawyers, mediators, mental health professionals, certified divorce financial analysts, and coaches.
A centralized and uniform technology platform, dtour.life, is used in cases.	Practitioners may use various technology solutions – or not – in their work on a case.
The team of professionals – and the process itself – is designed for the parties, based on their needs and finances.	The team of collaborative professionals is set: both spouses' collaborative divorce attorneys, a financial specialist, a divorce coach, and a mental health professional (like a child psychologist) who specializes in family issues.
The choice of professionals is client-driven; they can select who they like from the vetted professionals.	Collaborative professionals often work in a "pod," limiting either client's ability to choose a different professional.
No professional will compromise his or her confidentiality, or will change anything about their traditional role. So, if a case is contested, no one has to excuse themselves from the case.	Collaborative professionals do not have confidentiality between a professional and a client. They feel that full transparency will lead to a resolution. However, if that does not occur, clients will need to hire new professionals for any contested case, because confidentiality was compromised.

When designing the Amicable Divorce Process, one thing we learned about collaborative divorce was that professionals were changing the traditional collaborative process. The modified version has been termed "collaborative lite" or "quasi-collaborative." The change occurred because – in many circumstances – traditional collaborative team members were not needed or were not affordable.

In the amicable process, we have often found that divorcing couples do not initially meet with an attorney. Amicable-minded individuals are cautious of attorneys, because some have a reputation for driving up cost and conflict. Therefore, the first team member could be any one of a number of network professionals, from a counselor to a Realtor. The Amicable Divorce Network encompasses all professionals who help clients before, during, and after divorce.

Pursuing an amicable divorce itself does not cost anything. The process has even been utilized by the University of Georgia Family Law Clinic to assist low-income parties with divorce. On the other end of the financial spectrum, we have also seen couples with multimillion-dollar estates pursuing amicable divorce. Because the Amicable Divorce Network offers a streamlined and personalized process, any couple can find what they need with the network's professionals.

The Amicable Divorce Network provides a neutral platform via its website for potential clients to research attorneys and other team members. They can choose the specific professionals they identify with and want on their team.

On the other hand, with collaborative divorce, team members often are working in a pod of professionals. If one spouse hires a particular attorney in a collaborative divorce, the other spouse must work with the other attorney in the pod as well as that pod's financial, mental health, and other set professionals. Again, with the ADN, clients choose who they want to work with.

And in an ADN case, every professional involved does their job in the same way that they would in any other case. No professional will compromise confidentiality or will change their role in any way to accomplish a settlement. Because of that, no professional will be forced to exit the case in the event it becomes contested. When those involved in the case find that they are dealing with reasonable, like-minded professionals who aren't out to "stick it" to them, tensions diminish and everyone can work cooperatively toward resolution.

The Amicable Divorce Network is currently the *only organization in the world that vets professionals prior to membership for being experienced and resolution-focused, and for engaging in fair billing practices.* After a member is accepted and joins the network, they are trained in the Amicable Divorce Process, free of charge. Members are then given the opportunity to become an "amicable advocate" with Certified Amicable Divorce Professional

(CADP) designation training. After becoming a CADP, members can also obtain specialty designations in areas like finances, special-needs children, and LGBTQ+ families. Different specialties are offered each year.

Other industry organizations are either education-based or dues-based. Collaborative divorce certification is education-based; once an individual has taken the training, they are deemed "collaborative." We at the ADN have unfortunately found that not all collaboratively trained professionals are a good fit for our group (although many are!). Dues-based organizations simply make someone a member after they pay a specified amount.

With 90 percent of divorcing couples categorizing their divorce as uncontested, the Amicable Divorce Network feels it is most important to make sure that couples are paired with professionals who will honor the parties' desire to have a low-conflict divorce. In fact, couples seeking low-conflict divorce often use the search terms "amicable" and "collaborative" synonymously when searching for a professional.

As divorcing parties have become more informed about the destructive nature of adversarial litigation, they are increasingly choosing low-conflict options. The Amicable Divorce Network offers clients another tool in seeking an out-of-court resolution.

PART 4
Who Benefits from an Amicable Divorce?

Chapter 11
Gray Divorce
61

Chapter 12
LGBTQIA+ Divorce
66

Chapter 13
Cultural Diversity in Divorce
70

Chapter 14
Who Can Benefit from the Amicable Divorce Process?
73

Chapter 11
Gray Divorce
by Andrew Hatherley

A "gray divorce" refers to someone who is divorcing over the age of 50. As someone getting divorced later in life, you face a unique set of challenges. Mainly, you don't have the time to rebuild your finances like someone getting divorced in their thirties or forties. This may mean working longer than you planned with a reduced standard of living. It may mean adjusting your retirement plans – or you may already be retired and forced to go back to work.

Here are some of the common concerns and questions I hear from potential clients:

"My husband managed all our retirement investments. I need help there."

"Will I need to continue working to make ends meet?"

"How will my Social Security be affected by divorce?"

"Will I need to re-enter the workplace?"

"If my ex-wife and I sell the house, where will I live?"

"How do I get a mortgage if I don't meet the income guidelines for a loan?"

All these concerns boil down to a core concern: "Am I going to be okay?"

My focus as a financial advisor and Certified Divorce Financial Analyst (CDFA®) specializing in gray divorce came as a result of my own difficult divorce experience. After my divorce, I decided that the most valuable benefit I could give my clients would be to educate them – to teach them about mistakes I made during my divorce. That led to me to start *The Gray Divorce Podcast*.

What's Behind the Gray Divorce Revolution?

Here are six of the reasons for the rise in gray divorce:

1. Divorce is increasingly accepted in our society.
2. A growing share of older adults are in second or third marriages – and remarriages are more likely to end in divorce than first marriages.
3. There is an increased participation of women in the labor force. Divorce is a more feasible option when women have the economic freedom to support themselves outside of marriage.
4. Increased life expectancy decreases the likelihood that marriages will end through death, and increases the exposure to the risk of divorce.
5. The rise in the personal development industry encourages people to follow their dreams, or to end damaging relationships and start anew.
6. Children have left the house and are no longer a buffer or distraction. Couples are interacting more often, sometimes to the detriment of the relationship.

Whatever the cause of a gray divorce, the key issue is that you are rebuilding your financial and personal life late in the game. Here are some issues to understand.

The Two Rs: Retirement Plans and Real Estate

The primary home and retirement plans are often the two largest assets in divorce. For people divorcing later in life, retirement plans are often quite substantial assets, and there is often a lot of equity in the home as the mortgage has been paid down.

However, consider that older people are typically moving from an asset *accumulation phase* to a *distribution phase* where assets must now support them through their retirement years. This is why property division late in life is so important. You no longer have 30 or 40 years to re-accumulate assets.

With retirement plans in divorce, the IRS allows the tax-free transfer of an IRA or qualified plan from one spouse to another. A qualified domestic relations order (QDRO) will split a qualified plan, whether it is a defined contribution plan (typically 401ks), or a defined benefit plan (pensions). If you need some money, you can avoid the 10 percent penalty if you are under age 59 1/2 by taking money directly from the 401k pursuant to a QDRO.

One thing to note about pensions: like a 401k, a QDRO can split a pension. But if you and your spouse decide not to split the pension, the income stream from that pension can be expressed in terms of a present value. This amount can be used to exchange for other assets.

One thing that older divorcees, particularly those in their sixties and older, should know is that home equity conversion mortgages, commonly known as reverse mortgages, may provide a creative solution to cash flow and or financing issues later in life.

Spousal Support

Most states have statutes that list factors that courts consider when making spousal support awards. Generally, the criteria affecting the calculations for alimony are:

- The total combined income of both spouses from almost all sources.
- The capacity of each spouse to pay.
- The needs of each spouse.

Judges usually have discretion in awarding alimony. Some states use guidelines for alimony while a few use a formula to calculate alimony. Because alimony closely follows the tricky negotiations surrounding issues of property division, alimony itself – the amount due annually and the length of time one spouse pays it – is unpredictable.

Some questions that often arise around alimony and gray divorce:

1. **What is the normal retirement age?** Traditionally it's been thought of as age 65. But people are living longer than ever. There are issues of employability and health concerns, particularly for the older

population. Increasingly, we are seeing the desire to keep working to have meaning and purpose in our lives. Of course, there is also the need to keep working to meet life expenses, if necessary.

2. **When is early retirement legitimate?** Courts may react negatively to one spouse retiring early if it is likely to have a negative effect on the cash flow of the supported spouse. Some courts won't modify spousal support without an adequate explanation of good faith by the retiring party.

3. **When is modification warranted?** Courts have been unpredictable in their rulings to grant modifications regarding alimony based on the regular retirement age of the payor. Some spouses getting divorced late in their sixties or seventies expect permanent alimony, but this is becoming much less common. Only a handful of states may grant permanent alimony.

Social Security

People going through a gray divorce should make it a priority to understand the rules about a divorced spouse's Social Security benefits to maximize retirement income. Social Security benefits are a key component of retirement income and probably the most misunderstood.[1]

What's important to know is that if you are 62 or older and were married to your ex for 10 consecutive years or longer you may be able to collect up to half of your former spouse's Social Security benefit based on their earnings history. But you will only get a divorced spouse benefit if it exceeds your own benefit based on your own earnings record. You will not receive both benefits combined. When someone qualifies for two benefits, the Social Security Administration pays the higher amount.

---

1 https://www.kiplinger.com/retirement/how-gray-divorce-affects-social-security-benefits

Other eligibility criteria include:

- Your ex qualifies for retirement benefits or Social Security Disability Insurance (SSDI).
- Both you and your ex must be at least age 62 before you can claim as an ex-spouse.
- You must not be remarried.
- You and your ex must be divorced for two years or longer, or your ex must already be claiming retirement benefits.

Conclusion

In a gray divorce, you simply have less time to recover financially. You need to do everything you can to ensure that your divorce settlement puts you on a solid foundation to grow both personally and financially after divorce.

There is life after divorce, even gray divorce – *especially* gray divorce! Put your hard-earned years of experience to good use and build the best life possible for your next chapter.

Andrew Hatherley CDFA®, CRPC®
Host, The Gray Divorce Podcast
Certified Amicable Divorce Professional
Las Vegas, Nevada
Greenville, South Carolina

Chapter 12
LGBTQIA+ Divorce
by Dennis G. Collard

Despite great progress, many LGBTQIA+ people still face threats and violence, workplace hostility, rejection by family and friends, and many other challenges in society. Many members of the LGBTQIA+ community are not able to lean on their family members during a divorce, because their family did not support their union in the first place. That lack of approval and support can make a divorce even more difficult.

On the legal front, nationwide marriage equality only became law in 2015, as a result of the *Obergefell v. Hodges* case. And it was only in 2003 that certain acts of physical intimacy became legal under *Lawrence v. Texas*. Certain employment protections for people in the LGBTQIA+ community did not arrive until the *Bostock v. Clayton* decision in 2020.

So, considering the long arc of civil rights struggles, protections for LGBTQIA+ people are relatively recent. And – with some exceptions, of course – there is a long history of the courts and the greater legal system treating the LGBTQIA+ community with insensitivity and prejudice. To make matters worse, the traditional divorce process shatters support systems by forcing friends and family members to take sides. That can be devastating to an LGBTQIA+ person who relies on such special relationships for support. In a broad sense, traditional divorce pits the parties against each other in adversarial litigation. One party is the plaintiff, and the other is the defendant. Litigation encourages a hostile approach; what LGBTQIA+ people need is exactly the opposite.

The Amicable Divorce Network (ADN) replaces litigation with a structured, private parallel process. It greatly reduces the stress on LGBTQIA+ people who might worry that the legal system will not understand their unique struggles during divorce. The Amicable Divorce Process is a safe place for LGBTQIA+ people to bring their sensitive family law issues to professionals who understand and celebrate them. Amicable Divorce Network professionals have the practical knowledge to help LGBTQIA+ individuals navigate a way forward.

Going to court is like walking onto a stage where intimate facts are revealed. With centuries of prejudice written into the law, standing before a court as an LGBTQIA+ person can be frightening. What if I am coming out, or transitioning, and my soon-to-be-former spouse uses my sexual orientation or gender identity against me? Will the judge be biased against me, or simply not understand me? What if I am transgender, and my name in court documents does not match my actual gender identity? Will I be taken advantage of because my "legal" marriage was delayed? Will I lose my children? Will I receive the same courtesy and understanding that straight, cisgender people receive?

Cisgender (people whose gender identity matches the sex on their birth certificate) and straight people do not have these basic fears, because their sexual orientation and gender identity (SOGI) is the "norm." Divorce is hard enough. Apprehension about presenting one's SOGI compounds the stress. Therefore, the out-of-court nature of the Amicable Divorce Network process is of great benefit to the LGBTQIA+ community. If a divorcing couple remains in the ADN process, they will never step into a courtroom or be questioned before a judge regarding their case.

Divorce can bring out the worst in people, but the ADN process removes legal concepts and information that are sometimes used as weapons in litigation. For example, legal technicalities and gaps in the law are sometimes used by a "legal" parent to exclude (or "de-parent") the other parent from a child's life. Such action is the worst kind of weaponization of legal prejudice. To be blunt, the ADN process does not tolerate the kind of hostility that drives attacks on parenthood. Rather, within the safety and sensitivity of the ADN process, the parties and lawyers are respectful of parenthood. The rights of both parents can be solidified; parenthood is not attacked, nor at risk.

The ADN process also fosters and encourages financial creativity. For many LGBTQIA+ people, a legal marriage and divorce will allow for division of retirement, alimony, and other assets. But for some couples who are breaking up, the many challenges of being LGBTQIA+ simply never allowed for the formalization of a "legal" marriage early on. Many relationships started before marriage equality, meaning that the accumulation of marital property was delayed until the legal marriage.

And, many LGBTQIA+ people simply do not enter a legal marriage, due to lack of family support or other factors. A delayed legal marriage – or the lack of one – can put one of the parties at a great disadvantage when it comes to the division of hard-earned assets or to awarding financial support. Litigation encourages the "monied" spouse to hoard assets and deny support.

The ADN process allows for problem-solving that is not driven by legal brinkmanship. Rather, the professionals involved can help guide the process to an equitable result – even if the LGBTQIA+ couple was not "legally" married, or if the legal marriage was delayed.

The ADN process also provides a non-adversarial environment that is conducive to addressing relationships with nontraditional gender roles. As much as we try to break free of them, gender stereotypes influence family law. But many same-gender couples face the opposite problem – a lack of gender role differentiation. So, paradoxically, the lack of preconceptions based on gender can present a challenge.

One of the parties might be reluctant to identify as more or less dependent than their spouse, or deserving of benefits that might – accurately or inaccurately – be associated with one gender or the other. The ADN process gives the divorcing couple the time, space, and support necessary to break through gender prejudices. The spouses can be seen as individual people with unique roles in the marriage.

Two real-world examples help illustrate how the ADN process can apply to members of the LGBTQIA+ community:

PART 4: WHO BENEFITS FROM AN AMICABLE DIVORCE?

Twenty-five years ago, long before marriage equality, two women were married in a religious ceremony and changed their last names to a new married name. They combined their assets, and they planned and invested together. They had children by using donor sperm and artificial insemination. The woman who did not provide the egg or womb never legally adopted the children. The parties were legally married in 2015, after the Obergefell decision; however, the couple filed for divorce in 2024. One woman could have claimed that the pre-Obergefell assets in her name were not in the marital pot. And the other woman could have claimed that she was the sole parent, because there was no adoption by the other woman. An adversarial litigation process would have destroyed this family, as each woman had legal ammunition to use against the other. Instead, within the Amicable Divorce Process, the assets were divided in an equitable way (despite the delayed "legal" marriage) and the parental rights of both women were solidified.

An opposite-gender straight couple were married and had a child. The former husband then came out as transgender and announced their intention to transition. And so, what had been a husband/father and wife/mother combination was becoming two wives/mothers. In traditional divorce, an incredibly intimate and scary time for the transitioning party could have become a nightmare; she could have been attacked for being trans. Instead, the ADN process provided a team of lawyers, mental health professionals, and a neutral accountant to make the divorce as "normal" as possible. Family therapy was provided to help the child shift from having a mom and dad to having two loving moms.

Because the Amicable Divorce Process is private and respectful, concepts of mutual respect and support can remain intact, even when the road gets bumpy. The ADN process cannot guarantee an "easy" divorce, but it can guarantee a dignified process that is fostered by professionals who care deeply about the needs of the LGBTQIA+ community. In fact, the Amicable Divorce Network considers equality and respect for all to be one of its most basic tenets. Divorcing couples can be free to be themselves fully, to be vulnerable and share their anxiety, and to know that the process will not be adversarial or public.

LGBTQIA+ stands for lesbian, gay, bisexual, transgender, queer, intersex, and asexual, and the "+" stands for all of the other wonderful varieties of sexual orientation and gender identity (SOGI). Everyone has a sexual orientation (for example, lesbian, gay, straight, bi) and a gender identity (such as male, female, nonbinary), either of which may be fluid or not fit into any current terminology. In a legal setting, the terms "sex" and "gender" are often used interchangeably, but the term "sex" is generally centered on perceived biological characteristics at birth (which may be unclear), while "gender" encompasses concepts of self, identity, and expression (sometimes described as "what's in your brain").

Dennis G. Collard
Family Law Attorney
Registered Mediator/Arbitrator
Certified Amicable Divorce Professional
Atlanta, Georgia

Chapter 13
Cultural Diversity in Divorce
by Neena Saxena

For couples with diverse cultural or religious backgrounds, divorce can become even more complex than usual. It is vital for such couples to proactively safeguard their individual and shared cultural and religious identities. By employing strategic legal tools, cultural sensitivity, and mutual respect, diverse couples can ensure that their heritage and values are honored during and after the divorce.

Respecting and retaining individual cultural identity can be achieved through an amicable divorce. With an emphasis on collaboration and communication, divorcing spouses from diverse racial and religious backgrounds can benefit from an amicable process. By fostering a cooperative environment, the Amicable Divorce Process reduces potential racial and religious conflicts, and promotes understanding.

Diverse racial families should not count on the courts to protect their interests. In the United States, 28 states do not have any Black justices on the bench – and across all state high courts, only 17 percent of justices are Black, Latino, Asian American, or Native American. Those low percentages are problematic for divorcing couples who come from diverse backgrounds.

Culture and religion play pivotal roles in shaping a family's identity and practices. They influence parenting styles, celebrations, moral values, dietary habits, and community interactions. When a couple decides to divorce, cultural aspects can cause conflict if not carefully addressed.

Preserving cultural and religious practices is particularly important for children, because it helps maintain their sense of identity and continuity despite familial changes. The court system, however, may not automatically prioritize those considerations. Because of that, it is essential for couples to advocate for their values. Be aware that certain jurisdictions' court systems may not have the knowledge or forethought to consider a family's cultural and religious priorities, even if that issue is explicitly raised by the parties or their counsel. Moreover, certain special cultural, ethnic, or religious dates may not line up with Christian-oriented school calendars for holidays.

The Amicable Divorce Process offers benefits in racially and religiously diverse contexts, and can prevent an unnecessary escalation of tensions. One of the most effective ways to protect cultural and religious values is through a well-drafted settlement agreement. Couples can specify provisions related to religious upbringing, participation in cultural events, or observance of traditions. For instance, they can outline how children will celebrate religious holidays, attend places of worship, or participate in language and heritage education. By including those types of details, couples can ensure that their particular values are legally recognized and enforceable.

In any divorce case involving children, child custody arrangements can be very challenging. But when you try to determine how the children's culture and religion will be preserved, post-divorce, that can create further friction. Through the Amicable Divorce Process, the spouses can educate their attorneys, the mediator, or other professionals involved in the process. They can explain why those distinct cultural, ethnic, or religious aspects are integral to their family's identity.

Those discussions can then lead to parenting plans that explicitly address how the children will be exposed to their specific heritage and culture, and how they will celebrate certain holidays. Plans could include agreements about attending religious schools, maintaining dietary practices, or celebrating cultural festivals.

For families with children, an amicable approach ensures that both parents can work together to raise their children in a nurturing environment that values diversity and respect. If a divorce becomes contentious, it is highly unlikely that the court system's resolution will give priority to the couple's culture or religious practices. Therefore, an amicable divorce minimizes the risk of conflicts escalating. An amicable divorce provides a platform for each partner to uphold their cultural and religious values without fear of disrespect or condemnation.

Neena Saxena, Esq.
Attorney, Patterson Moore Butler
Certified Mediator with the Georgia Office of Dispute Resolution
Certified Guardian ad Litem
Certified Amicable Divorce Professional
Atlanta, Georgia
Boston, Massachusetts

Chapter 14
Who Can Benefit from the Amicable Divorce Process?
by Tracy Ann Moore-Grant

An amicable divorce and the Amicable Divorce Process is a beneficial process to many families.

Special needs children: Families with special needs children will benefit from the flexible timeline, child focus, and accessibility to experts to prepare a Special Needs Trust.

Complex and high asset cases: These families benefit from the private process as details about the family assets are not aired in a public courtroom or docket. Parties can also take the time and care needed to value assets, hire proper financial experts, and determine results on their own timeline.

Mental health: Anyone with mental health issues including depression and anxiety will like the low-conflict process as well as the fact that the process can be done from the comfort of home if needed and slowed down, or sped up, as may be needed.

Anyone who desires a child-focused, economical, low-conflict, and personal process will benefit from the use of the Amicable Divorce Network and its professionals.

Chapter 15
Preparing Emotionally
by Katheen Shack

Divorce is 95 percent emotional and 5 percent legal. Coping with your emotions starts long before the legal divorce process begins, and emotional turmoil can linger for months after the papers are signed. But there are steps you can take to proactively manage your emotions during a divorce. When faced with a change like divorce, you want to look at it as objectively as possible, even though that may be difficult. Have faith that you will successfully move through it. You will be stronger for having survived such a life-changing event!

Begin by taking an inventory of your thoughts and feelings. Are they grounded and realistic, or are they distorted and agitated? Are you optimistic and solution-focused, or pessimistic? Are you struggling with feelings of guilt or shame? Guilt can cause you to feel like you have no right to ask for what you need in a divorce. It may cause you to negotiate unbalanced, unrealistic settlements that you will later regret.

Get in touch with your thoughts and feelings by meditating or relaxing, journaling, sharing with others, and going to individual counseling. It helps to share your hopes, needs, expectations, and vulnerabilities with supportive and objective people. You can talk with friends, family members, a support group (or two!), and professionals who you trust.

Create a gratitude list to help remind you of the people and the aspects of your life that you are grateful for. Remind yourself of your strengths. As A.A. Milne wrote, "Promise me you'll always remember that you are braver than you believe, and stronger than you seem, and smarter than you think."

Harness your thoughts. To minimize your anxiety, look at facts ("what is"), instead of making faulty assumptions ("what if?"). When you take charge of your thoughts in a crisis, it will help you to feel empowered instead of anxious, weak, and immobile.

Take control of your behaviors. Once you've assessed your thoughts and feelings, taking control is best achieved by decreasing anxiety-provoking behaviors and by increasing anxiety-reducing behaviors. What does that look like?

- Minimize viewing negative, often inaccurate, stories on social media about bitter divorces.
- Avoid conspiracy theories.
- Ask for help when you need it and listen to experts who have accurate information about the divorce process.
- Do more of what helps you feel in control of your thoughts, feelings, behaviors, and environment.

People thrive on structure and routine. Set a daily routine for yourself and your family; maintain a structure during the divorce. Go for a walk; be active. Eat healthy and get enough sleep. Maintaining or developing your spiritual path may also ease your anxiety; it can remind you to never lose faith. Have patience with others, give others the benefit of the doubt, and promote cooperation.

Gather as much information as possible. Knowledge can be empowering and calming. Talking with professionals and others who have been through divorce can help you feel prepared and proactive, even prior to the legal process. Gathering financial information aids with setting realistic expectations for post-divorce budgeting, and can bring peace of mind.

Will This Grief Get Better?

You may be experiencing erratic emotions or have difficulty concentrating. In the early stages of the grief and recovery process, it can be challenging to think clearly or to make good decisions. That's normal during the divorce process; the emotional impact of divorce is as significant as the grief someone experiences when a close family member dies. The death of a marriage – and hopes and dreams that went into it – requires grieving in order to heal.

Even though it may seem like the emotional upheaval is endless, the feelings will fade typically within two years of the initial separation. Some people may experience the stages of grief in quick succession; others may experience them gradually in the divorce process. And, you may bounce back and forth between the stages as different situations trigger emotions.

Honor the grief, allow yourself to walk through it, and find healing. High-conflict divorce usually occurs when at least one spouse resists grieving and becomes stuck.

There are five stages of grief. According to psychiatrist Elisabeth Kübler-Ross, the grief stages are denial, anger, bargaining, depression, and acceptance. Each of these has benefits and risks.

1. **Denial** blunts the initial shock and pain of a separation or divorce. It numbs the pain until you can face the necessary tasks. However, if you get stuck in the denial stage, you may not be open to hearing about your options. Denial leads to being unprepared; for example, you may not be ready for an upcoming mediation or hearing because you refuse to acknowledge that you need to gather information or hire an attorney. Your emotions may also block your logic; you may not be able to make decisions, and mediation or negotiations may end up not being successful.

2. **Anger** can give you the energy to be actively engaged in the divorce process and can enhance your decision-making abilities. For instance, if an affair has happened, then anger about the betrayal can motivate you. You will be likely to maintain boundaries and take the necessary steps to complete the divorce process. However, if you are stuck in anger, you will likely make poor judgments, engage in futile conflict, and behave in ways that your children see as negative. People stuck in the anger stage are bitter, resentful, uncontrolled, and self-destructive. Fights over children or property can be propelled by angry feelings. Moreover, angry people may exhibit expensive, destructive, dangerous

actions and want unnecessary or questionable legal maneuvering. Angry people run a higher chance of being fired by their attorney.
3. **Bargaining** is helpful when there is a chance that the relationship can be saved. During the bargaining stage, discernment counseling, couples counseling, or separation may help. However, being stuck in this stage when your spouse has moved beyond reconciliation will look like you're trying to gain control. If the other person has moved on, trying to continue your marital connection and influence, making desperate promises, trying to reconcile, or even making sexual overtures will be seen as aggressive and counterproductive. Negative behaviors in this stage can be expensive, destructive, and dangerous. And as in the anger stage, people stuck in the bargaining stage often engage in unnecessary and questionable legal maneuvering in an attempt to maintain control.
4. **Some depression** is normal, and necessary to grieving. Sadness is a healthy emotional response to the ending of an important relationship. But if your depression interferes with a basic level of functioning and blocks progress in the divorce, you will need to see a counselor. Or you may possibly want to consult a psychiatrist. It is important to have a professional determine whether you have clinical depression, so that you can take steps to manage it. Spouses who are parents need to be able to manage their own mental health so that they can be present and involved with their children. It is crucial to keep your children from taking on the role of caretaker while you are going through a divorce.
5. **Acceptance** is when you are able to acknowledge the reality of divorce and embrace the readiness to move on. It can lead to heightened communication between spouses, facilitate co-parenting cooperation, and help make long-term planning possible. It is the most productive stage for successful mediations and negotiations.

Self-Care Is Crucial

Take time to care for yourself. Self-care can include meditating, praying, exercising, doing projects and hobbies, going to counseling, reading, doing a puzzle, devotionals, or listening to music. Trying a new recipe or watching a funny movie can relieve stress. Maintaining a gratitude list will remind you of the positives in your life on the difficult days.

Be present with those you love. Cherish your healthy relationships. Play with your children and pets. Stay connected and active with family and friends, support groups, and colleagues.

Turn your divorce into an opportunity. It is a time to self-reflect and make necessary changes. It may also be a time to recover from some unhealthy habits. People who are hurting tend to make shortsighted choices based on emotional reactions. Often, those decisions do not consider others' best interests. Working through your emotions and learning to manage them will help you be able to "ride the roller coaster" while making sound decisions for yourself and your family. Do not lose faith in the end of the story!

Kathleen Shack, MS, LMFT
Family Solutions Counseling
Certified Gottman Couples Therapist
Certified Discernment Counselor
Certified Amicable Divorce Professional
Divorce Coach
Divorce Mediator
Alpharetta, Georgia

Chapter 16
The Psychological Stages of Divorce
by Stephanie Robins

If you're sitting here reading this, chances are you are contemplating divorce or already in the midst of it. Let me start by saying that you're not alone, and it is completely normal to feel overwhelmed, confused, or emotionally drained. After all, divorce is something no one plans for. When you got married, you didn't imagine that one day you would look for a guide to help you navigate the end of that relationship. But life happens; and sometimes, even with the best intentions, marriages don't work out how we had hoped.

As a licensed clinical social worker for over 25 years, I've helped individuals, couples, and families navigate the emotional challenges that come with divorce. It has been a privilege to walk with people through every stage of this journey. I've seen firsthand how understanding the emotional side of divorce can make all the difference to how smoothly the process unfolds – not just emotionally, but legally as well.

In this chapter, we will explore the psychological stages of divorce – how they can affect you, and, more importantly, how you can manage them to make better decisions during the legal process.

The Emotional Roller Coaster: An Overview of the Stages

Divorce isn't just about dividing assets or signing papers. Emotionally, it's a process that often mirrors the stages of grief. These stages don't necessarily come in order; you might bounce between them as you go through the process. They include:

1. **Denial:** "This can't be happening to me."
2. **Anger:** "How could they do this to me?"
3. **Bargaining:** "Maybe if I change, things will go back to the way they were."

4. **Depression:** "I can't handle this; I feel so lost."

5. **Acceptance:** "It's time to move forward and rebuild my life."

Recognizing where you are in these stages is incredibly important because each stage brings its own emotional challenges that can impact your legal decisions.

The Pre-Divorce Stage: When Denial Takes the Lead

Before divorce is even on the table, many people spend time in the **pre-divorce stage**, where feelings of dissatisfaction start creeping in, but they're pushed aside or ignored. You might find yourself withdrawing emotionally from your partner, avoiding tough conversations, or throwing yourself into work or other distractions to avoid facing the reality of the situation.

Take Sarah, a former client of mine. She came to therapy because she felt "stuck" in her marriage. Sarah loved her husband, but felt emotionally distant as if they were living two separate lives under the same roof. She hadn't yet considered divorce because the thought terrified her. In our sessions, we explored her feelings and helped her acknowledge that the emotional distance wasn't something that would magically fix itself. This realization was hard for her but necessary for moving forward.

The **pre-divorce stage** is often filled with denial because it's scary to admit that your marriage is in trouble. If you're in this stage, the first step is acknowledging the truth of your emotions. Therapy can be beneficial here because it gives you a safe space to process these feelings without rushing to a decision.

Disillusionment: When Resentment Starts Taking Over

Once the cracks in the relationship become undeniable, the next stage is often **disillusionment**, where frustration and resentment build up. This is where I see a lot of clients, like John, come in. John was angry – really angry. He felt like he had sacrificed so much for his marriage only to have it fall apart. In our sessions, he would vent about all the small things his wife did that drove him crazy; and his resentment had built up to the point where they could barely communicate.

If you're in the **disillusionment stage**, it's easy to get stuck in resentment, focusing on how unfair things feel. But here's the thing: staying stuck in resentment can cloud your judgment when making important legal decisions. John, for example, wanted to fight for full custody of his kids – not because he thought it was best for them, but because he wanted to hurt his wife. Through therapy, we worked on shifting his focus from anger to what was, indeed, best for his children. In the end, he was able to create a more balanced custody arrangement.

If you're feeling this way, it's crucial to recognize that your emotions – while valid – can impact your legal decisions. Slowing down and seeking help from a therapist or mediator can help you avoid making decisions out of spite that you may regret later.

The Initiator and Responder: Two Different Journeys

In every divorce, there's often an **initiator** and a **responder**. The initiator is the one who first suggests ending the marriage, while the responder is typically caught off guard. This dynamic creates an emotional imbalance that can seriously affect the divorce process.

The initiator has often already moved through some of the emotional stages before even bringing up divorce, while the responder may still be in shock or denial. This was the case with Amanda and Jake, another couple I worked with. Amanda had been emotionally detaching for over a year before telling Jake she wanted a divorce. When Jake heard the news, he was devastated, still very much in denial, while Amanda was ready to move forward.

In these cases, communication becomes difficult. The initiator might be eager to finalize things, while the responder needs more processing time. As Amanda and Jake discovered, having a therapist to help mediate these conversations can bridge the gap and keep things moving forward while the responder works through their emotional process.

How Emotions Influence Your Legal Decisions

Your emotions don't just affect your feelings – they affect your decisions. For example, **anger** can drive you to make decisions out of spite, like pushing for more assets than you need, or fighting over custody to get back at your ex. On the flip side, **guilt** can cause you to give up too much, perhaps agreeing to a financial settlement that isn't fair just because you feel bad about the situation.

One of my clients, Tom, was so guilt-ridden over his role in his marriage's breakdown that he was ready to give his wife everything – half of his retirement, the house, and even full custody of their children. In our sessions, we worked on separating his guilt from the practical decisions he needed to make. Tom realized that giving up everything wouldn't make things better for anyone, including his kids, and he was able to come to a fairer agreement.

It's important to remember that emotions like guilt or anger are temporary; but the decisions you make during divorce can affect you for years to come. Take your time, get professional advice, and make sure your choices are driven by logic, not emotions.

Acceptance: The Light at the End of the Tunnel

Finally, we reach the stage of **acceptance**, where you begin to detach from the marriage and look toward the future emotionally. This is where natural healing begins. You can make decisions more objectively, cooperate more efficiently, and focus on building a new life.

This stage isn't about giving up – it's about moving forward. One of my clients, Marissa, came to me feeling completely drained. She had been through the denial, anger, and depression stages; but after several months of therapy, she reached a point where she was ready to move on. We worked together to help her create a vision for her post-divorce life. She took up new hobbies, started focusing on her career, and rebuilt her support network. Marissa was proof that while divorce is hard, it can also be the start of something new and exciting.

Conclusion: You've Got This

Divorce is tough – there's no sugarcoating that. But by understanding the emotional stages you're going through, you can make better decisions for yourself and your future. Take your time, seek help when needed, and remember there is a light at the end of the tunnel. You will get through this. And on the other side, there's an opportunity to rebuild and create a life that brings you peace and happiness.

Stephanie Robins, LCSW, CADP
Certified Amicable Divorce Professional
Alpharetta Family Therapy
Alpharetta, Georgia

Chapter 17
The Role of Mental Health Professionals
by Stephanie Robins

Going through a divorce is never easy; but an amicable divorce – where both parties choose to work together toward a low-conflict and efficient resolution – can make the process far less painful and stressful. Achieving an amicable split involves more than just legal agreements; it also requires managing the emotional and psychological aspects of ending a significant relationship. Parties may feel they need to let go of difficult feelings and emotions and need an outlet to do so. This is where the support of a mental health professional becomes invaluable. Even when both partners are committed to a cooperative process, divorce still triggers strong emotions that can complicate decision-making and communication. A mental health professional helps guide you through these challenges, supporting you in navigating the divorce with clarity, emotional stability, and long-term well-being in mind.

How a Mental Health Professional Helps You Through an Amicable Divorce

Divorce is a significant life change, and even in amicable situations, emotions can run high. Mental health professionals play a critical role in helping you manage these emotions, develop healthier communication skills, and move through the process with less stress. Their goal is to support your emotional well-being and help you make decisions that align with your long-term goals and values.

One particularly valuable service that mental health professionals provide is **discernment counseling**. This form of brief therapy, discussed more thoroughly in another chapter, should be seriously considered by couples.

If you have children, **co-parent counseling** can be a game-changer. A mental health professional works with you and your ex-spouse to establish a cooperative, co-parenting relationship, with the focus squarely on your children's well-being. This process helps reduce conflict between parents, which in turn minimizes the emotional impact of the divorce on your children. Whether it's through teaching effective communication strategies or mediating difficult conversations, mental health professionals ensure that you and your ex-spouse can work together to provide a stable, loving environment for your children.

You may also benefit from working with a **divorce coach**, who provides emotional support and helps you stay focused throughout the divorce process. Divorce coaches assist with communication skills, stress management, and goal-setting, helping you keep a clear head during legal proceedings and negotiations. They can also help you visualize your life post-divorce and set realistic, empowering goals for the future.

How Do You Know if You Need a Mental Health Professional?

You may be wondering if you need a mental health professional during your divorce, especially if it's amicable. The truth is, even amicable divorces can bring up intense emotions, and a mental health professional can provide invaluable support. Here are a few signs that you might benefit from working with one:

Overwhelming emotions: If you find yourself feeling anxious, depressed, or unable to manage your emotions, a mental health professional can help you process these feelings and develop coping strategies.

Communication issues: Even in amicable divorces, communication can break down. If you and your spouse are struggling to have productive conversations, a therapist or divorce coach can help facilitate better communication and conflict resolution.

Concerns about children: If you're worried about how the divorce is affecting your children, a mental health professional can provide guidance on co-parenting and help ensure that your children's emotional needs are met.

Feeling stuck: If you're having trouble moving forward or feel overwhelmed by decisions, a mental health professional can help you gain clarity and find the strength to make decisions that align with your values and future goals.

If any of these resonate with you, seeking support from a mental health professional can make the divorce process more manageable and emotionally healthier.

Qualifications of Mental Health Professionals

Mental health professionals involved in amicable divorces are highly trained, with expertise in helping individuals manage the emotional complexities of divorce. They are not only equipped with clinical knowledge, but they also specialize in understanding family dynamics, communication patterns, and trauma – all of which can arise during the divorce process.

Here are the key types of mental health professionals you might encounter in an amicable divorce:

Licensed clinical social workers (LCSWs): These professionals hold a Master of Social Work (MSW) degree and specialize in family dynamics, emotional trauma, and divorce-related issues. LCSWs are skilled in helping clients manage transitions and emotions, often acting as mediators as parent coordinators in high-conflict situations.

Licensed Marriage and Family Therapists (LMFTs) have a master's degree in Marriage and Family Therapy with a focus on couples and family systems. LMFTs are skilled in helping couples transition from a married relationship to a healthy co-parenting relationship, working with all members of the family system (including the children) as they transition into their new normal, and helping blended families create harmony.

Licensed professional counselors (LPCs): LPCs have a master's degree in counseling and focus on helping individuals and couples work through emotional and psychological challenges. In the divorce process, they provide therapeutic support and coping strategies to help you manage stress, anxiety, and difficult emotions.

Psychologists (PsyD, PhD): Clinical psychologists hold a doctoral degree and have extensive training in diagnosing and treating mental health issues. They are often called upon when more complex mental health concerns arise during divorce, such as depression, trauma, or anxiety. Psychologists can also conduct assessments, particularly in cases where child custody evaluations or psychological fitness are in question.

Divorce coaches and parent coordinators: These professionals focus specifically on helping individuals navigate the divorce process. A divorce coach helps with emotional stability, communication strategies, and goal-setting, while a parent coordinator works to resolve parenting conflicts and establishes cooperative co-parenting strategies. Credentials for both roles vary greatly by jurisdiction.

Each of these professionals brings a unique set of skills to the table, but they all share the common goal of helping you manage the emotional toll of divorce and make decisions that support your long-term well-being.

Benefits of Using a Mental Health Professional in Divorce

There are many benefits to working with a mental health professional during an amicable divorce:

Reduce emotional conflict: By offering guidance and emotional support, they help you manage your feelings and keep conflict with your ex-spouse to a minimum.

Improve communication: Mental health professionals teach effective communication strategies, which are crucial for peaceful negotiations and future co-parenting.

Support long-term well-being: They help you focus not only on immediate challenges but also on building a healthy, emotionally stable, post-divorce life.

Assist with parenting: For divorces involving children, mental health professionals help develop co-parenting strategies that focus on minimizing conflict and supporting your children's emotional health.

How Mental Health Professionals Collaborate with Other Divorce Experts

Divorce isn't just a legal process – it touches every part of your life, including your emotional, financial, and family dynamics. That's why mental health professionals often work closely with attorneys, financial planners, and other experts involved in the divorce process. This collaborative approach helps ensure that all aspects of the divorce are handled with care, addressing both the legal and emotional sides of the transition.

When mental health professionals collaborate with **lawyers**, they provide critical emotional insights that can help attorneys approach negotiations with greater understanding. Divorce can be highly emotional, even in amicable cases, and emotions like anger, sadness, or fear can complicate legal discussions. A mental health professional helps reduce emotional tension, allowing both parties to stay focused on solutions rather than getting stuck in conflict. By teaching effective communication strategies and helping clients manage their emotions, mental health professionals ensure that legal negotiations remain productive and that both parties feel heard and understood.

In collaboration with **financial planners**, mental health professionals help individuals make financial decisions that are rooted in long-term well-being rather than in-the-moment emotional reactions. Divorce often brings up anxieties around money, and it's easy to make decisions out of fear or stress rather than logic. A mental health professional helps you process these emotions and encourages you to take a balanced, thoughtful approach to dividing assets, alimony agreements, and planning for your financial future post-divorce.

By working alongside these professionals, mental health experts create a holistic support system for you, helping you navigate the divorce process with clarity and emotional stability. This collaboration ensures that all aspects of your divorce, from legal agreements to financial planning, are handled with your emotional health in mind.

Incorporating a mental health professional into your Amicable Divorce Process ensures that you are emotionally supported, making it easier to make thoughtful, clearheaded decisions as you transition into the next chapter of your life.

Stephanie Robins, LCSW, CADP
Certified Amicable Divorce Professional
Alpharetta Family Therapy
Alpharetta, Georgia

Chapter 18
Tips for Managing Stress
by Ashley Pepitone

Managing stress during any life transition is crucial for your emotional, physical, and mental health. There are actions you can take to navigate the complexities of divorce with resilience and grace. Here are some to consider:

Acknowledge Your Emotions

You can't change what you avoid – so it is important to experience and acknowledge your emotions. You may experience a mix of emotions: sadness, anger, relief, fear, and guilt, but also hope, joy, and relief. It is okay to experience all of them. Allow yourself to feel and process your emotions. Journaling, talking to a trusted friend, or seeking therapy can provide healthy outlets for expression.

Next, remember that every human emotion is based on one of two core emotions: fear or love. It helps to see what is under your emotions. When you feel *negative* emotions, recognize them for what they are at their root. They are all based in fear. Be honest with yourself about what you fear at that moment. Maybe you are feeling anxious and angry – perhaps what you fear is the financial outcome of your case. Identifying the actual cause of the emotion is the first step.

Once you identify the source of the fear, you can just sit with it for a bit and then take action. Maybe the next step is to schedule a call with a financial advisor to come up with a plan. If you are feeling sad and betrayed, and you realize that the root fear of these feelings is loneliness, a walk and chat with a close friend might help.

Remember that the bad moments are just that – moments – and there are good ones to enjoy as well. Give yourself the gift of grace, and be proud of the progress you are making. Recognize that these *positive* emotions are rooted in love – and love is always something to celebrate.

Prioritize Self-Care

Taking care of yourself is not selfish; it's essential. Here are some self-care practices to incorporate into your routine, for your mind, body, and spirit.

For the Mind:

Mindful Media Consumption Limit your exposure to things like true-crime podcasts and documentaries, movies with dark and twisted plots, music with sad or angry lyrics, and even (maybe especially) the news. Be mindful that the sound vibrations of music affect thoughts, emotions, and body systems. Consider replacing them with inspirational podcasts, motivational books, and positive or classical music.

Mel Robbins' "Let Them" Theory If a person in your life is not showing up for you the way you need, stop wasting your time and energy forcing them to match your expectations. Instead, "Let them be themselves because they are revealing who they are to you. Just let them."

This goes for any person with whom you interact: friends, family, colleagues, and, especially, your soon-to-be ex.

WAIT: Why Am I Talking? *You do not have to attend every argument you are invited to.* If your ex sent you an inflammatory email or text, take a beat and determine if it requires a response. If so, maybe *Received* is sufficient. If a more detailed response is required, maybe delegate it to your attorney. If a detailed response is required and it must come from you, give yourself enough time to make sure you are responding and not reacting.

Daytime vs. Nighttime Books Self-help books are wonderful, but you need sleep. Let your brain rest at night – this is not the time to get fired up with self-improvement brainstorms. If you like to read at night, remember that novels are great for bedtime. Save everything else for the morning and daylight hours.

Emotional Freedom Technique (Tapping) EFT or *tapping* is a way to help you shift your emotions. The basic technique requires you to focus on the stressful emotion – fear, anxiety, a memory, an unresolved problem – while keeping your mental focus on this issue. Use your fingertips to tap five to seven times on each of nine meridian points[2] on the body. Tapping on these meridian points – while concentrating on accepting and releasing the emotion – will access your body's energy, restoring it to a balanced state.

For the Body:

Food, Caffeine, and Alcohol Food is medicine. No one diet is right for every body, so it is important to be cognizant and mindful of what you are

---

[2] The meridian points: top of head, eyebrow, side of eye, under eye, under nose, chin, collarbone, under arm, side of hand ("karate chop" point).

eating and how it makes your body and mind feel. If you pay attention to how your food makes you feel, you can learn a lot. The physical effects of caffeine in your body from your quad-shot latte may undo your good efforts. Carefully consider the impact of everything you put in your body. Alcohol is a depressant. Period. If you want to feel happier, or at least try to avoid sadness and depression, reduce or eliminate it.

Flip Your Dog, Not Your Lid. Try an Inversion! Inversions are postures where your head is lower than your heart. There are inverted yoga poses that are accessible to all ranges of mobility. There are numerous physiological and psychological benefits of inversions, including:
- Improved circulation
- Support for your lymphatic system
- Heating or energizing the body
- Cooling or relaxing the body

Try an inversion before bed – like legs up the wall. This can relax your mind, balance blood pressure, and improve digestion, circulation, and sleep patterns.

Meditative Movement Movements that are repetitive and rhythmic can help your body move from the flight or fight state to a rest and digest state. Running, walking, yoga, tai chi, dance, and even coloring are all examples of meditative movements that can activate your parasympathetic nervous system and help lower cortisol levels. Engaging in one of these activities, even if only for a short period, helps you connect your body, mind, and spirit.

For the Spirit:

Start with Gratitude First thing in the morning, as you are waking up, think of something for which you are grateful. You can train yourself to do this by recording a cue on your phone and using it as your alarm. Gratitude journaling can be extremely effective for reducing stress and anxiety.

Celebrate Your Wins We have a tendency to gloss over our accomplishments. It is easy to check the box and focus on the next problem. It is important to stop and give our good work the spotlight it deserves. Brag about it. Journal about it. Give yourself and your team recognition for a job well done, before you move on to the next issue.

Meditation, Prayer, or Journaling This does not have to be religious, but rather quiet, reflective time with yourself. Guided meditations can be helpful and require little effort. The Calm app, YouTube, and podcasts are great resources.

Grounding and Sungazing Grounding, or earthing, involves direct contact with the Earth's surface, like walking barefoot on grass or soil. It can balance the body's electrical charge, reduce inflammation, improve sleep, and promote overall well-being. Sungazing, practiced safely during the first hour after sunrise or before sunset, is believed to have potential benefits like increased energy, better eyesight, and enhanced mood.

NSDR: Non-Sleep Deep Rest NSDR refers to activities or practices that promote relaxation and rejuvenation without requiring traditional sleep. These include mindfulness meditation, deep breathing exercises, progressive muscle relaxation, or calming hobbies like reading, drawing, or listening to music. During these restorative practices, the mind and body enter a state of relaxation where stress hormones decrease, heart rate slows, and muscle tension releases. Unlike sleep, which involves distinct sleep stages, non-sleep deep rest focuses on consciously relaxing the body and mind to promote mental clarity, emotional balance, and overall well-being. This type of self-care helps to replenish energy levels.

Yoga Nidra Yoga Nidra is a guided relaxation and meditation practice that induces deep relaxation while maintaining a state of consciousness. It's believed to reduce stress, improve sleep, enhance self-awareness, and promote overall well-being.

Breathwork Practices Our breath is an incredibly powerful tool that we can use to change our emotional and physical experiences. There is a continuous feedback loop through the nervous system. When we breathe intentionally, we can reduce fear and the fight or flight response, and in turn, reduce cortisol and other stress hormone levels in our bodies.

How are you breathing right now? When you breathe, what is moving? Your mouth? Shoulders? Nose? Belly? As you go through this breathing practice, try to notice in your body where you are holding tension and negative emotions. It's often in our face or jaw, and for women it's very often in our hips. Try to send the breath there and tell your body it's okay to release that feeling as you exhale.

Final Thoughts

Divorce is a difficult chapter, but it doesn't define your entire story. You will emerge stronger and more resilient if you prioritize wellness and embrace change. Use this time to nurture yourself and build a foundation for a fulfilling new beginning.

Ashley Pepitone
Founding Attorney, Pepitone Family Law
200RYT, Certified Practitioner
Certified Amicable Divorce Professional
Atlanta, Georgia

STEP 1
GATHER INFORMATION AND BUILD A TEAM

Chapter 19
Hiring a Divorce Attorney
by Tracy Ann Moore-Grant

First it is important to stress that you should hire a divorce attorney to represent you. Many seeking a low-conflict result, like amicable divorce, are hoping to avoid attorneys altogether. However, this is not advised. Just like you would hire an expert to fix your car, you should hire a lawyer to handle your divorce. Divorces involve property, taxes, retirement, kids, and more and should be handled properly and with care. We vet lawyers in the Amicable Divorce Network so that they do not fan the flames of conflict and increase cost for your family. There are unfortunately many family law attorneys who increase conflict because the harsh truth is that the more conflict, the more money they make. These lawyers are not approved for our network.

The choice you make in hiring your divorce attorney is an important decision, and often comes at a stressful time. Your attorney is the professional who will guide you through the divorce journey, and you certainly want to find someone who is a good fit. Because you are reading this book, you are interested in finding a resolution-focused professional who is not going to drive up costs and escalate conflict.

Common Questions About Lawyers

Can one lawyer represent both parties?
Generally no. A lawyer's job is to represent their client's interest, and they can only have one client. Advising opposing parties, no matter how agreeable, on what is best for them is not.

> Please note using one lawyer is permitted in England and Wales in some circumstances. UK parties seeking this service should inquire with a solicitor member of Amicable Divorce Network

Can a lawyer draw up paperwork for us both to sign?
Yes. This is often done in an uncontested divorce. However, if one spouse does not have a lawyer, they can reach out to the ADN to secure an attorney for assistance, advice, and document review. We suggest that both spouses look to the Amicable Divorce Network for attorneys to ensure that both professionals have the same approach to the case.

Can we just use a lawyer to act as a mediator and tell us what the law is?
No. A lawyer is an advocate and advisor. A mediator is a neutral non-advising professional. It is suggested that one party meet with a lawyer to get all legal questions answered. If the parties have a dispute on how to resolve an issue after receiving legal advice, a neutral mediator can assist guiding a solution.

Hiring a Lawyer

Hiring an attorney to handle a divorce can provide significant benefits. Overall, an attorney can see that the process is handled effectively and that your rights are protected. But on a more basic level, the lawyer will make sure that the necessary paperwork is completed properly, that it will be accepted by the court, and that it will be approved by a judge.

Many divorcing couples don't realize that even people with the best intentions may come up with an agreement with documents and terms that may not comply with the law in their jurisdiction. Failure to comply with legal requirements will cause the paperwork to be unacceptable (and therefore, no divorce could be granted). Documentation that cannot be accepted will also delay the case and could potentially increase costs and tension among all involved. There are key reasons to consider hiring an attorney for your divorce case:

- **Knowledge of divorce laws** It is important to know that laws and rules vary by jurisdiction and to get advice on your case.
- **Objective advice** Lawyers should be able to provide unemotional and practical advice for your situation.
- **Protecting your rights** Your lawyer is your advocate to help you understand and protect your rights.
- **Managing complex issues** Amicable Divorce Network members are experienced at handling complex issues and advising you properly.
- **Reducing stress** Handing your issues over to a lawyer can be a very good feeling and assist with turning down the temperature in a case.

It is important to know that the Amicable Divorce Network vets all members. The network makes sure that its professionals are resolution-focused, experienced in their field, and engage in fair billing practices. A good place to start looking for your lawyer is the Amicable Divorce Network membership directory at AmicableDivorceNetwork.com and DivorceAmicably.com. As you review the directory, you might find many professionals in your area, a few, or even none. You may need to dig deeper or go farther afield to find the right attorney for you.

Hiring the Right Kind of Lawyer

Many search to find the "bulldog" or "shark" divorce attorney. This is understandable; divorcing spouses are upset, and they want someone to "fight" for them and protect them during such a difficult time. As noted in the chapter on divorce myths, seeking an attorney solely on the basis of an aggressive record or reputation is a costly mistake.

When looking for a lawyer, an individual who is thinking about divorce should assess the attorney's experience, evaluate their advice, and consider their skillset. If you hire an attorney for their ability to project your anger into the court system, you may feel some temporary happiness in seeing your spouse antagonized – but in the long run, the cost can be devastating. Hiring a lawyer's anger is the most costly thing you can pay for in your divorce.

A lawyer who does not resolve conflict – but rather fights every battle – is engaging in a time-consuming fight on your dime and it only benefits their pocketbook.

Let's look at an example that would involve health insurance. In this particular jurisdiction – and pursuant to the amicable divorce agreement to maintain status quo – it would not be permissible for one spouse to drop the other from their health insurance policy without that party's knowledge and consent. However, in this incident, during open enrollment in November, the wife – who covers the family on her insurance – only enrolls herself and the children. The husband is left off the policy. When the husband is notified that he is no longer on the policy, he calls his attorney.

With an attorney employing the "bulldog" approach, the lawyer would first ask the client (the husband) to provide all information possible about the issue. The lawyer would then spend one hour drafting a motion for contempt (cost, $400) and the attorney's paralegal spends time preparing it, filing it, serving it on all parties, and requesting a hearing date (cost, $250). At that point, the lawyer also sends a scathing letter to the other spouse's attorney, noting how improper and uncalled-for the omission was (cost, $200).

The other attorney receives the motion and reviews it, along with the letter, and sends the documents to their client, the wife (cost, $200). The wife's lawyer calls the wife and has a conversation with her about the issue (cost, $200). It is soon evident that the wife did not intend to violate any laws or agreements, and had believed the omission was permissible, as the husband had mentioned getting insurance via his employer. Nevertheless, the wife's lawyer has 30 days to respond to the other party's motion.

The wife's lawyer prepares a response to the motion (cost, $400); a paralegal files it and sends it to all parties, including opposing counsel (cost, $200). The court sets the motion for a hearing on February 15, the following year. The lawyers and paralegals prepare for court (cost, $1,500 each), and everyone shows up to court at 9 a.m. on February 15. The parties wait about four hours to have their hearing (cost, $1,200 to each party).

After the hearing, the judge finds that the wife should not have taken the husband off the policy. However, the judge also notes that it was a misunderstanding and not a willful action. He issues an order that the wife get the husband back on the policy, if she can. The judge does not award fees to the husband because the action was not willful.

The judge then asks the husband's attorney to draft the order from the hearing. The husband's lawyer does that (cost, $400) and the attorneys communicate back and forth (cost, $400 each) until they can agree on the order's wording. It is submitted to the judge on March 15. The judge signs the order and it is finally filed in the system on April 15.

For this incident, the total cost to the parties with the confrontational approach was $8,450, and the resolution of the issue took five months.

With an attorney taking the "amicable" approach, the husband's lawyer would immediately reach out to the wife's lawyer via email, noting that the husband was dropped from the health insurance policy (cost, $80). When the wife's lawyer gets the email, the lawyer calls the wife (the client). They discuss the situation and confirm that the omission from the policy was a mistake. The wife's lawyer then tells her to add the husband to the policy, as it is still open-enrollment time (cost, $200). The wife's lawyer emails the husband's lawyer, explaining that there was a mistake, and also provides proof that the husband was added back on the policy (cost, $120). Total cost to the spouses with the amicable approach was $400 and the adjustment was handled quickly.

In an amicable divorce case, evidence is still gathered and negotiation takes place. But zealous advocacy for the client in no way means that the attorney is required to be difficult, rude, or insulting. In fact, those kinds of behaviors are contrary to a client's best interest – they do nothing but increase the cost of the lawyer's service and delay results. Amicable lawyers assess a situation, advise on the most likely and reasonable results, and work toward a quicker resolution.

What to Look for in a Lawyer

Some people are hesitant to ask others who have been through a divorce about their experience, but you should not feel ashamed. If you know someone who has been divorced, ask them about the attorney they used – and if they were pleased with their representation. A personal endorsement from a client is a good way to determine if a particular lawyer might be someone who you would want to have a consultation with. Keep in mind that there are other things to consider:

Are they both an attorney and a mediator? These professionals often have a settlement-oriented perspective, as they hold two roles in the system.

Do they hold special designations or work with children? If you are looking for someone with expertise in children and divorce, check if they also work as a guardian ad litem (GAL) or work in the juvenile court. If so, it is evident that they have a passion for, and knowledge of, issues regarding children.

Are they a member of organizations that emphasize mediation, amicable resolution, or collaboration? Organizations with such keywords often offer advanced training in divorce settlement and negotiation. Lawyers often list their organizations on their biography page.

Be aware of marketing techniques. If you notice a law firm promoting itself on Google (it will say "sponsored" online), billboards, or other advertising, that is not necessarily a bad thing. To be competitive in the market, many attorneys advertise. However, make sure you are doing enough research. Read the Google reviews for the attorney you would like to meet with, and also look for information about the attorney on Martindale.com (which rates lawyers by incorporating opinions of them from other attorneys and judges and is a reliable resource).

After you have identified a few lawyers who are good candidates, you will want to schedule consultations ("consults") with them. It is recommended that you meet with two or three attorneys, in order to evaluate their different approaches.

When calling law offices, do not be put off if the lawyer charges for a consult. When an attorney meets with you, it creates a conflict situation for them and their entire law firm. At that point, because they are consulting with you, they cannot ever represent your spouse, be your mediator, or hold another role in your case. They will be rendering legal advice to you and creating a professional relationship.

Tips for Scheduling Your Consult

- If you are calling a law firm for a specific attorney, make sure your appointment is with that attorney and not a different member of the firm.
- Be open to meeting online. Many attorneys now work from different locations or home offices. It may be easier to get a quicker appointment if you are open to meeting on the Zoom or Teams platforms.
- Ask how much time is being set aside for the consult. An hour is typical; but if you feel you need less time, ask if the consult fee is "apportioned," meaning that you would pay only for the time spent. If you feel that you need more time, make sure they are available for longer than the time initially scheduled.

Preparing for Your Consult

When making your appointment, ask if there is anything the lawyer or the office wants you to bring to the consultation. Each attorney has a different procedure, and if they do want something from you, please be prepared. Otherwise, here are some points for preparation:

- Bring any prenuptial agreement or postnuptial agreement you may have.
- Bring a list of questions that you have. (There are more ideas for questions below.)
- Bring any documents that you want the lawyer to review. Make copies of anything important; give the lawyer the copies (not the originals).

- If you wish to keep your consult a secret, be prepared to pay for the consult in cash. Credit card and check purchases leave a footprint in your accounts.

Before meeting with an attorney, it is not only important to get your papers in order but also to organize your thoughts and goals. What do you hope will happen in your divorce? What is the most important issue to you? Identify your values and your goals for the case.

Goals are items like a desire to stay in the marital home, being provided a certain amount of support, or approval of a particular custodial schedule with children. Values are things like having a good co-parenting relationship after the divorce, being in a financially secure position, or making sure that the settlement is fair.

Take a few moments to identify your top goals and values:

Goals	Values

Below are some questions to reflect on, along with ways to approach them with the lawyer. The lawyer's answers will help you to know if they are aligned with your goals and values.

Questions to ask yourself before your consult	How you can ask the lawyer about this topic
What is the level of conflict you expect in your case, and how do you want your case handled? Do you desire low to no conflict, or are you willing to go to trial on all issues? (Hopefully not!)	"My goal is to have a low-conflict divorce. Can you honor my desire to keep this case peaceful?"
What is your budget to complete your divorce case?	"My budget allows for me to spend (insert dollar amount) on this divorce. Is that a realistic budget for my case?" (Ask why, or why not.)
Do you have full financial transparency with your spouse? Is there anything you need from them?	"How can you help me gather the information I need about my spouse's finances, so that I know I am evaluating a full financial picture?" "What can I do to help reduce my costs during the process?" "Are there any other professionals or experts that we need in order to assist with the financial piece of my case?"
Do you plan to bring up issues of potential fault in your divorce like adultery or emotional abuse? (See the separate section on the fault issue.)	"I feel that my spouse is guilty of (insert issue). If that is brought up in my case, do you think it will help me reach my (financial, custody, timeline, budget) goals? How will bringing up these issues impact my cost/case timeline/conflict level?"
About 90 percent of family law cases settle outside of court. Is your desire to stay out of court? If so, is the lawyer skilled in low-conflict resolution?	"What percentage of your family law cases settle?" "What would you say prevents cases from settling?"
What is your expected timeline to have your case resolved and finalized?	"Do you think this case will be over by (insert deadline)?" "Are there any tasks I can do to make things move faster?" "What is the mandatory waiting period in (insert your jurisdiction)?"

Here some other great questions to ask during the consult:	"Based on my goals in this case, do you think my expectations are realistic?"
	"I value (insert value) for my divorce case. What steps can we take to make sure my values are honored?"

Red flags

Your consult is with a paralegal. Some firms use a consult with a paralegal as a way to get clients in the door, but then will say a legal conflict with your spouse was not created because you only met with a paralegal. Your legal consult should be with a lawyer.

The lawyer guarantees results. Lawyers should be familiar with the legal process, laws, and judges in their jurisdiction. However, it is unethical for a lawyer to guarantee a particular outcome.

The lawyer only talks about litigation. Again, 90 percent (or more) of family law cases are settled. If the lawyer talks only about your case going to court, and does not focus on settlement offers or mediation, then they are only offering you their litigation skills. They are not skilled in resolution. It would be a good idea to meet with a second lawyer and present the same facts to see if they advise a different path.

Hiring the right lawyer for you is a bit like dating. It is fine to take time to make a decision and have multiple consults. Moreover, you could have a consult with a great attorney and still find that it does not feel like a fit for you. Trust your gut – and choose the attorney that feels best for the type of divorce you want to have.

Chapter 20
Using Divorce Technology
by Storey Jones

The direct correlation between the advent of technology and the introduction of more client-centric divorce models, like the Amicable Divorce Process, is exciting to see. Technology makes a complicated data- and document-driven process immediately more transparent, less time-consuming, less expensive, and more accurate – all of which far more effectively serves families during this transition.

The dtour.life technology platform serves as the digital infrastructure for divorce, offering an exceptional user experience with features designed to help you easily get started, manage the process, and reach a resolution alongside your professional team. This applies no matter what type of divorce you are facing and regardless of your comfort level with a computer. Here are just a few highlights of how dtour.life will contribute to your Amicable Divorce:

1. **Flexible design:** dtour.life is designed to accommodate all types of families, financial situations, and levels of conflict and/or divorce processes.

2. **Family background:** The platform guides you to easily build a report containing all family and biographical information, saving you time and money before the first consultation and throughout the process.

3. **Net worth report:** dtour.life helps you easily build a net worth report, providing a clear picture of assets and debts.

4. **Income and expense sync:** The secure bank sync feature allows you to link all financial institutions for an accurate picture of transactions and a cash flow statement. This feature alone significantly advances your divorce toward a sustainable settlement while providing valuable insights as to how to best plan for your future.

5. **Parenting plan tool:** The platform includes a tool to work collaboratively in order to develop a list of co-parenting agreements.

6. **Document repository:** The drag-and-drop document repository allows you and your team to organize all paperwork, making it accessible to everyone involved without the need to email endless PDFs.

These primary features, along with many others, such as the ability to comment, add notes, and develop settlement scenarios, make it easy for you to work proactively with your team. This ensures they have all the information they need, saving you time and money while giving you control over decisions that you make today and for your future.

Storey Jones
Founder, dtour.life Divorce Management Platform
New York, New York

Chapter 21
How to Talk to Your Spouse About Divorce
by Alexandra Geczi

Speaking to your spouse about divorce can feel terrifying – for good reason. How will my spouse react? What if I'm making a mistake? How will we tell our children, friends, and family? Is this the point of no return?

It's natural to feel anxious and overwhelmed by these concerns. Fortunately, by approaching the conversation with care, you can minimize conflict, promote mutual understanding, and lay the groundwork for an amicable separation.

Step 1: Reflect on Your Decision

Before initiating a conversation about divorce, it's important you feel confident in your decision.

Clear Mindset

I conduct debriefs at the end of my cases – and in those calls, I ask clients what advice they would offer another person considering divorce. They often stress the importance of mindset. They tell me that what guided them through the dark moments of the divorce process was staying clear and firm about the reasons for divorce and understanding that it was the right decision. Good advice – because like anything difficult in life, if you are clear and set on the direction you want to go, then the conversations to get you there become easier.

Emotional and Physical Preparation

If you are uncertain about moving forward, then consider whether you've exhausted all other options to address your marital challenges, such as counseling or open communication. Also, consider looking inward. Perhaps you are struggling with mental or physical health issues that are making things more difficult. Engage in self-reflection, therapy, or conversations with trusted friends. Check your bloodwork for nutritional and hormonal imbalances, and speak with your healthcare provider about things that may contribute to how you feel. Maintaining good mental or physical condition can make things clearer – and allow you to communicate with your spouse from a place of calm.

Your Spouse's Condition

Consider your spouse's emotional and physical state as well. If your spouse is under significant stress – from work, health concerns, or family obligations – it may not be the best time to initiate the conversation. Waiting until both of you are in a relatively stable place can help ensure that the discussion is productive and respectful. However, if your spouse seems perpetually stressed, then there may never be a good time, and it may be best to proceed with the conversation.

Step 2: Choose the Right Time and Place

Where and when you have the conversation can significantly impact how it unfolds.

Environment

Pick a neutral, private location where both you and your spouse can speak freely without fear of interruption. Avoid initiating the conversation in public settings or high-stress environments. A quiet moment at home or in a neutral space like a park can provide privacy. Choose a place that allows for easy escape in the event either of you gets upset and one of you needs to leave. If you have a therapist, seek their advice as to the best place. Consider breaking the news at the counselor's office, if appropriate.

Timing

Timing is important as well. Avoid starting the conversation during high-pressure moments, such as right before work or while handling a family crisis. Instead, look for a calm, uninterrupted time when both of you are relatively relaxed and can focus on the discussion. If you have children, pick a time and place when the children won't be there.

Step 3: Use Clear, Compassionate Communication

The words you use and the way you communicate your decision will set the tone for the rest of the divorce process. Strive for compassion and clarity.

Starting the Conversation

Begin the discussion gently but directly. Avoid ambiguous language or beating around the bush, which can lead to confusion. For example, you might say, "I've been reflecting a lot on our relationship, and I feel that we need to have a serious conversation about our future." This approach is honest while still being sensitive to your spouse's emotions.

Stay Calm and Focused

It's natural for your spouse to get upset. They are entitled to feel their emotions. Acknowledge these emotions without becoming defensive. Stay calm and avoid letting the conversation devolve into an argument. Use "I" statements to express your perspective, such as, "I feel like we've grown apart," rather than pointing fingers with "You" statements like, "You never listen to me." If your spouse becomes too emotional, it may be best to end the conversation. You can let them know that you will reengage the discussion after they've had a chance to process things and calm down. Giving them space can de-escalate tension and foster a sense of mutual respect.

Avoiding Blame

Refrain from assigning blame or rehashing past grievances. Focus on irreconcilable differences or the mutual realization that the marriage isn't working. This keeps the conversation from becoming adversarial and prioritizes moving forward constructively.

Making Threats

Avoid making threats. If your spouse makes threats, like taking the children or leaving you homeless, stay calm and remind yourself that they are probably feeling scared and uncertain – and making threats helps them feel in control. It may also be helpful to speak with an attorney before having the conversation, so that you understand your rights and can stay calm.

Step 4: Be Honest, But Avoid Overloading with Details

Honesty is important, but sharing too much information can overwhelm your spouse and intensify their emotions.

Balance Transparency with Sensitivity

Clearly communicate your reasons for wanting a divorce, but avoid listing every complaint or issue in the marriage. Instead, focus on overarching themes, such as personal unhappiness or incompatible goals.

Focus on the Future

Rather than dwelling on past problems, shift the conversation toward the future. Discuss what you envision for both of your lives moving forward, and how you hope to approach the divorce process with respect and cooperation.

Step 5: Discuss Next Steps

Once you've shared your decision, it's helpful to outline potential next steps to provide a sense of direction.

Exploring Options Together

If possible, suggest exploring peaceful resolution methods like amicable divorce or mediation. These approaches prioritize cooperation and minimize the adversarial aspects of divorce. It may be helpful to gather information about these options beforehand so that you are prepared to answer questions and provide specific details.

Setting Boundaries and Expectations

Establishing boundaries during this time can help maintain stability. For instance, if your spouse can engage in rational dialogue, discuss how you'll communicate during your separation, whether you'll remain in the same household for a period, and how financial responsibilities will be divided. If you have children, it's important to discuss how you will speak to the children about the situation so that you are on the same page. Consider engaging a counselor or parenting coach to help.

Outline the Path Forward

Discuss practical next steps, such as meeting with divorce attorneys or attending counseling to facilitate the transition. These options can help create a roadmap for navigating the process.

Step 6: Give Space and Time to Process

Divorce is a significant emotional event, and your spouse will need time to process what you've shared.

Emotional Space

Expect an emotional reaction, whether it's sadness, anger, or disbelief. Allow your spouse the space to experience and express these feelings without rushing them toward acceptance. The initial conversation may last just a few minutes, and you may need to revisit the topic later to have a more in-depth discussion. Remember, you just threw a bomb into their lives, and their primary focus will be on surviving that impact.

Pacing the Conversation

Conversations about divorce can be an ongoing process rather than a one-time discussion. Don't expect to tell your spouse about your decision and then jump into negotiations over everything. You may be ready to end things, but for your spouse, this may all come as a shock. They may be afraid and angry. You each need time to process. You may also need to engage professional help to get you through these difficult conversations. It's important you remain calm and patient with yourself and your spouse.

Conclusion

Talking to your spouse about divorce is seldom easy – but with preparation, compassion, and clarity, it can be handled in a way that minimizes conflict and respects both parties. Approaching the conversation thoughtfully not only sets the tone for a more amicable divorce, but it also honors the relationship you've shared.

Alexandra Geczi
Founder of Alexandra Geczi PLLC
Certified Mediator
Certified Collaborative Law Attorney
Certified Amicable Divorce Professional
Dallas, Texas

Chapter 22
How Lawyers Bill Their Time
by Tracy Ann Moore-Grant

Understanding how lawyers bill their time can help the divorcing parties move forward with confidence in how their case is being handled. But one of the biggest fears people have when approaching divorce is the cost and conflict that lawyers will add to an already tense situation.

That fear is justified. What the public often does not know is that family law professionals – and lawyers in particular – often have a minimum billable hour requirement to meet in order to keep their job with their firm or earn bonuses. In other words, if more tasks are created in your case, the more drawn-out your case will become, and it will be easier for the lawyer to meet their billable hour requirement.

Many people only get divorced once, and therefore have no reference point to know if their selected professionals are overbilling or increasing conflict. Unfortunately, in the family law realm, many professionals engage in overbilling – either by charging more time or cost for services or by creating unnecessary activities or conflict in a case. Some lawyers do try to diffuse tensions and look for solutions, but others stoke the flames to increase tensions (and their bills).

Conflict in a family law case is inevitable. How conflict is handled for the parties is essential to their entire divorce process.

The Amicable Divorce Network (ADN) was formed to vet lawyers and other professionals so that divorcing spouses can feel more comfortable about the people they hire. Prior to ADN membership, the professionals are screened to ensure that they try to minimize conflict, are resolution-focused, and engage in fair billing practices.

Before meeting with a lawyer, or deciding who to hire, it is important that you know what you can afford and are willing to pay for your divorce. Do you have money saved, or will you need to use a credit card? If someone is loaning you money or assisting with the cost, what are they willing to pay? It is important to know your limits and your budget before beginning the process.

After you have your budget defined, communicate that information to each professional whom you are considering for your case. Whether it is a lawyer, a financial professional, or a coach, be clear in what you can afford for the services. Ask if the needed work can be completed within your budget.

It is important to know that lawyers generally have two different methods of billing for their services – retainers and flat fees.

Retainers

An **evergreen retainer** or **replenish retainer** is a type of payment arrangement between a client and a lawyer. It is a deposit or advance fee paid to the lawyer, which the lawyer draws from as legal services are performed. The key feature of an evergreen retainer is that the client is required to replenish the retainer account regularly, usually once a month, to maintain a set balance. Replenishment ensures that funds are always available to cover ongoing legal work.

The main characteristics of an evergreen retainer are:

- **Replenishment requirement** – The client must maintain the retainer at a specific minimum monetary level. If the balance drops below that level due to work completed by the lawyer, the client is required to replenish it.
- **Continuous funding** – The availability of continuous funding ensures that the lawyer is paid promptly for services and costs rendered. The lawyer won't have to chase payments or pay out-of-pocket for costs.
- **Trust account** – The retainer funds should be held in a trust account or escrow account until the lawyer earns them by performing the agreed-upon legal work.
- **Transparency** – The lawyer should provide an accounting of the work done and the corresponding amounts deducted from the retainer. A

bill should come in advance of a request for you to replenish, and the bill should identify who did the work on your case (a lawyer, paralegal, etc.), the time spent, and a description of the task, so you can understand the charge.

The benefits of an evergreen retainer include:

- **It provides financial security for the lawyer** and reduces the risk of non-payment for services, and clients should get full details of the work done on their case.
- **It helps avoid unexpected large legal bills for the client** by encouraging regular billing, while still providing an accounting for funds spent. The client will pay exactly for the services and costs in their case.

Evergreen retainers are common in complex or ongoing legal matters, such as family law and divorce cases when legal needs and costs can be unpredictable.

Breaking Down the Hours

When there is a replenish retainer, that means the lawyer – and the lawyer's staff – is keeping track of their time, and billing you by the hour. In an hourly billing system, time is broken down into fractions in a couple ways. Usually, everyone in the same office will handle their time in the same manner. The two hourly breakdowns are:

- **An hour is divided into 10 segments.** That means the legal team is billing **six minutes at a time.** So, a simple yes-or-no email, billed at the smallest billing fraction, is one-tenth of an hour, or six minutes. If the attorney's rate is $300 per hour, six minutes is $30 under this system.
- **An hour is divided into four segments.** That means the legal team is billing **15 minutes at a time.** A simple yes-or-no email billed under this method (with one-quarter of an hour as the smallest billing fraction) is 15 minutes. If the attorney's rate is $300 per hour, 15 minutes is $75 under this system.

PART 6 : HOW DO YOU PREPARE FOR A DIVORCE?

A good way to save money and to get organized is to send the lawyer your questions in one email. If you have multiple questions, start the email draft and add your questions. Whether you send all of your questions at the end of the day or the end of the week, you have consolidated your questions and saved time and money. Some lawyers will charge one-tenth of an hour per email, instead of assessing how long it took them to answer an email.

Another tip is to be clear on who administers what tasks in the office. Emailing a paralegal directly for something that they can handle (rather than emailing the attorney) might get you a direct and cheaper answer more quickly. When in doubt, ask! How your funds are handled, and how your lawyer – or any other professional on your case – bills their time should be transparent to you.

The hourly rate for attorneys also varies greatly by location. Urban areas generally charge more than suburban and rural areas. When scheduling consultations, don't be shy about calling several locations to ask for hourly rates and how lawyers bill their time. You can also ask for the rates of the other attorneys in the same office to compare them.

Beware of the **empty retainer**. A new retainer structure has emerged in family law that is known by professionals as the "empty retainer." With the empty retainer, a lawyer will say that the retainer is, for example, $5,000 – but $2,500 of that may simply be to retain the lawyer as your lawyer. The other $2,500 is the actual retainer fee that you will receive services for. Although the empty retainer does prevent the attorney from ever representing your spouse or holding another role in the case (like a mediator), it is not the industry standard to charge an empty retainer.

Flat Fee

A **flat fee retainer** for a divorce case is a payment arrangement where a client pays a single, upfront amount to the lawyer to handle specific tasks, or the entirety of the divorce proceedings. Unlike hourly billing or an evergreen/replenish retainer, the flat fee is fixed and does not vary. The amount is not tied to the actual time that the lawyer spends on the case.

Here is how the flat fee retainer works:

- **Scope of services** – The lawyer and client agree on what the flat fee covers before the case begins. Examples of covered services might include: filing the divorce petition; representing the client during mediation or court hearings; drafting a marital settlement agreement; or handling all of a simple, uncontested divorce. The flat fee usually excludes additional or unforeseen services (for example, complex litigation or appeals, drafting of deeds or QDROs), which might require separate fees.
- **Upfront payment** – The client pays the agreed flat fee before legal work begins. That ensures that the lawyer is guaranteed compensation for their services.
- **No ongoing billing** – Since the fee is fixed, the client does not receive bills based on hourly rates or the number of hours worked.
- **Cost predictability** – A flat fee provides cost certainty to the client, helping them more easily budget for legal expenses.

The common scenarios for flat fee retainers in divorce cases may include:

- **Uncontested divorce** – Both parties agree on key issues (like asset division, custody, and support) and the divorce will require minimal legal work.
- **Limited scope representation** – Flat fee retainers are often appropriate when the lawyer handles only a specific aspect of the divorce (for instance, drafting legal documents or offering legal advice).
- **Mediation support** – The lawyer may only be hired to advise the client during mediation sessions, without extensive court involvement.

There are some key considerations when looking at the flat fee retainer structure:

- **Complex cases** – Flat fees are typically not suitable for contested divorces or situations involving high-conflict disputes, significant assets, or custody battles, as those types of cases can be unpredictable

in terms of time and resources. Some attorneys do offer a flat fee for cases with more complex factors, however, so if a flat fee is attractive to you, it is something you should explore.
- **Written agreement** – The retainer agreement should clearly outline the scope of services and specify whether additional costs might arise (such as court filing fees or expert witness costs). You should receive a clear understanding of what is included – and what is not – in the flat fee payment.
- **No-refund policy** – Most flat fees are nonrefundable, even if the case resolves quickly, if it changes course to a different type of case, or if the lawyer does less work than expected. Clients should make sure they understand the terms of the agreement.

A flat fee arrangement is most beneficial when both the client and lawyer have a clear understanding of the divorce case's complexity and scope. Some clients like the flat fee type of payment, because it allows the clients to know up front what the overall costs will be. They do not have to deal with monthly billing, and they can clearly and easily budget their divorce costs. Other clients prefer to pay exactly for the time spent on their case, and so a flat fee is not desirable to them.

Of the two types of payment methods, a flat fee is less common in family law matters. If it is not a fee structure that your chosen professional usually offers, they probably won't set up a flat fee arrangement just for you. Don't be put off if it's not an available option.

Potential Billing Issues

Regardless of the fee structure, as a client, you have every right to understand all of the actions being done on your case – and by whom. If you receive a bill that you do not understand, or you feel there was an error, address it as soon as possible. Lawyers are human too, and the time for a case is entered manually. It is possible that the wrong case or wrong amount of time was put on your bill.

If you get into a situation where you can no longer afford your lawyer or a particular bill, make sure you communicate that as soon as possible. The lawyer may suggest that different actions be taken in your case, or they may set up a payment plan. Not communicating your financial issues to your lawyer can only lead to challenges in the attorney-client relationship.

Chapter 23
Building a Solid Divorce Team
by Nanette Murphy

The journey through divorce does not have to be faced alone, nor does it have to be a path filled with confusion and distress. It certainly can be a challenging time. However, by assembling a dedicated team of professionals you can alleviate anxiety, foster empowerment, and find clarity.

It is essential to recognize that the process often requires a multi-faceted approach. Assembling a team of professionals can provide comprehensive support that addresses both the legal and emotional aspects of divorce. Divorce professionals generally fall into a few major categories:

- Legal
- Alternate Dispute Resolution
- Mental Health
- Financial
- Mortgage and Real Estate
- Coaching
- Wellness Professionals

Let's explore the various key players you might consider including in your support network:

Divorce Lawyer

The divorce attorney is your legal advocate, ensuring that your rights are protected throughout the process. They provide essential guidance on legal matters, such as asset division, spousal support, and custody arrangements. A skilled attorney will help you navigate the complexities of the law, ensuring that you are informed about your options and that your interests are safeguarded. Having a knowledgeable attorney on your side can reduce a significant amount of stress. It is up to the attorney to handle the legal intricacies, while allowing you to focus on your emotional well-being. It is important to know that your attorney is in charge of the legal advice and guidance and can often be one of, if not the, most expensive professional on the team. To save time and money, it is important to call on the correct team member for the problem at hand. Using an attorney as the only member of your team can put you in a position of only getting a *legal* perspective. Your divorce actually has many different pieces, and you should utilize the right professionals for each issue.

Divorce Coach

Many have not heard of a divorce coach, but a divorce coach is at the heart of your support network, guiding you through the process's emotional and practical complexities. A divorce coach empowers you to take charge of your situation, providing guidance and encouragement as you work toward creating the life you envision.

Unlike a divorce attorney, who is primarily focused on the legal aspects of the process, a divorce coach addresses the organizational and emotional hurdles that arise. The main goal of a divorce coach is to empower you. The divorce coach can help you to gain clarity about your situation and guide you in making informed decisions. Ultimately, you will reclaim control over your life.

A divorce coach provides a variety of services, tailored to meet your needs. The coach can offer emotional backup during a tumultuous time, helping you articulate your feelings and fears in a safe and nonjudgmental environment. A coach can help you develop coping strategies, build resilience, and foster a sense of self-worth that may have diminished during your marriage. A coach can also help sort through all of the information in a divorce case, help you get organized, and guide you to the next step in the process.

Additionally a divorce coach will assist you in setting realistic goals, and together you'll create actionable plans to achieve those goals. Whether it's managing the logistics of your divorce, addressing financial concerns, or preparing for co-parenting, a coach will help you break down the overwhelming process of adjusting to your new life into manageable steps and can direct you to additional resources or professionals to assist you. A structured, organized and supported approach not only reduces anxiety; it also empowers you to be proactive in shaping your future.

Benefits of Working with a Divorce Coach?

Here are several key benefits that can significantly improve your experience during this challenging time:

Emotional support A divorce coach offers expertise – as well as a compassionate, empathetic presence – during one of the most trying times in your life. A coach provides a safe space for you to express your feelings, fears, and frustrations – all without judgment.

Clarity and direction When faced with the chaos of divorce, it can be challenging to see a clear path forward. A divorce coach helps you gain clarity about your goals and aspirations, and can assist you in creating a personalized action plan. A structured approach reduces the feeling of being overwhelmed and will enable you to focus on what truly matters.

Skill development A divorce coach equips you with essential skills for effective communication, negotiation, and decision-making. These skills are invaluable not only during the divorce process, but also in your daily interaction with others. By sharpening your ability to advocate for yourself, you will feel more confident in navigating your new life.

Empowerment One of the greatest benefits of collaborating with a divorce coach is the sense of empowerment that comes from taking control of your own circumstances. Rather than feeling like a passive participant in the divorce process, you will learn to advocate for yourself. You will make informed decisions and actively shape your future. And your newfound empowerment can be transformative – it can allow you to emerge from the divorce with new strength and confidence.

Save money You may wonder if a coach will add to the expense of your divorce. Actually, hiring a divorce coach can ultimately save you money in several significant ways. A coach can help organize your case, focus your decision-making, and help guide you through the process efficiently.

Financial Advisor

It is helpful to have a financial advisor; specifically, a CDFA (certified divorce financial analyst). Divorce can have profound financial implications, and it is essential to seek the guidance of a CDFA, who may also be able to serve as your financial advisor to help you gain a clear understanding of your financial landscape, assess your assets and liabilities, and develop a plan for your financial future. A CDFA can provide insights into budgeting and division of assets, and a financial advisor can assist with retirement planning and investment strategies – ensuring that you are well-prepared for the changes that lie ahead. By working with financial professionals, you can develop a sense of financial security and confidence. You'll know that you have a solid plan in place.

It is also important to consult with a CPA and/or tax professional before finalizing any divorce terms. You will want to fully understand any present and future tax consequences of your settlement.

Mediator

If you and your spouse are open to collaboration, a mediator can facilitate productive discussions and help you reach agreements on contentious issues, such as asset division and child custody. Mediation provides a more amicable and cost-effective alternative to traditional litigation, allowing both parties to work toward mutually beneficial solutions. A mediator's role is to ensure that communication remains respectful and constructive, fostering a cooperative approach. Cooperation can significantly reduce conflict and stress.

Therapist, Counselor

The emotional toll of divorce can be overwhelming. Navigating a divorce can be an incredibly complex experience, and having both a therapist and a divorce coach can provide well-rounded support. There are good reasons for employing both professionals.

Different focus areas A therapist primarily addresses emotional and psychological issues, helping people process feelings such as grief, anger, and anxiety. They provide a safe space for exploring deep emotional wounds and past traumas that may affect one's mental health. In contrast, a divorce coach focuses on practical aspects of the divorce process, helping individuals set goals, create action plans, and develop strategies for moving forward.

Emotional support vs. practical guidance Again, while a therapist is equipped to help you work through complex emotions and mental health challenges, a divorce coach provides constructive guidance and accountability. Taking a dual approach will allow you to manage both your emotional well-being and the logistical aspects of divorce.

Skill development A divorce coach often teaches skills related to communication, negotiation, and decision-making, which are vital during the divorce process. Meanwhile, a therapist can help you build emotional resilience and coping strategies. Together, they can empower you to handle both the emotional and practical challenges of divorce more effectively.

Holistic healing Combining therapy and coaching allows for a more holistic, "big-picture" approach to healing and growth. A comprehensive support system can lead to a more successful transition into post-divorce life.

Real Estate Agent

If the divorce makes it necessary for you to sell your home or find new living arrangements, a real estate agent with experience in divorce situations can be an indispensable resource. They can guide you through the intricacies of the real estate market, helping you make informed decisions about property sales or purchases. A skilled agent can alleviate the stress of navigating the housing market; the goal is to see that you secure the best possible outcome in your transition.

Child Custody Specialist

For those with children, a child custody specialist can provide crucial guidance. A custody specialist can navigate custody arrangements and ensure that your children's best interests are prioritized. Moreover, they can help facilitate discussions between you and your spouse, providing resources to promote effective co-parenting. A specialist can also help prepare you for custody evaluations and court appearances. Preparation with the specialist will help make certain that you are well-informed and confident when advocating for your children's needs.

Support Group

Connecting with others who are experiencing similar challenges can be incredibly comforting. Divorce support groups provide a sense of community and understanding, allowing you to share feelings and gain insights from others who have walked a similar path. Engaging in a support group can help you feel less isolated and more empowered, as you realize that you are not alone in your struggles.

A Path of Renewal and Resilience

When you contemplate or prepare for divorce, feeling anxious and uncertain about the future is entirely natural. However, by assembling a team of qualified professionals tailored to your unique needs, you can ease some of that anxiety and start to build a sense of empowerment. You can always turn to a member of your team for the best advice and use the expertise of the professional in your area of need. By utilizing professionals in different industries, you know that you are getting the right information from the correct source.

Remember that you are not alone in your journey. With the right support system in place, you can emerge on the other side of divorce, ready to embrace a new chapter in your life. The future holds promise and opportunity. With each step you take, you'll move closer to reclaiming your power and creating the life you desire.

Be open to the possibilities that lie ahead. You possess the strength to not only survive, but to thrive in your new reality. The journey may not be easy, but trust in the support of your team – especially your divorce coach – as you take those crucial steps toward a brighter, more fulfilling future.

Nanette Murphy
Divorce and Life Reinvention Coach
Live Life Now LLC
Certified Amicable Divorce Professional
Amicable Ambassador Michigan
Detroit, Michigan

Chapter 24
Creating a Child-Centered Divorce
by Traci A. Weiss

While unwinding a marriage will have some impact on the children, there are ways to navigate the process that can minimize the disruption and stress the divorce takes on them. Here are some guidelines.

Co-Parent from the Start

Do what you can to co-parent from the start. You had the children together, and you will both continue as their parents after the divorce is over. So, your children will be better off the sooner you can think about the other party as the parent of your children as opposed to the other party as your spouse. Both parents should encourage the children to love and continue to have a strong relationship and bond with the other parent. Just because they may not be the best spouse, or even the best parent, doesn't mean they can't be a good parent and an important presence in the children's lives.

The most adversarial custody battles typically come from a place of fear about the role each parent will play in the lives of the children going forward. Making the best efforts to co-parent, and including the other parent in important decisions, events, and time with the children, will alleviate those fears. This will give you the best chance to achieve a Parenting Plan that works for all of you.

Be Reasonable and Realistic

People often become fixated on the terminology around child custody: Will they have sole custody? Primary? Joint? What really matters is a plan that details decision-making authority and a parenting time schedule that gives the children similar access to each parent that they had when the family was intact. The focus should *not* be on what time each parent has with the children, but rather what time the *children* have with each parent.

A good Parenting Plan will allocate these things in a way that best serves the children. Both parents should approach the crafting of the Parenting Plan with the idea that their children's needs, schedules, and interests are fluid. The hope is that after the divorce is finalized, the children will have a routine, and the Parenting Plan can be set aside in a drawer and never looked at again. That is possible if each parent is willing to give and take as needed, as schedules change and things come up.

Make Decisions from a Child's Perspective

Many parties fight tooth and nail for a particular holiday schedule or a provision in a Parenting Plan, not realizing they are fighting for what is best for *them* and not their child. When making decisions, try to look at things from the child's perspective. Does the motivation for the decision-making center on what is best for the child or what is best for you? It is important to look at decisions that involve children and take a step back – and separate your emotions from the decision. What will the schedule be like for the child? Will this decision benefit the child? How much time will the child spend in a car? Looking at these topics and removing your personal feelings from the process can help you focus on making decisions that are best for the child.

Don't Lean on the Children

It's your job as parents to protect and support your children – not the other way around. While many children will have questions about the reason for the divorce and the dynamics of the process, they do not need to be told details – particularly those that may negatively impact their relationship with the other parent.

If you need someone to talk to, a therapist is always a good idea during such an emotionally charged time. Talking to friends and family may inflame the situation – and you do not want anything you say about your spouse to be overheard or repeated to the children. Speaking to a therapist is a safer option. And if the children have been exposed to acrimony between their parents, or are struggling with the divorce, a good therapist is helpful for them too. Even very young children can benefit from play therapy. Provide them with a safe space where they can share their feelings without worrying if they are upsetting either parent. This is not just your breakup – it's theirs too.

Traci A. Weiss
Family Law Attorney
Guardian ad Litem
Certified Amicable Divorce Professional
Atlanta, Georgia

Chapter 25
Types of Co-Parenting
by Michael Cohen

When you divorce, you don't divorce your children. Nor do you and your spouse end your relationship as parents. After your divorce, how you handle your ongoing relationship as parents is the most critical thing you will do. Your behavior will affect your children's emotional and mental health. If you can both find a way to be healthy co-parents together – perhaps even better parents than when you were married – you can mitigate the impact that your divorce will have on your children, and on yourselves. You can help bring about healing for your family.

As a divorce mediator in Lake Forest, Illinois, and as a father who went through a divorce, I have seen firsthand the impact a divorce can have on children. It is why I became a divorce mediator – to help couples continue to be healthy parents during and after their divorce. When you divorce, you can either "parallel parent" or "co-parent." Let's elaborate on both methods.

Parallel Parenting

Parallel parenting means that you each are the best parent you can be, *individually*, but without coordination. Often, there will be little to no sharing of information or collaborating about your children.

Parallel parenting is often employed when the parents can't talk to each other in a healthy manner, or when they can't put their children first because they can't stop focusing on the reasons for their divorce. Sometimes this dynamic can't be avoided, but parallel parenting is generally discouraged.

Even in healthy marriages, children find gaps between Mom and Dad to get what they want. The more aligned parents are, the closer they can stand together on any issues that may come up. The more unified the parenting message, the better the chance is that the parents can raise their children under a single umbrella that encompasses the values, work ethic, and mental health standards that both parents envision.

However, when parents divorce and they must parallel parent, they don't communicate with each other that much about the children. Therefore, they are not able to work together for their children's benefit.

Children are very smart. Because the divorced couple is parallel parenting, the children immediately see that there is a large gap between Mom and Dad. They can find room in that gap to develop bad habits, not work as hard in school, and have unhealthy relationships. Parallel parenting can lead to children showing distinct effects of the divorce in their development, and it can create immense guilt in both parents because of the impact that the divorce has on their children.

Counter-Parenting

Counter-parenting refers to a dysfunctional dynamic in co-parenting, where one parent intentionally undermines or works against the other parent's decisions, values, or parenting style. This behavior often arises in situations of high conflict, such as post-divorce or separation, and can negatively impact the child's emotional well-being and stability.

Key characteristics of counter-parenting may include:

1. **Inconsistency in rules:** One parent may disregard rules set by the other, such as bedtimes, screen time limits, or diet preferences.
2. **Criticizing the other parent:** Openly disparaging the other parent in front of the child, which can create loyalty conflicts or confusion for the child.
3. **Blocking communication:** Avoiding meaningful discussions about the child's needs or refusing to share important information about their life, such as school updates or health matters.
4. **Encouraging bad behavior:** Deliberately enabling or overlooking behaviors that the other parent disapproves of, in an attempt to "win" the child's favor.
5. **Legal conflicts:** Using custody arrangements or court processes as tools to undermine the other parent.

Counter-parenting contrasts with healthy co-parenting, which prioritizes collaboration, consistency, and the child's best interests. This toxic pattern can create stress for children and weaken their sense of security.

If you're experiencing counter-parenting, a therapist or mediator can provide tools for setting boundaries and minimizing its effects on you and your child.

Co-Parenting

When you co-parent, both parents communicate regularly about the children. Communication allows both of you to know what the children are doing and how they are feeling, so you can both support their specific needs. Communication also opens the door to working together to truly parent and find the best ways to raise your children.

More importantly, co-parenting shows your children that you are still standing next to each other as their parents, which in turn greatly mitigates the impact your divorce will have on your children.

When you co-parent, the parents are flexible and supportive of each other. My clients often ask what they should say when the other parent needs help with the children. "The answer is always 'yes,'" I say, "if you're able to help." Remember, these are *your* children and this is *bonus* time with your children. Take it – help your former spouse, and enjoy some additional time with your children. Not only is helping each other good for you and the children, but it also opens the door for your former spouse to be flexible to help you when you might need help.

When parents co-parent together, their children see that Mom and Dad are on the same page. Together, you are able to minimize any perceived gaps between you. A united goal and consistent messaging will allow you both to have a joint, directive role with your children. You'll be better equipped to help them develop into the children you both always envisioned they would be.

Another benefit of co-parenting in a healthy way is that *your* mental health will be enhanced. Working together may be difficult to do immediately after your divorce, but the sooner you can collaborate as co-parents, the sooner you can minimize stress you might feel when crossing paths with your former spouse. And you just might make other divorced couples jealous of how well you both work together for the benefit of your children.

What if you and the other parent can't find a way to communicate and collaborate? All is not lost. You can still give your children the appearance of co-parenting; for example, by texting each other updates about the children just before every transfer of supervision (what activities the kids did, what they enjoyed, how they were feeling, etc.). That information allows the other parent to open discussions with the children about their time with you, which shows the children that Mom and Dad are united in their desire to work together for them. It also allows each of you to have a greater understanding of how your children are doing, even when they are with their other parent.

You can also agree to be civil during transfers or when you're both at the children's events. A show of cordiality or friendship would be to your children's benefit. For example, if the children see you both being nice to each other, being comfortable near each other, and seemingly friendly, they will be less agitated and more emotionally content. The alternative – letting them see that their mom and dad can't be near each other, let alone speak to each other – would be emotionally detrimental for them. Sometimes, getting along requires "taking the high road," but it is all for your children's well-being.

Tips for a Healthy Co-Parenting Relationship

- During your divorce journey, you will discuss whether you want full or joint physical and legal custody. Ask your divorce professional the different ways to parent to determine the best for you.
- If your divorce is being mediated, work with your mediator to outline co-parenting guidelines that you both will respect and adhere to. A divorce mediator can help you outline a plan with rules, deadlines, and boundaries that will guide you as parents.
- Keep your children front and center in everything you do. Remember that you are the adults and they are the children. Show them that you can both be adults and be the parents that they deserve.
- Take pride in successes. Post-divorce, it is not easy to communicate as a couple; but if you mediate, you can more easily do so (because your divorce mediator will help you build healthy communication habits). When you find yourselves doing something positive for the children together, recognize each other's efforts, thank each other, and tell each other how much you appreciate that you're able to put the children first.
- Don't get frustrated if emotions get the better of you from time to time. It happens. Put your children back in front, take the high road, be the better person, and know that your children deserve Mom and Dad working together for them.

Final Thoughts

- No one in the world will ever care more about your children than both of their parents.

- No one in the world will receive more joy from the way your children develop than both parents.
- Enjoy the feeling – know that you and your children's other parent share something very unique and special.
- Work together – be the parents that you always wanted your children to have.
- Your children will thank you immensely for your efforts at harmony, because the alternative often creates challenges for children. Put your children first.
- PS – When you become healthy co-parents, you actually learn how to move past your divorce in a healthier way, with less baggage and more pride. In turn, that will allow you both to more quickly move toward your next phase in life, with a more healthy outlook.

Michael Cohen
Certified Public Accountant
Divorce Mediator
Lake Forest, Illinois

Chapter 27
How to Have a Child-Centered Divorce
by Kathleen Shack

Research shows that children are profoundly affected by divorce. They will think about their loss – their family's breakup – almost every day. They will have an increased risk of academic, behavioral, and psychological issues.

Anxiety is the primary psychological distress that children will experience, long-term. Physical ailments may also occur more frequently – and last longer. Studies show that children of divorce have higher rates of: long-term expectation of failure; fear of loss; fear of change; and fear of conflict.

As children, they are likely to experience feelings of abandonment and confusion about why their parents are not together. Those feelings can lead to long-term attachment and abandonment issues. Later on, they may tend to make poor adult relationship choices, giving up hastily when problems arise – or, they may avoid relationships altogether. They are likely to view premarital sex and cohabitation more favorably.

Nevertheless, parents are able to counteract many of those risk factors.

Parental conflict is the biggest predictor of poor outcomes for children of divorce. Children do not want conflict between their parents. Children need stability and peace to thrive. Young children expect their parents to have supernatural abilities and to overcome their issues.

Older children, however, begin to understand that some adult issues are not easily resolved. They may come to realize that if their parents live in two separate homes, it may lead to a more peaceful environment for them. Older children are also more able to see each of their parents as individuals and recognize toxic or abusive situations. In those scenarios, you often may see the children supporting a decision to divorce.

Studies show that children from high-conflict homes whose parents got divorced ultimately have fewer negative impacts on their long-term mental health than if the unhealthy family had stayed intact. In other words, the children often do better when removed from the unhealthy environment. Unhealthy environments include family homes where there is emotional or physical abuse, substance abuse, and psychological issues with emotional dysregulation.

How can parents counteract the increased risks for their children? Divorced parents need to create a stable, safe home environment by modeling healthy self-care. That is achieved by participating in individual counseling, and going to divorce support groups or co-parenting counseling as needed. Such individual work helps each adult be as emotionally stable as possible, which, in turn, helps them to be healthy parents.

Adult stability allows the child to remain a child, and not become a parental confidant or replacement. Children of all ages tend to feel frightened, anxious, or burdened by parents' neediness, so it is imperative that you take care of your own mental health. Moreover, children tend to be as resilient as the parents are, and they look to their parents to model appropriate behavior and emotional regulation.

Stable parents show that they are dependable; they do not expose the children to adult conflict or badmouth the other parent. They keep children out of the middle. Healthy parents do not use their children as messengers or spies, and they do not feel threatened when the children are with the other parent.

It is important for children to be able to openly talk about their parents in each home and to love both parents. They need to remain connected with both parents' families and remain involved in both parents' lives. And, both parents need to have consistent, meaningful contact with the children.

Children need to be allowed to express their feelings about the divorce and the family changes. Be aware that you will want to share upcoming major changes – such as moving – with the children, so that they can emotionally prepare. Do not burden them with adult issues such as court proceedings, custody, dating, or finances.

Healthy divorced families co-parent well, and they put the children's needs above their own individual adult issues. In a healthy post-divorce environment, both parents are involved in parenting and respect and value each other's roles. They exhibit flexibility with a problem-solving attitude, and they seek solutions instead of arguments.

Ways to keep conflict to a minimum include: maintaining healthy boundaries with your child's other parent; sticking to your financial agreements; making sure you have a clear and complete parenting plan; and keeping any changes to the co-parenting schedule to a minimum. Understand and manage your anger and develop a business-like attitude in discussions with the other parent.

Using a digital platform such as OurFamilyWizard for communication and scheduling is very helpful. Agree on a way to consistently give each other updates about the children. Create a mechanism to make decisions and resolve disagreements. Consider using a counselor, mediator, or parenting coordinator to help you as needed.

PART 7 : HOW DO I HAVE A CHILD-CENTERED DIVORCE?

Being healthy co-parents starts at the very first discussion – when you tell the children that you're getting a divorce. Ideally, both parents will be involved in that conversation, and all of the children will be told at the same time. Keep in mind that there will probably be an ongoing series of small talks after the main discussion. But before the meeting with the children, you will need to decide what you're going to say, and also have answers to the questions that the children might have.

It is important to tell them that divorce is a decision that you made together. Presenting the news in a united way helps the children to not blame either parent. Instead, they will be allowed to love each of you without adult issues getting in the way. Above all, make it clear that the divorce is not the children's fault. Plan a follow-up chat with the children a few days after the initial talk. Ask your children what they think divorce means, and correct any misperceptions they may have.

Children need to spend time with each parent, and that schedule needs to be determined by the parents. Explain the plan for spending time with each parent and what the living arrangements are going to be in each home. For young children, it is beneficial to help them make a color-coded calendar that shows when their parenting time is with each parent. Have such a calendar readily accessible to them in each house, and in their school bag.

You need to convey key items to the children, and they should be adjusted for the children's age and level of understanding. But regardless of the children's age, you should shield them from the details and reasons for the divorce. Doing that will help your children to avoid assigning blame. Assure them that you tried to make things better but that the marriage was impossible to fix. Emphasize that you are still a family – just a different kind of family than you used to be. Children need reassurance that both parents love them and are going to be available. They need to be told they can continue to love everyone in the family.

Let the children know that you understand their feelings. However, they need to be told very clearly that Mommy and Daddy will not get back together again. When putting your new home together, give the children a chance to explore and get a feel for the new place. Make your new home a comfortable, inviting place for your children, where they will have their own private spaces. Get the children involved in choosing decor and items for their new rooms. Be available whenever they have questions or need to express their thoughts and feelings about the changes ahead.

You don't have to have all the answers right away. Counselors who work with divorcing families can help you navigate what to tell the children, based on their developmental stages. Encourage your children to talk with someone other than yourself and facilitate the meeting. It may be a play therapist (for younger children), a counselor, a teacher, a church group leader, or other trusted adults.

Kathleen Shack, MS, LMFT
Family Solutions Counseling
Certified Gottman Couples Therapist
Certified Discernment Counselor
Certified Amicable Divorce Professional
Divorce Coach and Mediator
Alpharetta, Georgia

Chapter 27
Your To-Do List for a Child-Centered Divorce
by J. Ashley Heredia

Would you like an amicable, child-centered divorce? The points below provide guidance on what NOT to do to help achieve that outcome (and what TO do instead)!

Don't Speak Negatively About the Other Parent

Children internalize negative comments made about their other parent, which can affect their self-esteem and sense of security. Negative comments usually undermine trust in co-parenting. That can make cooperation between the parents difficult, which is essential after the divorce.

Instead, speak positively or neutrally about the other parent in front of the children. Don't vent your negative emotion in front of your kids; discuss your frustrations with a therapist or another trusted adult. Continue to remind the children that both parents love them and that the divorce is not their fault.

Don't Involve Children in Adult Conflicts

Children should not be involved in divorce-related conflicts. Specifically, children should not be placed in the role of messenger, confidant, or decision-maker. Children who are exposed to adult disputes or issues may feel guilt or fear, or may develop loyalty dilemmas. Such internal conflicts in a child can lead to anxiety, depression, or behavioral problems. In addition, burdening children with adult matters can damage their trust and their bond with the parent involved.

Each parent should communicate directly with the other parent rather than through the children. Moreover, legal issues, financial concerns, or custody disputes should never be discussed in front of the children. Ultimately, both parents should work to protect the children's innocence by keeping their lives focused on school, friends, and hobbies.

Don't Overshare or Use Social Media to Vent

You may be tempted to vent about your divorce on social media or to friends and family. However, social media posts can be used as evidence in court to show hostility, poor judgment, or lack of cooperation in your case. Sharing too much information about your divorce can create bias and spread misinformation. Doing that will only escalate tensions if information gets back to the other party. Oversharing is typically perceived as gossiping or attempting to inappropriately sway another's opinion – which a court will likely frown upon. Negative social media posts can amplify misunderstandings, fuel conflict, and embarrass your child. Plus, your child could potentially read this online in the future.

Avoid posting on social media about your divorce, parenting frustrations, or personal matters. Also, it's smart to adjust privacy settings; still, assume anything you post could be seen. You may even consider taking a break from social media completely during your divorce to focus on self-care.

Avoid Emotional Escalation

Emotional instability in divorcing parents creates a stressful environment for the children, negatively affecting their emotional well-being. Additionally, emotional outbursts can lead to impulsive decisions that may undermine your case, or potentially harm your relationship with your children. Lastly, anger and hostility typically provoke retaliatory behavior from the other party, prolonging and complicating the divorce.

Emotional escalation can be avoided in many ways. For instance, try to pause before responding to provocative messages or situations. Engage in stress-relief activities like exercise, journaling, or therapy. Ask that your case be mediated to resolve disputes in a structured, calm environment.

Refrain from Making Big Decisions About Kids Without Consultation

Major decisions during a divorce – such as relocating, altering a child's routine, changing a child's school, or making large purchases – can be seen as undermining the other party's rights or as destabilizing the family. Such sudden changes can potentially influence custody outcomes. From the children's point of view, major decisions can disrupt their sense of well-being, their educational experience, and their social life.

It is a good idea to discuss any significant potential changes with your attorney before acting. If possible, discuss with your co-parent as well to attempt to achieve a mutually agreeable result. Be mindful of court orders that may limit your ability to make unilateral decisions. In the end, it is best to work with your co-parent to ensure that decisions align with your child's best interests.

Don't Deny Access to Your Children Without Cause

The legal system prioritizes that children maintain relationships with both parents unless there is evidence of harm, or other serious safety concerns. Denying a child access to a parent without court approval or just cause can result in sanctions, custody modification, and negative inferences from the court.

Parenting schedules and agreed-upon visitation should be honored. Both parents should focus on ensuring that the child feels loved and supported. However, any concerns about safety or well-being should be documented and reported through legal channels. When in doubt, ask your lawyer about deviating from the Parenting Plan or withholding your child from the other parent.

Avoid Making Threats or Ultimatums

Threatening or pressuring the other party can be viewed as abusive and manipulative. Such actions will only escalate hostility and harm settlement discussions. Children who are exposed to hostility between their parents tend to feel unsafe or emotionally burdened.

Use neutral, respectful language in all communications. Try to focus on problem-solving rather than assigning blame or issuing demands. Consider family therapy or a divorce coach to help facilitate constructive conversations.

Don't Ignore the Emotional Impact

Divorce can be emotionally overwhelming for children; it can negatively affect their mental health and behavior. Children without emotional support during their parents' divorce may experience anxiety or depression, or may have difficulty forming relationships later in life. Failing to address your children's emotional needs can damage your bond with them and their trust in you. Remember that courts consider each parent's ability to meet the emotional and developmental needs of the child when assessing a child's best interests.

Watch your children for signs of distress – such as changes in behavior, poor sleep, or low academic performance. Reassure your children that they are loved, and that their feelings matter. You may also consider involving a child therapist to help your children navigate the divorce.

Don't Neglect Yourself

During a divorce, it is easy to become overwhelmed by stress, emotional turmoil, and uncertainty about the future. Taking time for self-care will help maintain your mental, emotional, and physical well-being. That time will allow you to approach the process with greater clarity and resilience. By prioritizing your own well-being, you create a more supportive environment for your children. An improved, stable outlook on your part will help your child feel more secure – and better able to cope with the changes.

So, schedule regular personal time, or "me time." Whether it's a small break of quiet time, a neighborhood walk, or an enjoyable hobby, treat those moments as non-negotiable appointments with yourself.

Also, set boundaries or limit contact with your ex-spouse to necessary or child-related communications. Stick to the facts when you have to communicate; try to remove the emotion. Reducing unnecessary conflict will free up emotional space to better take care of yourself.

Additionally, you might practice mindfulness or relaxation techniques, like deep breathing, meditation, or yoga. Those activities will help lower your stress levels and keep you feeling present rather than overwhelmed.

By avoiding these common pitfalls, divorcing spouses can reduce conflict, preserve their integrity, be better co-parents, and ensure that their child's needs remain the top priority.

J. Ashley Heredia
Founding Attorney, Heredia Family Law
Former Chair, the Family Law Section of the Atlanta Bar Association
Member, Family Law Section of the State Bar of Georgia
Atlanta, Georgia

PART 7 : HOW DO I HAVE A CHILD-CENTERED DIVORCE?

Chapter 28
Children's Developmental Stages and Divorce
by Kathleen Shack

Children experience the effects of divorce differently at different developmental ages. What follows is a guideline about the primary tasks that occur at each developmental stage and the effects of divorce. Signs of distress for each stage are listed, as well as guidelines for parents on how they can address the distress their children may be experiencing. It is recommended that children participate in counseling (play therapy for young children) to help them learn coping skills and deal with stress.

Developmental stage – 18 months to 3 years old
Primary task: Learn to be a unique, separate person while seeking parental approval.
What toddlers experience: • Toddlers are aware of parents fighting. They may act out or try to make parents stop. • They feel unsafe and stressed when a parent is unable to take care of them. • Magical thinking: They think they are the cause of problems. • Routine and predictability provide security. They are uneasy, stressed, and afraid without a routine.
Toddler signs of distress: Regressing, Withdrawal, Normal patterns of sleeping and eating may change significantly, May develop fears.
Parents should: • Maintain a consistent routine. • Reassure your toddler that you love him/her. • Avoid punishing the child for acting like a baby. • Don't force hugs on a child who is pulling away. However, be aware when your child is reaching out. • Set limits and be consistent. • Allow frequent parenting time with each parent.

Developmental stage – 3 to 5 years old

Primary task: Learn new skills; develop personality and independence.

What preschoolers experience:
- Preschoolers may believe they are the cause of the divorce.
- They feel frightened by immense changes. They fear abandonment.
- They fear they will never see the parent who moved out of the home.
- They may try to magically wish the divorce away.
- They may think they can get their parents back together.

Preschooler signs of distress:
- May say things that indicate that they feel responsible for the divorce.
- May become clingy.
- May regress.
- May become bossy, and try to control everyone and everything.
- May have increased anger or aggression.
- May become withdrawn.
- May worry about the other parent.

Parents should:
- Provide predictable, consistent routines. Don't make too many changes at once.
- When you leave, reassure them that you will be back at a specific time. Keep your word.
- Provide opportunities for the child to express feelings.
- Reassure the child that your love will never change.
- Reassure the child that he/she is safe and you will always take care of him/her.
- Keep the other parent informed about the events in the child's life. Both parents should attend special events for the child.
- Inform teachers or day care providers about any changes.

Developmental stage – 6 to 9 years old

Primary task: Family is very important. Family wholeness is where children find security, so that they can successfully venture out and develop their self-esteem and identity.

Children 6 to 9 experience:
- The child may have very strong feelings of sadness, anger, guilt, or loneliness.
- The child will miss the other parent when they aren't together.
- The child may have difficulty concentrating at school.
- The child may fear that one parent will stop loving them.
- The child may side with one parent – usually the one that's most needy.
- The child may try to provide emotional support for a parent who appears to be suffering.

Children 6 to 9, signs of distress:
- A significant change in grades or attitude about school.
- Spending a great deal of time withdrawn, crying frequently, or acting sad.
- A possible increase in physical symptoms.
- A lack of enthusiasm.
- Likely to test abandonment fear by acting out.

Parents should:
- Accept the child's feelings. Be available to listen.
- Never say demeaning things about the other parent in front of the child.
- Role-model self-care for the child's benefit.
- Let the child know that you want him/her to love, and spend time with, the other parent.
- Don't encourage the child's hopes of reunification.
- Tell and show the child that you love him/her.
- Try to keep both parents involved.

Developmental stage – 9 to 12 years old

Primary task: Become more independent.

Ages 9 to 12 experience:
- Conflict over what they want for themselves and others.
- The child may feel torn between parents.
- Most likely will feel anger, and it will usually be directed at one parent for "messing up my life."
- May feel ashamed or embarrassed by any public display of parental disagreement.
- The child will often worry about their parents, feeling tremendous responsibility for their well-being.

Children 9 to 12, signs of distress:
- Acting as if the divorce is of no consequence to them.
- Boys may exhibit poor school performance, or get into fights.
- Girls may bend over backward to try to please.
- A possible increase in physical symptoms.
- Possible premature sexual activity.
- Taking on an adult role in the family, which forces the child to side with one parent; guilty feelings.
- The child becomes angry if forced to choose a parent.

Parents should:
- Model self-care.
- Remain in the role of adult.
- Encourage children to be physically active.
- Stay aware of what is going on with school, and with their friends.
- Talk with the child about his/her feelings and what is happening.
- Do not badmouth the other parent or divulge adult information.
- Encourage the child to talk with someone other than yourself, and help facilitate it.
- Create an environment where your child is able to be a child.

Developmental stage – 13 to 18 years old
Primary task: Get ready to leave home and live responsibly.
What adolescents experience: • Adolescents may feel anxiety about leaving home. • They are often not realistic about the future. • They may feel responsible for the divorce. • They may believe that the parent who moved out no longer loves them. • They may worry about their future plans and having money. • They may feel rejected or neglected. • They may feel frightened or burdened by a parent's neediness. • They may resent their parents for messing up their life. • They are likely to feel embarrassed or ashamed about their parents' divorce.
Adolescent signs of distress: • Launching earlier than planned. • Talk of delaying their own plans so they can be at home to help out. • Fear about leaving home, because there will be no home to come back to. • Disappearing for longer periods into video gaming or the internet. • Being extremely negative and/or critical. • Increased sexual behavior. • Increased aggression. • Moderate to severe legal problems; substance abuse; school problems; running away; withdrawal; self-injuring behaviors.
Parents should: • Model self-care. • Offer love, encouragement, and support. • Remain in a parental role. Maintain clear expectations and consistent boundaries. • Encourage the teen to become independent. • Be discreet about your sexual activities. • Give the teen permission to know and love the other parent. • Tell your teen often that you love him/her. • Allow the teen's input regarding the schedule. • Don't take it personally if the teen chooses to spend time with the other parent. The same-sex parent is often preferred at this age. • Remain involved.

Developmental stage – 18 years old and over

Primary task: To explore possible directions and roles in life until finding one that feels like the right fit. Emerging adults focus on themselves as they develop the knowledge, skills, and self-understanding they will need for adult life.

What the emerging adult experiences:
- Fear of commitment.
- Distrust of the opposite sex.
- Fear of success.
- Apprehension about marriage.
- May have unresolved identity issues.
- Symptoms of mild depression.
- Difficulty regulating emotions.
- May try to fix the relationship between the parents.

Emerging adult signs of distress:
- Relationship issues: They may question whether to ever marry.
- Frequent job instability.
- Attachment issues.
- Excessive drug or alcohol use.
- Moderate to severe legal problems.
- Problems keeping up with classes at college.
- Withdrawal.
- Self-injuring behaviors.
- May stay home to fix or help instead of launching.
- May move far away from home to avoid parental issues.

Parents should:
- Both parents need to stay closely connected with adult children and continue to attend important events.
- Encourage children to launch and develop their sense of self.
- Do not use adult children as confidants to put down the other parent.
- Validate the adult child's struggles and monitor their functioning.
- Provide a warm environment for the young adult to visit; it should feel like a safe and comfortable home.
- Encourage the adult child to maintain boundaries, and not to be the counselor or mediator for the parents.

Kathleen Shack, MS, LMFT
Family Solutions Counseling
Certified Gottman Couples Therapist
Certified Discernment Counselor
Certified Amicable Divorce Professional
Divorce Coach and Mediator
Alpharetta, Georgia

Chapter 29
The Child's Perspective
by J. Ashley Heredia

What is divorce like for a child? I am both a family law attorney and someone who once was on the other side of a divorce – your child's side. My parents divorced when I was nine, and while their marriage was full of conflict and turmoil, their divorce was – surprisingly – not.

The direction of my life changed for the better when my parents decided to take a child-centered approach to their divorce. I hope that my story will inspire you to navigate your own divorce with the same care and thoughtfulness.

I had a somewhat turbulent childhood. My dad struggled with substance abuse, and both of my parents carried emotional wounds that fueled their many arguments. The arguments started out as tense, muffled, closed-door talks, but eventually became combative screaming matches. They happened mostly at night, when my parents thought I was asleep.

I am over 40 years old now, but I still have vivid memories of the fights between my parents. For example, I remember being huddled in bed with my glow-in-the-dark sheets pulled over my head and a pillow over my ears, trying to block out my parents' yelling. During another argument, I found my mom kneeling on her bedroom floor, crying. She was trying to pick up her sewing pins and needles that had been scattered around the room. The ceramic case that had once held her sewing supplies was shattered on the floor – another casualty of my dad's temper.

When my mom finally decided to divorce my dad, she could have turned the process into a battle; she could have used his past mistakes like a weapon against him. If my mom had sought to limit my dad's parenting time with me, the court would have probably sided with her. But she didn't do that.

And to my dad's credit, he didn't fight for a parenting arrangement that would differ much from our existing family dynamic. He openly acknowledged that my mom had been my primary caregiver and was the more stable parent. He was honest with himself and the court, agreeing to a Parenting Plan that reflected my mom's significant role in my upbringing, but also gave him the opportunity to have a safe and meaningful presence in my life.

My parents approached their divorce with humility and respect for each other. They kept my best interest at the forefront. Because of that, they resolved things quickly. They gave me the gift of stability at a time when my world could have easily been thrown into further chaos.

For me, the divorce wasn't devastating; it was relief. For the first time in years, I didn't have to tiptoe around my parents' conflicts or brace myself for their next argument. My relationship with each of them improved. My mom was no longer weighed down trying to hold everything together, and my dad could work on being the best version of himself without the stress of what had become a toxic marriage.

Many of my most cherished memories with my dad were formed after my parents divorced. Those memories are especially precious now, as my dad unexpectedly passed away about four years after my parents' marriage ended. Had my mom chosen another path in the divorce – had she fought to 1) remove my dad from my life or 2) severely limit our time together – I would not have seen the more kind, funny, and loving sides of him. I will always be deeply grateful to my mom for allowing me to have those experiences.

Years after the divorce, my mom asked me if there was anything she could have done differently. My answer surprised her: "I wish you'd left sooner." Like many parents, she thought she'd hidden much of their conflict from

PART 7 : HOW DO I HAVE A CHILD-CENTERED DIVORCE?

me, but as I always tell my clients, children are incredibly perceptive – and at a younger age than you might expect. I saw and felt much more than she realized that I did, even early on, when their disagreements were much less heated. My mom's attempt to hold it together "for her child's sake" only prolonged my stress and instability.

If you have children and are in the thick of a divorce or even on the brink of one, you are probably worried about how the process will affect your children. Remember that you can't shield your children from every hurt they may experience during the divorce – and that's okay. Like the divorce, life will challenge them in ways you cannot control, but those challenges will help shape them into stronger versions of themselves; into who they are meant to be.

What you *can* control is how you work through your divorce with your future co-parent. Approach the process amicably. The goal is to create a parenting schedule that prioritizes your children's well-being, while also preserving their relationships with both parents. Even if your spouse has made mistakes, even if you feel angry or betrayed, there's a way to move forward that focuses on what's best for your child.

My parents handled their divorce with dignity and two clear intentions. One, keep the health and happiness of their child as the top priority; and two, despite the circumstances of the divorce, maintain respect for each other.

Following those intentions resulted in a divorce that wasn't the end of my family, but rather turned out to be a peaceful, new beginning for all of us. With similar care and intent, that same outcome can be true for your family too.

J. Ashley Heredia
Founding Attorney, Heredia Family Law
Former Chair, the Family Law Section of the Atlanta Bar Association
Member, Family Law Section of the State Bar of Georgia
Atlanta, Georgia

Chapter 30
Complex Issues
by Tracy Ann Moore-Grant

Many have the misconception that if their divorce case involves a complicated issue or difficult spouse, the case must be litigated, and cannot be "amicable." That is simply not the case. The reality is that over 90 percent of family law and divorce cases settle without the need for a final hearing in court (we will just keep reminding you of that).

Moreover, many of those cases involved complex issues. Amicable cases that have been resolved have included issues such as multimillion-dollar marital estates, international property, mental health issues, complicated finances, jointly owned small businesses, addiction, and difficult personalities.

In an amicable divorce case, experienced professionals can guide you through those types of matters, using the same tools they would use in a litigation case. But in an amicable case, there will be a more efficient result. That is one of the reasons that the Amicable Divorce Network requires that its professionals be experienced to be members.

It's appropriate to think about each divorce problem as a lock – and that each lock has a key, or solution. The reality is that judges are not the only ones who have keys. The spouses themselves often have the keys to get issues resolved – and experienced professionals can assist with finding and using those keys, providing ideas and solving problems. Having the judge use their key to solve your problem is the most time-consuming, unpredictable, and costly way to do it.

When it comes to any issue in a divorce – complex or not – it is important that the parties first agree that there actually is an issue that needs a resolution. In the first phase of your divorce, you are doing information gathering, which involves each party making a list of all the issues that need to be resolved.

An issue could be something financial, like deciding who gets the IRA account; or, it could be something less tangible, like establishing safety parameters regarding a spouse's addiction. What is essential is that both parties agree to put the issue on the list. So, if one party thinks the other has addiction issues, and then that spouse denies there is a problem, this issue may take more work.

In the second phase of your divorce, you will do an information assessment. For example, in regard to the previously mentioned issue of addiction, perhaps one party needs to ask for an addiction assessment on the other spouse to prove their point. Or, perhaps the other spouse would agree to some testing to prove they are sober. Likewise, with an issue involving a marital small business, as long as both parties agree that all or part of the business is a marital asset, then the parties can move forward in Phase 2; i.e., getting the asset properly valued.

It is important to know that any issue can be solved outside of the court system with the right professionals and tools. Some key questions to ask your team:

- **Does my spouse agree** that there is an issue?
- If they do not agree, **what type of information can I provide** to show that this is an issue?
- **How can we resolve** this issue?
- **What is the time and cost** associated with the solution?
- **Will my spouse share** in the cost?

Remember, your team members are always there to support and assist you in resolving any issue, big or small. Rely on them for advice and guidance.

Chapter 31
Intimate Partner Violence
by Tori E. Owens

Domestic violence, or intimate partner violence, is never an easy topic to discuss. Yet, it is important to understand if it is happening to you, particularly when considering separation and divorce.

If you are approaching a divorce and domestic violence is involved, it is best to proceed with caution when handling things outside of the court system and pursuing an amicable divorce. It is important to be candid with your chosen legal professional and discuss options that apply to your particular circumstances.

Explaining Terminology

Domestic violence (abbreviated DV) is a broad term for a pattern of abuse and control that happens within romantic relationships, partnerships, and marriages. More recently, the term "intimate partner violence" (or IPV) has been used to replace domestic violence. "Intimate partner violence" emphasizes the close context of this type of abuse and includes LGBTQIA2+ relationships. Although either term is more than appropriate to use, for the purpose of discussion here, IPV will be the preferred term.

Forms of Violence

Unfortunately, there are countless ways to inflict violence upon another human being.
- Words can be used in **verbal** violence: name-calling, put-downs, yelling, screaming, threats.
- With **physical** violence, bodies and weapons can be used: pushing, shoving, hitting, slapping, hair-pulling, blocking, sitting upon/immobilizing, kidnapping.

- In **emotional and psychological** violence, mind games can be used: gaslighting, dismissing/discounting, belittling, blaming, undermining, blackmail, isolation.
- Violence can be used in **sexual and reproductive** contexts: rape, sexual manipulation or coercion, hiding or replacing birth control, intentional transference of sexually transmitted diseases (STDs).
- **Finances, assets, and debts** can be used: not allowing access to financial accounts, disallowing the partner's name on assets, applying the partner's name to all debt.
- **Religion or faith** can be used: using sacred text to threaten or oppress, using isolation of the religious community, threatening to name or use past disclosures (or "sins"), gender oppression based on religion.
- **Children** can be used: threats to run with children or gain sole custody, favoritism or unhealthy competition, pitting children against each other, preferential same-gendered treatment, threatening a child, child abuse.
- **Pets** can be used: threats to take away or kill a pet, refusing to feed or care for a pet, killing or harming a pet to make a point.
- **Social media, phones, and technology** can be used: doxing, spoofing, use of car apps to disrupt use of the vehicle, use of air tags and map apps for tracking, posting sexually explicit photos without consent.
- **Stalking** can be used: repeated predatory behavior to scare or frighten, watching, following, tracking, documenting, recording, calling, texting, emailing to the extent that it interferes with daily living.

Types of IPV

IPV crosses all social, economic, gender, language, racial, ethnic, sexual orientation, and religious lines. There are four types of IPV:

- **Intimate terrorism or intimate coercive control** is a pervasive pattern of coercive control and abuse that happens over the course of a relationship. Typically, the abuse increases in frequency and severity over time, and is most often kept secret.

- **Violent resistance** occurs when an abused partner fights back against an abuser within an intimate coercive controlling relationship.
- **Situational violence** describes a one-time violent incident that happens within a particular situation. It often occurs due to alcohol overconsumption, substance use, or extreme emotional or psychological stress. It is important to remember that a pattern of power and control does not exist for this type of IPV. This is a one-off.
- **Mutual combat** is just that – intimates mutually agreeing to fight. It might be quite strange for most of us to consider this as an option. Yet, if the partners see one another as equals, and there is no pattern of power and control, it would be left to them to decide the terms.

Lethality

"Lethality" is a term used to describe how dangerous a person is, or how violent they could become. There are a few things to consider when we assess for lethality in IPV:

- **Prior violence** of the abuser: How often, what type of violence, and how severe was it?
- There are **lethality indicators** such as stalking, choking/strangling, having access to a gun, or being unemployed. These lethality indicators, and others – if present, and depending on how many – tell us how likely someone is to be violent or even potentially kill.
- It is important to **trust the input** of the person being abused. They have firsthand information regarding the lethality of an abuser and what could happen next.
- Lethality assessments are a formal way of **measuring the risk of lethality**. Law enforcement, as well as DV/IPV hotlines and shelters, should have access to such surveys and be qualified to administer them. The assessments can be an important way to plan for safety when a spouse is considering leaving.

Safety Planning

Safety planning can be done at any point during coercive controlling relationships. However, it is imperative to have a plan when you are considering leaving, separating, or filing for divorce.

Starting a safety plan cannot be stressed strongly enough – the moment of leaving is the most dangerous time for someone being coercively abused and controlled. Safety planning includes considering information, looking at choices, making decisions, and establishing next steps so that you can keep yourself and loved ones safe during the leaving process.

Some key points for safety planning:

- Keep your phone charged, and on you.
- Maintain quick access to your car keys.
- Let those whom you trust know your whereabouts or daily schedule; check in regularly.
- Keep your gas tank filled.
- Have a small bag of belongings packed for you and your children, place it in your car or leave it with someone you trust.
- Keep documents, insurance cards, and money in a safe place.
- Call a local DV/IPV shelter or hotline to talk, access therapy and other services, or seek shelter.
- Speak with an attorney.

Resources

DV/IPV resources are available; the extent of resources varies, depending on where you live. Each resource is a good place to start to get more information about DV/IPV, local shelters and services, safety planning, and steps to healing.

Do not access any resources on your phone or computer if you are being monitored, or if it is not safe to do so. The following websites have quick exits available, but you will need to manually delete site information from your internet browser history after visiting them. For added safety, it is best to borrow a friend or relative's phone, or to access a computer at a local library.

For the United States:
- National Domestic Violence Hotline
  1.800.799SAFE (7233)
  Text BEGIN to 88788
  Chat and other resources: thehotline.org
- Bright Sky – US app

For Canada:
- sheltersafe.ca
- iHEAL app

For the UK:
- National Domestic Abuse Helpline
  0808 2000 247
  Chat is also available
- Bright Sky – UK app

Tori E. Owens
Licensed Professional Counselor
National Certified Counselor
Dahlonega, Georgia

Chapter 32
Personality Disorders
by Tori E. Owens

Narcissism is a trendy topic. When we journey through the divorce process, nearly anyone can present with narcissistic symptoms. Why? In moments of increased stress, grief, and anxiety about our family's futures, sometimes we are not quite our best selves.

There is a distinction, though, between understandable behaviors and feelings emanating from the difficult days of divorce versus the long-term manipulative and contentious behavior of a narcissist. The former happens for a limited period; the latter is a way of life, consistent over time.

Many parties facing divorce think that because their spouse has – or seems to have – a personality disorder (or is just very difficult to deal with), their case must go to court and a judge. That is not always the case; an amicable divorce may be possible.

Moving the case through the court system can increase costs and conflict; expense and stress can both be reduced if the case can be steered toward an amicable resolution. You should discuss options with your selected legal professional in order to make the best choice for your case.

The Amicable Divorce Network screens their professionals for membership. The professional joining the ADN must have a minimum of five years of experience; that means that they will have the skills necessary to deal with difficult people.

Definition of terms

First of all, it is important to define some terms:

- Our **mental health** impacts all of who we are and everything we do – our relationships, perceptions, attachment styles, jobs…you name it! Our mental health has to do with our well-being, emotions, thoughts, self-esteem, and self-confidence.
- A **mental health disorder** is a diagnosable set of symptoms that have an impact on our mental well-being. The symptoms disrupt or interfere with daily life, and they persist over time.
- **Personality disorders** are a particular category of mental health disorders. Personality disorders are about your perception – of yourself, the world, and your relationship with that world. The perception is concretized or unyielding, and it is not explainable by a person's culture. As an illustration, we all experience the world through a particular windshield. Most of us, for most of the time, realize the windshield is there. We can get around the windshield, describe it, name how it changes our perception, and even create a new windshield. When you

have a personality disorder, you don't realize you have a windshield, and that means you don't know there's anything wrong.

What Is Trauma?

Trauma is what happens to us. It's the awful, extreme stuff like intimate partner violence. It can also be a car accident, surgery, or a bullying incident. Trauma often has a way of being seared into our memory. Yet, trauma is also about what we needed and didn't receive: attachment, security, stability, support. Begin to think about trauma in little ways, not just the big obvious ways. Remember also, traumas are not comparable among individuals. What is traumatic for one person may not be for another, and vice versa.

Fight or Flight Response

When our brain registers something traumatic or life-threatening, it will trigger the **"fight or flight"** response. It is a remarkable temporary response, overriding all other brain and bodily functions, with the sole intent of keeping us alive. There are countless combinations of how we respond to a crisis in any given moment. The way we might respond hinges on our past personal traumas, how we grew up, our family-of-origin traumas, historical traumas (what our ancestors experienced and passed down), who is around us, life stressors, our physical well-being and immunity, our mental health, our support system, etc.

The defensive mechanism of "fight or flight" has been expanded over the years to include other responses: **freeze, fawn,** and **flop.** Here are brief explanations for each of the five basic responses:

- **Fight** – Physical attack, protection, aggression. More broadly, "fight" can also include debating, negating, challenging, or arguing.
- **Flight** – Running away, fleeing, hiding. In an everyday sense, "flight" can be moving often without need, quitting jobs and starting another, or ending relationships suddenly.

- **Freeze** – Paralysis, "deer caught in the headlights," inability to act. "Freeze" can also look like indecisiveness for fear of repercussions; or, not being able to talk during high stress or conflict.
- **Fawn** – Not making waves, sidling up to the danger, people-pleasing, a belief that keeping things smooth will prevent bad things from happening. Often, children – or those without physical strength – will automatically take on the "fawn" position.
- **Flop** – Apathy, submission, surrender. In everyday life, "flop" can look like depression, wanting to sleep all day, or having little or no energy.

Trauma and Personality Disorders

How do trauma and the "fight or flight" responses connect to personality disorders?

Trauma can change how we see ourselves, how we attach to others, or how threatening the world around us can seem. Trauma will change our brains, our bodies, and our spirits.

Personality disorders have roots in trauma and become a way of being and interacting with the world. Our brain, the environment, genetics, and traumas all factor into building that windshield mentioned earlier. What began as an effective mechanism to defend and protect can become – when triggered repeatedly by traumas – more defined and immovable over time. What was intended to be a temporary protective response becomes the way we live every day and with everyone.

Personality Disorder Clusters

There are three separate personality disorder clusters.
- **Cluster A** (odd and eccentric) – *paranoid, schizoid, and schizotypal*
- **Cluster B** (dramatic and erratic) – *antisocial, borderline, histrionic, and narcissistic*
- **Cluster C** (anxious and fearful) – *avoidant, dependent, and obsessive-compulsive*

Our focus is on **Cluster B,** the dramatic and erratic type, since these symptoms manifest most often in relationships. There are some general characteristics for all four of the Cluster B personality disorders:
- Dramatic and emotional
- Underlying impulsivity and erraticism, jeopardizing the well-being of self and others
- History of trauma
- Familial patterns of personality disorders in general, of a particular cluster, or of a specific personality disorder
- Genetic relationship between this cluster, mood disorders, and substance use disorders
- Extreme caretaking figures: the absence of physical/emotional connection with a caregiver, and/or a highly demanding caregiver

Let's take a closer look at the four disorders within Cluster B:
- **Antisocial** – The "go-to" is aggression and fights; history of unlawful behavior; deceit/lying; inability to sustain financial obligations; lack of empathy; dismissal of others' feelings.
- **Borderline** – Triggered by real or perceived abandonment; vacillates between extremes of love and hate; instability in facial expressions, moods, and self-image; history of suicidality; intense anger; self-damaging tendencies; feelings of paranoia.
- **Histrionic** – Attention-seeking; emotionality; sexually provocative; focused on physical appearance; shallow and shifting emotions; theatrical; misperceives deeper levels of intimacy in relationships.
- **Narcissistic** – Grandiosity and need for admiration; lack of empathy; sense of entitlement; exploitative; arrogant; haughty; fantasies of unlimitedness (success, brilliance, love, etc.).

On our worst days, we might exhibit behavior that could look like any one of these, but that would be temporary. For anyone with a diagnosable Cluster B personality disorder, this type of behavior is a way of life. There is consistency in the impulsivity and erraticism – no matter if the times are good or bad.

Personality Disorders in Relationships

With any one of the Cluster B personality disorders, symptoms most often show up in the context of relationships. Operating with a personality disorder is an adaptive way of life, developed and hardened over time. This type of interaction with others was quite effective at one time – it was a way to get needs met. Very probably, it was the only way to get needs met.

Because these are trauma-based disorders, everyone is being assessed quickly and constantly – a hyper-reading of tone, breathings, body language, and word usage. Things can switch up instantly based on those hyper-readings, whether they are accurate or not, and the switch-up will always be with self-preservation in mind.

When children are involved, unrealistic expectations abound for the parent with a personality disorder. Children will not be able to organically journey through developmental stages. More is always demanded of them, they become parentified and tend to the emotions of the parents, or they are left to fend for themselves.

Giving exists in only one direction – toward the parent with the personality disorder. This is not a relationship of reciprocity. Everyone is being assessed for opportunity. Relationships are transactional and exploited to get what is needed.

Don't Forget

If you are in a relationship with someone exhibiting Cluster B symptoms, life can be exhausting. The struggle can feel endless at times. It is essential that you take care of yourself in all necessary ways. This is what we call self-care.

Get a therapist. Talk to someone regularly who understands personality disorders and how symptoms show up in relationships.

Practice meditation, contemplation, prayer, or some other grounding technique. Walk in the grass barefooted. Touch the trees. Pet your dog or cat. Develop your own sense of being and root in. Know who you are.

Don't react emotionally to being hyper-read or having your buttons pushed. A person with a personality disorder behaves this way with everyone they encounter. In this regard, you aren't special, which means it's not your fault. Creating distance between you and the cause of why they do what they do will help you develop your own flow. You will no longer yield to their erraticism.

One Last Thing...

Typically, when addressing the topic of personality disorder, the focus is on how we might interact with someone exhibiting those symptoms. However, if you are reading this and find yourself described in this cluster, or feel that you might need mental health help, reach out to a therapist. Don't hesitate.

Tori E. Owens, MA
Licensed Professional Counselor
National Certified Counselor
Dahlonega, Georgia

Chapter 33
Handling Addiction in Amicable Cases
by Tracy Ann Moore-Grant

Addiction is an issue that involves many Amicable Divorce Network (ADN) cases. *Addiction* is a broad term that, applied to the out-of-court and private nature of the ADN process, makes it ideal for when one party's employment could be negatively impacted by an addiction issue, or the parties simply want to keep the matter private. Additionally, the Amicable

Divorce Process is flexible and the timeline is customized. This allows for parties to design a timeline that works for their circumstances, which may include a period of treatment, testing, temporary agreements, or professional evaluations.

> It is important to note that if at any time you feel physically unsafe due to addiction issues, or any other, you should take immediate action to protect yourself and any minor children including calling 911. Safety far outweighs the desire to handle things out of court.

As long as both parties agree that addiction is an issue, it is one that can be resolved outside of the court system. If one party believes the other has an addiction problem, and the other denies there is any issue, you should discuss this with your lawyer. In this circumstance, it could be that additional evidence is needed to prove this is an issue or further discussion needs to occur.

Addiction takes many forms. When it comes to a divorce, the addiction issues come to the forefront when they negatively impact the marital assets and or a party's ability to properly care for minor children. When choosing to pursue making addiction an issue, speak with your lawyer about whether it is worth it in your case. For example, if your spouse has a gambling addiction and has lost $100,000 of marital assets to gambling, they may acknowledge this and be willing to credit that amount to you in the settlement. This makes further action on the issue unnecessary. Most addiction issues, however, are not that straightforward.

Addiction can manifest in various forms, generally categorized into substance addictions and behavioral (or process) addictions. Here's an overview of the different types:

1. Substance Addictions

Substance addiction involves a physical or psychological dependence on specific chemicals or drugs. Common forms include:

- **Alcohol addiction:** Dependence on or misuse of alcohol.

- **Nicotine addiction:** Dependence on tobacco products.
- **Drug addiction:** Abuse of illegal drugs or misuse of prescription medications, such as:
  - **Opioids** (e.g., heroin, prescription painkillers)
  - **Stimulants** (e.g., cocaine, methamphetamine, ADHD medications)
  - **Cannabis** (marijuana)
  - **Hallucinogens** (e.g., LSD, ecstasy)
  - **Sedatives or tranquilizers** (e.g., benzodiazepines)
  - **Inhalants** (e.g., glue, paint thinners)
- **Caffeine addiction:** Excessive dependence on caffeine-containing products.

In a divorce action, it is unlikely that nicotine or caffeine addiction would be worth pursuing as neither are illegal. But always check with your lawyer. When it comes to substance addictions, there are several tools available that can be used to monitor substance abuse:

Substance abuse evaluations: a comprehensive assessment conducted by a trained professional to determine the extent of an individual's substance use and its impact on their mental, emotional, and physical health, as well as their relationships and overall life functioning. The goal is to assess whether a substance use disorder (SUD) is present, the severity of the condition, and appropriate treatment options.

Soberlink: a real-time alcohol testing device that attaches to a person's cell phone. The schedule for testing can be determined by the parties and could be random or coincide with child visitation time.

Drug/substance abuse testing: testing exists for every type of drug whether legal or not. A party can go to a lab in person and take a blood, hair follicle or urine test. These tests can look at substance use sometimes months into the past. Testing has also made great strides into the future and parties can now do testing by mail with a urine test. Although results are not reported in real time, some benefits are that the test is DNA matched so no other urine can be used. The test can provide markers for all substances including the presence of prescription medications someone may need to address a companion issue. The technology and testing ability in this area is progressing quickly.

2. Behavioral Addictions

Behavioral addictions involve a compulsive engagement in activities despite negative consequences. These include:

- **Gambling addiction:** Compulsive participation in gambling activities.
- **Internet addiction:** Excessive use of the internet, including:
  - **Social media addiction**
  - **Online gaming addiction**
  - **General internet use**
- **Sex and pornography addiction:** Compulsion toward sexual activity or pornography consumption.
- **Shopping addiction:** Compulsive spending and shopping behaviors.
- **Food addiction:** Dependence on the consumption of certain types of food, often high in sugar, fat, or salt.
- **Exercise addiction:** Excessive and compulsive engagement in physical exercise.
- **Work addiction (workaholism):** Compulsion to work excessively, even at the expense of personal health or relationships.

In divorce the most common behavioral addictions addressed are gambling, sex and pornography, and shopping addictions as these impact the marital finances and or a person's ability to parent. Just like substance addictions, evaluations are available to determine if a person has one of these addictions. Recommended treatment plans are available. Compared to substance addictions, however, there is no black and white test to determine if someone is on the path to recovery. For behavioral addictions, treatment may involve therapy, medication, and/or ongoing treatment.

There are many other addictions that fall under the addiction umbrella, be it behavior, substance, or both. If you have a concern about your spouse's behavior that is not listed here, it is a good idea to consult with your lawyer and potentially even a psychological professional. A spouse may have a serious issue, but if it is not relevant to your divorce case, there is no reason to put it in your legal proceeding. However, it could be handled otherwise outside of the divorce process.

Handling Addiction Issues

In addition to the testing and therapy mentioned above, there are some other tools that may be helpful in your process to help work through addiction issues, such as:

For Children:

A graduated parenting plan: In this scenario a parent may begin with little or no supervised contact with minor children, with visitation increasing over time as the parent reaches milestones in their recovery as articulated in the plan.

A temporary agreement: Parties can agree to try out an arrangement on a temporary basis before making it final in the court system. They can try a course of treatment, a period of testing, or a similar solution either to investigate if it works for them or to just have something in place while they work out final issues.

For Finances:

Forensic accounting: A financial professional can evaluate the financial records to identify funds used toward an addiction so an accounting can be made for negotiations.

Dividing finances early: If there is a concern about the squandering of finances despite the Amicable Divorce Network Status Quo Agreement, parties can always agree to divide some or all financial accounts before a Final Order. It is important to note this cannot be done with 401k, pension, or IRA accounts; but a spouse can be removed from a credit card, and liquid assets can be divided if all involved parties agree.

If you have concerns about addiction issues in your case, consult with your legal professional to determine the best route for you.

Chapter 34
Pet Custody
by Karis Nafte

Divorces are emotionally charged, no matter what – but when you add a pet to the picture, things can get even more heated. To prevent your dog or cat from becoming a pawn in a larger power struggle, address their future as soon as possible when you begin your divorce process. Ideally, your pet's future home should be determined solely on what's best for *them*, not as a bargaining chip in negotiations.

Frame the discussion entirely around your pet's best interests. Consider these factors:

Which home best suits your pet's personality and routine? Does your pet thrive in a quiet home or an active one? Consider their energy level, breed-specific needs, and any medical, dietary, or behavioral issues. Which environment minimizes disruption to their established routine? Look at your work schedules; consider who has more time and flexibility to provide daily exercise, feeding, grooming, and veterinary appointments.

Sole custody, meaning one person takes the pet, is often the simplest solution. It's less complicated for the pet, who will settle into one home more easily; and also for the two people, who would otherwise have to stay in close contact with each other. Deciding on sole custody requires an honest consideration of the pet's needs, a realistic look at the owner's capabilities, and the ability to focus on the animal's well-being.

Sharing the pet may seem like the best compromise initially, but it doesn't always work in the long run. It requires a high degree of cooperation and communication. The two parties should realize that sharing the pet will make it necessary for them to be in contact, post-divorce. A trial period (for example, six months) is highly recommended to see if a sharing arrangement is feasible and stress-free for both owners and the pet.

A written agreement on pet custody should be included as part of your divorce settlement. It should include custody arrangement specifics, financial responsibilities, plans for emergencies, and clarity about who will retain ownership of the pet if either party can no longer take care of it.

Remember, the goal is to create a stable and loving environment for your pet, minimizing stress during a challenging time. Open communication, compromise, and a high priority on your pet's well-being are crucial.

If a dog, cat, parrot, lizard, or any animal is an issue in your case, please bring it up with your lawyer along with all other issues in dispute. The attorney will need to prepare to discuss, and potentially negotiate, custody, visitation, and financial terms about your pet. They will need information and time to prepare for this issue, as with any other factor in your case.)

Karis Nafte
Author, Who Keeps the Dog: Navigating Pet Custody During Divorce

Chapter 35
Going Public with Your Divorce
by Stephanie Robins

Divorce is a personal journey, and when it's time to share that journey with others, knowing how and when to do so can feel overwhelming. Not only are you dealing with your feelings, but also you are managing the reactions of those around you. This guide will walk you through announcing your divorce to family, friends, children, and the public. It will also address your emotions leading up to and after sharing the news, the challenges of timing, and how to handle tricky situations – like someone asking for more sensitive information than you want to share.

Preparing Emotionally to Announce Your Divorce

Let's discuss how you feel before diving into when and how to share your divorce news. Divorce, even when it's the right choice, is emotionally exhausting. You may be experiencing a roller coaster of emotions – sadness, fear, guilt, relief, or anxiety about the future. These feelings are normal and can make the thought of telling others daunting.

Leading up to the conversation, you might experience:
- **Fear of judgment:** You may worry about how people will react – whether they will judge your decision or make assumptions.
- **Sadness and grief:** Even if the divorce is necessary, it still represents the end of a chapter, which can bring up feelings of loss.
- **Relief:** On the other hand, you might feel relieved that you no longer have to pretend things are okay.

After telling people, expect a mix of emotions:
- **Relief:** Once the news is out, you may feel a weight lifted off your shoulders. You won't have to keep up appearances anymore.
- **Vulnerability:** Sharing something as personal as a divorce can leave you feeling exposed, especially if others respond unexpectedly.
- **Sadness or guilt:** Even if things go smoothly, you may still feel sadness over the situation, or guilt about how it affects others, especially children.

It is important to recognize these emotions. Give yourself time to process them, and avoid rushing to share the news before you're ready.

Disadvantages of Telling Too Soon

There's a balance between feeling emotionally prepared and choosing the right moment to tell people. If you share your divorce news too early, several challenges can arise:
- **Uncertainty:** If key issues like child custody, living arrangements, or finances haven't been decided, telling people too early may lead to more questions than you can answer, increasing your stress.

- **Premature advice:** Well-meaning friends and family may offer unsolicited advice, often based on incomplete information.
- **Increased stress:** If you're still emotionally processing the decision, sharing the news before you're ready can add unnecessary pressure, making you feel like you need to perform emotionally for others before you're prepared.

Waiting until you have key logistics determined can give you more control over the narrative and help you feel more grounded in your decision.

Telling Your Family: Your family may be the first group with whom you think you will share the news, and they can offer a great deal of support. However, feeling anxious about how they'll respond is also natural.

When to Tell Them: Once you've made decisions about key issues, like living arrangements and child custody (if applicable), it's time to share the news with your family. Avoid telling them too soon, as they might press for details you're not ready to share.

How to Tell Them: Start with close family members in a private setting. Be straightforward, but avoid oversharing. You might say, "After careful consideration, we've decided that divorce is the best decision for us. It wasn't easy, but we believe it's the right path forward." Reassure them that you're doing what's best for you and, if applicable, your children.

What to Expect: Family members might express shock, sadness, or even anger. Give them time to process the news, and don't feel pressured to provide more details than you're comfortable sharing.

Talking to Friends: Friends can be a vital source of emotional support, but it's important to approach this conversation thoughtfully.

When to Tell Them: Start with your closest friends – those you trust to offer support. There's no need to make a broad announcement right away. Take it one step at a time.

How to Tell Them: Be honest; but again, avoid sharing too much detail. You might say, "I wanted to let you know that we've decided to divorce. It's been difficult, but we believe it's the best choice for us." Set boundaries around what you're comfortable discussing, and don't hesitate to let friends know if you need time before answering personal questions.

What to Expect: The reactions from your friends may vary. Some will be supportive, while others might not know what to say. Be patient and give them time to process the news, just as you did with your family.

Breaking the News to Your Children: Telling your children is one of the most emotionally charged steps. How you handle it can have a lasting impact on their well-being.

When to Tell Them: Once you and your spouse are aligned on key decisions, like living arrangements and custody, it's time to talk to your children. Both parents should ideally be present, presenting a united front.

How to Tell Them: Keep the conversation age-appropriate and reassuring. Younger children don't need to know every detail; they just need to know that both parents still love them and that the divorce isn't their fault. You can provide a bit more context for older children, but avoid placing blame. Stick to statements like, "Mom and Dad have decided to live in separate homes, but we both love you very much, and that won't change."

What to Expect: Your children may feel sad, confused, or angry. Be patient and open to answering their questions, but avoid burdening them with too much information.

When the Other Parent Tells the Children Without You

If your spouse tells your children about the divorce before you've had a chance to discuss it together, it can cause confusion. In this case:

- **Stay calm** and talk privately with your spouse to express the importance of handling these matters together.
- **Reassure your children** and make sure they understand that the divorce is not their fault. Offer them the chance to ask questions and share their feelings.

Sensitive Reasons for Divorce: Should You Share Them?

Sensitive reasons for divorce, like infidelity, substance abuse, or mental illness, require careful thought. While you may desire to explain yourself, oversharing can create more challenges.

- **Children:** Avoid sharing sensitive details with children. Instead, focus on making them feel safe and loved.
- **Family and friends:** You may feel pressured to explain why, but too much detail can lead to uncomfortable conversations or even people taking sides. Stick to statements like, "We've had issues that we couldn't work through, and this is the best decision for us."
- **Public or acquaintances:** Keep it simple: "We've decided to divorce after much consideration. It's a difficult time, but we appreciate your support."

What to Do When Someone Asks for the Reason

Curiosity often leads people to ask, "What happened?" Have a response ready, such as, "We've been through a lot, and this is the best choice for us." If they press, kindly remind them it's a private matter. Setting clear boundaries will help you navigate these situations.

When to Tell the Public

There's no rush. Some people wait until the divorce is final, while others prefer to share sooner. Once family and close friends know, consider if and how you want to make a more public announcement.

How to Tell the Public

Keep it short and respectful: "After much thought and consideration, we've decided to divorce. We remain committed to co-parenting and appreciate your privacy."

Final Thoughts on Announcing Your Divorce

Announcing your divorce is emotionally challenging. You're not only managing your feelings, but also preparing for the reactions of others. You can reduce stress and create a supportive environment if you consider when and how to share the news. Remember, you don't owe anyone the whole story; setting boundaries is essential. Focus on your emotional well-being and the well-being of your children. You're already taking the necessary steps toward a brighter future.

Stephanie Robins, LCSW, CADP
Alpharetta Family Therapy
Certified Amicable Divorce Professional
Alpharetta, Georgia

Chapter 36
Staying Clearheaded
by Stephanie Robins

During divorce you are making decisions that will shape your future, all while navigating through a whirlwind of emotions. It's a difficult balancing act. On the one hand, you are trying to protect yourself and your family; and on the other, you're navigating feelings of anger, guilt, fear, and sadness. It's completely normal to feel emotionally overwhelmed during a divorce; but allowing those emotions to drive your decisions can lead to long-term consequences that may not serve you well.

This chapter offers practical advice on how to stay clearheaded during the divorce process, allowing you to make thoughtful, rational decisions that protect your future.

Why Emotional Decision-Making Can Hurt You

Divorce involves a lot of critical decisions – how assets will be divided, where you will live, and how much time you will spend with your children. Making these decisions while caught in an emotional storm can lead to outcomes you may regret later. For example, when driven by anger, you might make choices to hurt your spouse, such as fighting for full custody, when shared custody might be better for your children. Conversely, guilt might cause you to give up too much, like surrendering financial security or time with your kids. Fear can push you into accepting an unfair settlement just to finish the process quickly.

These emotions are valid – and real – but can lead to decisions that do not reflect your best interests. Understanding this will keep you from making choices you might regret later.

How Emotions Can Affect Your Decisions

Anger: When angry, the desire to *win* can become overwhelming. You might focus on punishing your spouse instead of thinking about what's best for you or your children. This approach often leads to increased conflict, longer legal battles, and higher costs. The focus on revenge can cloud your judgment, preventing you from making practical decisions that serve your long-term goals.

Guilt: It's common to feel guilty about the end of the marriage, especially if you believe you're to blame. This guilt might lead you to overcompensate – giving up more than you should. For instance, you might offer more money than necessary in a financial settlement or agree to less parenting time. Decisions made out of guilt rarely reflect fairness, often leading to an imbalance that can affect you and your children in the long term.

Fear: Divorce can be scary, particularly when you're uncertain about your financial future or how your relationship with your children will change. This fear might push you to make hasty decisions to avoid the discomfort of ongoing negotiations. However, decisions made in haste, especially around finances or custody, often result in outcomes that don't serve you well over time.

How to Stay Clearheaded During Divorce

1. Recognize Your Emotions

The first step in avoiding emotional decision-making is recognizing your feelings. Take a moment to check in with yourself: Are you angry? Sad? Scared? Acknowledging your emotions can prevent them from dictating your decisions. By recognizing these feelings, you can pause before making significant choices, giving yourself the time to reflect and make decisions based on logic, not just emotion.

2. Give Yourself Time

Divorce doesn't have to be rushed. You're dealing with complex legal and financial issues, and it's important to give yourself time to think things through. When emotions are running high, it's easy to feel like you need to resolve everything quickly. But taking time to process your feelings and consider your options will help you make more thoughtful decisions.

If you are in the heat of an argument or feeling overwhelmed during a negotiation, give yourself a break. Stepping away from the situation lets you clear your head and return with a more level perspective. Slowing down allows you to make decisions that reflect your long-term goals, rather than based on temporary emotions.

3. Seek Professional Support

Divorce is complicated; you don't have to go through it alone. Leaning on professionals such as therapists, financial planners, and attorneys can help ensure that your decisions are based on facts and practical considerations rather than emotions.

- **Therapists** can help you process the emotions that come up during divorce, allowing you to make decisions without being driven by anger, guilt, or fear.
- **Financial planners** provide guidance on the long-term impact of your financial decisions, ensuring that you're not giving up too much or agreeing to a settlement that could harm your future financial security.
- **Divorce attorneys** offer a clear perspective, ensuring you understand your rights and helping you make sound, legal decisions.

These professionals act as a buffer, providing objective advice that keeps you grounded and focused on your long-term well-being.

4. Focus on the Future

It's easy to get caught up in the emotions of the present, but it's important to remember that the decisions you make today will impact your future. Ask yourself, "How will this decision affect me in five or 10 years?" For example, clinging to a property out of emotional attachment might feel comforting. But maintaining that property may not be financially viable in the long run.

Shifting your focus from immediate emotional relief to long-term stability will help you make choices that benefit you and your family over time. Divorce is a transition; and while the emotions you feel today are intense, they will pass. Make sure that your decisions now set you up for a stable, fulfilling future.

5. Find Healthy Ways to Process Your Emotions

It's essential to process the emotions during a divorce, but you must find healthy outlets for them. Instead of letting your emotions dictate your decisions, find ways to release and manage your feelings in a way that does not interfere with your divorce process.

- **Therapy or counseling** can be an invaluable resource for working through the grief, anger, and sadness that come with divorce.
- **Journaling** can help you organize your thoughts and feelings in a private, safe space.
- **Exercise** is a great way to reduce stress and clear your mind, making it easier to reason.
- **Talking to supportive friends or family members** can provide emotional relief; but make sure they are offering you constructive, not reactionary, advice.

If you handle your emotions in a healthy manner, you'll be better equipped to approach your divorce with a clear head.

Conclusion

Divorce is undoubtedly one of the most challenging emotional experiences – but that does not mean your emotions have to control your decisions. You can avoid making choices you will regret later if you recognize your feelings, give yourself time, seek professional support, and focus on your future.

Remember, your decisions during your divorce will shape your future for years to come. Staying clearheaded and thinking long-term, you can protect your well-being and confidently move forward.

Stephanie Robins, LCSW, CADP
Alpharetta Family Therapy
Certified Amicable Divorce Professional
Alpharetta, Georgia

Chapter 37
Avoid These Common Mistakes
by Stephanie Robins

Because divorce is so emotional, people often make mistakes that end up complicating the process and causing long-term damage. Recognizing these missteps can help you avoid unnecessary hardship and stay focused on your well-being and your children's future.

Rushing Through the Divorce Process

It's completely understandable to want the divorce over as quickly as possible. Divorce is draining, and the thought of extending that pain can feel unbearable. However, rushing through the process often leads to hasty decisions you'll regret later. You might agree to a settlement that doesn't serve your best interests or overlook crucial details that could have serious financial consequences. Take your time, consult professionals like your attorney or a financial advisor, and make sure you're fully informed before making decisions. Many want out of the marriage quickly and don't pursue getting all of the information available or do not want to go to the time to get complicated assets valued. The more thought and care you put into the process now, the better your outcome will be down the road. The divorce agreement is final and binding and you only get one bite at the apple. Pause and take the time to make the best agreement for your future. If you are unsure what to do, ask the appropriate member of your team "Do you think this is the best settlement for me?" or "If we gathered (insert type of information), how long would that take and how do you expect that to impact my settlement?"

Not Being Fully Truthful with Your Attorney

Divorce can stir up feelings of embarrassment, shame, or fear, especially concerning personal matters. Some people make the mistake of withholding information from their attorney because they're embarrassed or think it might hurt their case. However, your attorney can only help you if they have the full picture. Keeping secrets or leaving out important details can hurt your legal strategy. No matter how uncomfortable the truth may be, it's essential to be completely honest with your attorney so they can provide the best possible representation. Remember, what you tell your attorney is confidential, so you do not need to fear that they will share this information.

Vilifying Your Spouse and Wanting Your "Day in Court"

People want to vilify their spouse, hoping to "win" by having their day in court. Publicly shaming your spouse may feel satisfying, but it rarely leads to your desired outcome. Court battles are long, expensive, and emotionally exhausting. Judges often have limited time and do not let parties get into many of their grievances. Focusing on revenge rather than resolution will prolong the conflict, cost an incredible amount more, and delay healing. Instead of framing your spouse as the villain and pursuing emotional justice, stay focused on achieving the best possible outcome for yourself and your children.

Comparing Your Divorce to Others

One of the most common mistakes is comparing your divorce to others and expecting the same outcome. Every marriage and divorce are unique, with different factors at play, including finances, assets, and child custody arrangements. Just because your friend received a particular settlement or outcome doesn't mean your situation will turn out the same. Avoid the comparison game and work with your team to develop a strategy that fits your circumstances and your goals and values that you identified when starting your case.

Ignoring Professional Advice

With divorce comes a flood of advice—from friends, family, and sometimes even social media. While these sources may have good intentions, it's crucial to prioritize the advice from your selected team members, who have the best information about your facts and circumstances. Some people fall into the trap of thinking they know better or letting emotions guide them, leading to disregarding expert advice. Your attorney is your advocate and knows the legal system far better than anyone else. Failing to listen to them could cause costly legal setbacks or jeopardize custody agreements. Trust the expert you've hired to guide you through this complicated process. Google is no substitute for professional advice.

Failing to Stay Organized or Provide Information to Your Attorney

Divorce is an emotional and logistical process that requires gathering and providing essential documents, such as financial statements, tax returns, and asset information. One common mistake is failing to stay organized or promptly providing this information to your lawyer. This can slow down the process and hurt your case. Being disorganized or withholding key details—intentionally or not—will likely lead to delays or unfavorable outcomes. Make it a priority to stay on top of your paperwork and communicate regularly with your attorney.

Oversharing on Social Media

It's tempting to vent your frustrations or seek validation from friends on social media during your divorce. But what you post online can come back to haunt you. Negative comments about your spouse, photos that suggest reckless spending, or images of partying or new partners can all be used against you. It's better to stay off social media altogether during this time, or at least be extremely mindful of what you share. Everything posted online can be used in court because social media is public, so think twice before hitting "post."

Making Big Life Changes Too Soon

Making drastic life changes during this time can create more problems. Whether moving to a new city, quitting your job, or jumping into a new relationship, these big decisions can cause additional stress and instability. It's important to maintain stability, especially if you have children. Wait until the dust has settled before making any major changes, giving yourself time to heal and adjust to your new normal.

Attempting to Reignite Intimate Relations with Your Ex

The lines can get blurred when emotions run high. One common mistake is attempting to rekindle intimacy with your soon-to-be ex. While it may feel comforting or provide a temporary connection, this decision can significantly complicate the divorce process. It may send mixed signals to your spouse or be used as leverage in court, particularly in cases involving child custody or division of assets. Maintaining clear boundaries during the divorce process is best to avoid further confusion and emotional complications.

Neglecting to Plan for the Future

It's easy to forget to plan for the future when you are overwhelmed with the divorce process today. However, life post-divorce requires careful financial and emotional planning. Consider everything from housing to job security, retirement, and how you'll co-parent your children. Working with a financial advisor and other professionals can set you up for success. Failing to plan for the future can leave you unprepared and struggling to rebuild your life after the divorce is finalized.

Overburdening Friends and Family

It's essential to have a support system during your divorce, but relying too heavily on friends and family for emotional support can strain your relationships. Constantly venting or asking for advice might overwhelm them, especially if they feel caught in the middle. Instead, consider seeking help from a therapist or support group, where you can process your emotions in a healthy, neutral environment. This can help preserve your relationships and provide a more constructive outlet for your feelings.

Refusing to Compromise

Divorce negotiations require compromise. Being too focused on "winning," or not agreeing to something simply because the other person wants it, can prolong the process and increase conflict, adding to the emotional toll and financial strain. Staying flexible, especially regarding custody, asset division, or visitation schedules, is essential. Remember that digging your heels in will make things more difficult for everyone involved, including your children. Focus on what's truly important and your goals, not what you think your spouse's goals are, and be willing to meet your spouse halfway to minimize the damage.

Jumping to Conclusions and Spying on Your Spouse

In the emotional whirlwind of divorce, jumping to conclusions or trying to "catch" your spouse doing something wrong is tempting. Spying, stalking, or obsessively monitoring their location can lead to more harm than good. Whether it's checking up on them to find evidence of infidelity or attempting to use this information as leverage, these behaviors only heighten anxiety and conflict (and may be illegal). Focus on staying calm and letting your chosen team handle concerns about your spouse's actions.

Overreacting and Escalating Conflicts

Living under the same roof during a divorce can be incredibly stressful, and arguments can quickly escalate. Outbursts of anger, physical confrontations, or damaging property are all behaviors that can have lasting consequences. In some cases, these actions result in police involvement, and any domestic violence allegations, even if exaggerated or false, can influence custody decisions. The best course of action is maintaining your composure and avoiding conflict, especially in front of your children. When in doubt, walk away and calm down.

By avoiding these common mistakes, you can protect your well-being, maintain healthy relationships with your children, and emerge from your divorce ready to move forward. It's a process that requires patience, thoughtful decision-making, and emotional resilience. But with the right mindset and support, you can navigate this challenging time and set the stage for a better future.

Stephanie Robins, LCSW, CADP
Alpharetta Family Therapy
Certified Amicable Divorce Professional
Alpharetta, Georgia

Chapter 38
To Date or Not to Date?
by Stephanie Robins

First, let's talk about dating *during* the divorce process. It might seem like a great way to boost your spirits, but there are pros and cons to consider.

The Upside of Dating During Divorce

Emotional support: Let's face it – divorce can be lonely. Some people find comfort in a new relationship during this stressful time. Having someone new around can be a welcome distraction and boost your self-esteem.

Rediscovery: After years in a marriage, it can feel refreshing to rediscover who you are through dating. Trying new things and connecting with different people can help you explore what you truly want in a relationship moving forward.

Dipping your toe in the dating pool: If you've been married for a long time, dating can feel like an entirely new world. Getting out there while still technically married might seem like a way to "test the waters" and see what it's all about.

The Downside of Dating During Divorce

Emotional roller coaster: Divorce is one of life's most emotionally taxing experiences. Add dating to that mix, and things can get even more complicated. If you're not in the right headspace, a new relationship can become a way to avoid dealing with your emotions, which is not healthy.

Legal complications: Depending on where you live, dating during divorce could impact your case, especially if child custody, alimony, or financial settlements are still up in the air. Your soon-to-be ex or their attorney might use this against you, claiming you are unfit or acting irresponsibly. Always be honest with your lawyer and make sure you ask them about any implications you may expect legally if you date before being divorced.

Children's reactions: If you have kids, their emotions are already in flux during the divorce. Bringing someone new into their lives too soon can add to their confusion and pain. Children often need time to adjust to the changes before accepting a new relationship.

What About Dating After the Divorce?

Once the ink is dry on your divorce papers, the dating question might pop up again. You are free to move on, right? Well, sort of. While dating post-divorce is less complicated legally, there are still some things to consider.

The Upside of Dating After Divorce

A clean slate: The divorce is final, and you've come out the other side. Dating now can symbolize a fresh start. You've left the legal stress behind and can explore relationships with a clearer mind and heart.

You know yourself better: Divorce can teach you much about yourself – what you want in a partner and what you're willing to tolerate. With this new understanding, dating after divorce might lead to healthier, more fulfilling relationships.

Less stress for your children: Once the dust settles and your kids adjust to their new routine, introducing someone new into their lives will likely feel smoother than during the divorce process. Kids tend to do better when there's stability, and dating after divorce provides that element.

The Downside of Dating After Divorce:

Lingering emotions: Even after the paperwork is signed, the emotional baggage of a divorce can hang around. You might think you're ready to move on, but dating could be more of a distraction than a genuine connection if those wounds remain fresh.

Pressure to move on: Society often pushes the idea that you must "move on" quickly after a divorce. You might feel pressured to date again before you're truly ready, whether it's from family, friends, or even your internal clock. Don't let this pressure rush you – healing takes time.

Children still need time: Your kids might need more time to adjust than you realize. While dating after divorce is undoubtedly less chaotic than during, it's still important to carefully ease your children into this new phase of your life. They've been through a lot, too.

So, When Should You Start Dating?

Deciding when to date again after a divorce is deeply personal. There's no magic number or set timeline. Instead, ask yourself these questions to help gauge if you're ready:

1. **Am I emotionally ready?** Do you feel stable and content without needing a new relationship to make you happy? If dating feels like an escape or distraction, consider holding off for a time.

2. **Have I processed my divorce?** Understanding what went wrong in your marriage and learning from it is essential. This reflection will help you avoid repeating old patterns in new relationships.

3. **How will this affect my kids?** If you have children, their needs should be front and center. Think about how a new relationship might impact them emotionally. Will they feel neglected, confused, or anxious? Give them time to adjust to the new family dynamic before introducing someone new.

4. Will dating affect my divorce case? If your divorce isn't finalized, check with your attorney to understand how dating could impact custody or finances. Sometimes, waiting until everything is officially over is the wisest course.

Final Thoughts: Moving Forward, When You're Ready

There is no rush to jump back into dating – whether it's during or after your divorce. Giving yourself the time and space to heal and rediscover who you are is essential outside of your marriage. When you're ready, dating can be an exciting new chapter, but only if you've done the emotional work beforehand.

Ultimately, the right time to date is when you feel emotionally stable, legally clear, and ready to open up to new experiences without needing them to complete or fix you. Let your heart guide you, but don't forget to listen to your head. Take your time. There's no rush. When you're truly ready, dating can be the beginning of something beautiful – on your terms.

Stephanie Robins, LCSW, CADP
Alpharetta Family Therapy
Certified Amicable Divorce Professional
Alpharetta, Georgia

Chapter 39
Communicating Effectively with Your Spouse
by Holly Schymik

Divorce is often an emotionally turbulent time, and it's easy for conversations to spiral into disagreements. Yet, maintaining effective communication during the divorce process is crucial. Clear, respectful dialogue can help both partners manage the transition into new lives more smoothly, limiting misunderstandings and easing tensions.

Interestingly, poor communication is actually one of the leading contributors to divorce; studies suggest it factors into nearly 65 percent of separations. However, efforts to communicate effectively during the divorce process can pave the way for a more cooperative and less stressful resolution.

The Importance of Communication

Effective communication is more than merely speaking – it's about listening actively, understanding one another's perspectives, and responding thoughtfully. During a divorce, communication done well can:

- **Minimize conflicts** – Open, honest discussions reduce assumptions and misinterpretations that often fuel arguments.
- **Encourage mutual respect** – Respect in communication can de-escalate tension, making the process less contentious and more constructive.
- **Shape the future relationship** – How you communicate now can influence your interaction after the divorce, especially if you share parenting responsibilities.

By prioritizing healthy communication, both parties can establish an atmosphere conducive to cooperation – even when emotions run high.

Preparation Is Key

Good communication often begins with preparation. Before starting a discussion, think about what you want to achieve. Are you addressing parenting schedules, discussing property division, or setting emotional boundaries? Define your objectives clearly; jot down key talking points to ensure that you remain focused and avoid veering into unproductive territory. Knowing your goals helps structure the conversation and prevents it from derailing.

Setting Boundaries

To foster productive communication, set boundaries. Agree on topics that should be avoided if they tend to spark unnecessary arguments. Defining such limits can help maintain a more positive tone during discussions. For example, avoid criticizing past mistakes or reopening old wounds; doing so won't contribute to resolving current matters.

Communication Methods

Identifying the best method of communication for each topic can result in smoother conversations. Consider the following options:

- **Face-to-face discussions** – Face-to-face is usually reserved for complex or emotionally charged matters – like co-parenting strategies, where body language and tone are crucial.
- **Emails or texts** – Emails and text messages are useful for logistical or factual exchanges, such as confirming schedules or updating details. Written communication also provides a record and minimizes the possibility of miscommunication.
- **Co-parenting apps** – Digital platforms like OurFamilyWizard are designed to simplify communication between divorced or separated parents, and can be incredibly effective. Applications promote neutrality, structure, and clarity.

By tailoring the method to the topic at hand, you can reduce miscommunication and ensure that both parties feel comfortable.

Choose the Right Time, Right Place

It is very important to decide when and where to have discussions. Schedule significant conversations ahead of time, so that you can prepare mentally and emotionally. Select a location that minimizes distractions and stress for both parties. For instance, avoid having serious discussions in front of children, as that could add unnecessary strain and complicate their understanding of the situation.

Communication Guidelines

Focus on the following points for more effective communication:

- **Maintain respect and professionalism** – Approach each conversation with respect and professionalism. Refrain from personal attacks or

emotional accusations, as such language can escalate tensions. Setting a respectful tone establishes a foundation for constructive dialogue and deters defensiveness.
- **Practice active listening** – Listening is just as important as speaking. Truly hear what the other person is saying, without interrupting. A calm, neutral tone, along with open body language, encourages productive conversations. If emotions rise, take deep breaths or pause momentarily to reset. Active listening not only improves understanding but also demonstrates respect and eases the path to resolution.
- **Express yourself constructively** – When sharing concerns, use "I" statements to express how you feel rather than assigning blame. For instance, replace "You always ignore the kids' bedtime routines!" with "I feel overwhelmed when bedtime routines aren't followed." This approach fosters understanding rather than provoking defensiveness. Be concise and direct when sharing your thoughts to avoid misunderstandings.

Managing Emotional Triggers

Divorce discussions are often laden with emotions. Identifying your emotional triggers is a key step to navigating conversations calmly. If you feel emotions bubbling up, take a break. Stepping away temporarily can prevent conflicts from escalating. Lean on trusted friends, family members, or professionals when emotions threaten to take over. They can provide a sounding board, and can offer perspective and support.

Handling Disagreements

Disagreements will inevitably arise, but how they're managed makes all the difference. Keep the following tips in mind to address conflicts effectively:
- **Steer away from emotional exchanges** – Recognize situations or comments that tend to upset you, and prepare strategies for dealing with them. If conversations begin to spiral into arguments, pause and

regroup. Staying aware of your emotional responses can help move discussions back to a more constructive path.
- **Avoid escalation** – When conflicts threaten to intensify, consider involving a neutral third party, such as a mediator or counselor. Professionals trained in conflict resolution can facilitate understanding and guide conversations toward solutions. Mediators can be particularly helpful during complex negotiations related to finances or custody.
- **The power of apology** – Mistakes are bound to happen, especially when emotions run high. If you overreact or say something hurtful, own up to your actions and apologize sincerely. Acknowledging missteps and making amends can repair trust and de-escalate conflicts.
- **Resist impulsive reactions** – Avoid making phone calls or sending emails when you're upset or under the influence of alcohol. Impulsive reactions often lead to regret and intensified conflict. Instead, give yourself time to process emotions before communicating.
- **Avoid petty behavior** – It's tempting to involve friends or family members, vent frustrations publicly, or speak poorly of your spouse on social media. However, such actions can harm relationships and prolong the conflict. Focus on resolving issues directly with your spouse to maintain the integrity of the process.
- **Protect children from conflict** – Don't use your children as messengers or involve them in disputes. Children need stability and reassurance during a divorce, not the burden of mediating between parents. Keep adult matters separate from them to protect their emotional well-being.

Planning for Future Relationships

The way you communicate during the divorce sets the tone for your future relationship with your ex-spouse, especially if you share parenting duties. Maintaining a civil relationship with your ex is essential for your own peace of mind and your children's well-being. Consider developing a structured co-parenting communication plan that prioritizes your children's needs, while still respecting each parent's role in their lives.

Effective communication isn't just a short-term challenge – it's an ongoing necessity. Focus on building a foundation of cooperation and understanding that will benefit everyone.

Divorce presents countless emotional and logistical challenges, and communication can be one of the most difficult to master. However, making an effort to communicate effectively can significantly reduce stress and conflict, fostering smoother interactions. Respect, active listening, and clear boundaries can pave the way for calmer, more productive discussions.

By managing emotional triggers, addressing disagreements constructively, and focusing on future relationships, divorcing couples can achieve a more amicable separation. While the process is undoubtedly taxing, the skills developed during this period can improve future interactions, making life post-divorce more harmonious.

Holly Schymik, JD
Board Certified Family Law
Texas Board of Legal Specialization
Dallas, Texas

Chapter 40
Technology in Family Law
by Steven Bradley

Technology advances are moving quickly these days, and the process of divorce is moving right along with it. The Amicable Divorce Network process relies on technology to streamline the divorce process, share information, and allow online collaboration among professionals. In recent years, we have seen several advances that assist with the process of divorce:

Online mediation and counseling – Many are turning to online mediation as a method of dispute resolution. The days of everyone driving in traffic across town to arrive at a law firm for mediation are gone; the parties can now mediate from the comfort of their home. Or, they can attend an online meeting during their lunch hour without missing any work.

OurFamilyWizard – This online tool for parents sets the standard for co-parenting. It features a shared calendar, a portal for expenses and reimbursements, a communication tool with a tone meter, and now video calling. The technology in the platform makes it a one-stop application for everything co-parents need in the digital age.

dtour.life – Amicable Divorce Process is hosted by the technology platform dtour.life. The sophisticated program allows for collaboration among multiple professionals, budgeting, a marital balance sheet that is constantly updated, settlement scenarios, and much more.

Online counseling – Those seeking assistance and support can now attend counseling – as individuals or as a couple – from their computer. Remote online counseling sessions allow for more flexibility with time, and can still offer the same level of privacy found in traditional in-person therapy.

Digital document management – The digitization of legal documents has played a significant role in streamlining the divorce process. Online platforms allow couples to file for divorce, submit documents, and track case progress from the comfort of their own homes. There is less need for in-person meetings and court appearances, making the process faster and more efficient.

Real-time alcohol testing – Soberlink and other similar devices allow real time alcohol testing with the use of their device and a smartphone.

Virtual court hearings and mediations – The COVID-19 pandemic made it necessary to accelerate the availability of virtual court hearings; the virtual trend is likely to continue. Virtual hearings allow divorcing spouses to participate in legal proceedings remotely, which can be more convenient and less stressful than appearing in person. Virtual hearings also reduce the backlog in the court system, speeding up case resolution. The current availability of virtual hearings still varies greatly by jurisdiction. Virtual mediations are now also widely conducted.

Artificial intelligence-enhanced legal research and support – AI technology – the tool of the future – has also made it easier for people to access legal information and support, craft co-parenting messages, and consolidate information. Online legal tools, self-help websites, and virtual support groups provide valuable resources for those navigating the complexities of divorce.

Challenges and Considerations

While technology offers many benefits in the divorce process, there are also challenges and considerations to keep in mind. Not everyone is comfortable using digital platforms, and there may be privacy and security concerns. It is important for users to choose platforms that prioritize data protection and offer user-friendly interfaces.

Additionally, technology should not be seen as a replacement for professional legal advice or counseling. While platforms like OurFamilyWizard can facilitate communication and organization, they do not address the emotional and legal aspects of divorce. It is important to seek professional guidance when necessary.

As technology continues to evolve, it is likely that we will see even more innovations that make the divorce process more manageable, less costly, and less emotionally taxing for all involved. The Amicable Divorce Network is committed to harnessing the power of technology advances to streamline the divorce process to reduce both emotions and cost.

Steven Bradley
Safety and Technology Expert
OurFamilyWizard
Certified Amicable Divorce Professional
Dallas, Texas

Chapter 41
Using dtour.life in a Divorce
by Storey Jones

The direct correlation between the advent of technology and the introduction of more client-centric divorce models, like the Amicable Divorce Process, is exciting to see. Technology makes a complicated data and document-driven process immediately more transparent, less time-consuming, less expensive, and more accurate – all of which far more effectively serves families during this transition.

The dtour.life technology platform serves as the digital infrastructure for divorce, offering an exceptional user experience with features designed to help you easily get started, manage the process, and reach a resolution alongside your professional team. This applies no matter what type of divorce you are facing and regardless of your comfort level with a computer. Here are just a few highlights of how dtour.life will contribute to your Amicable Divorce:

1. **Flexible design:** dtour.life is designed to accommodate all types of families, financial situations, and levels of conflict or divorce processes.

2. **Family background:** The platform guides you to easily build a report with all family and biographical information, saving you time and money before the first consultation and throughout the process.

3. **Net worth report:** dtour.life helps you easily build a net worth report, providing a clear picture of assets and debts.

4. **Income and expense sync:** The secure bank sync feature allows you to link all financial institutions for an accurate picture of transactions and a cash flow statement. This feature alone significantly advances your divorce toward a sustainable settlement while providing valuable insights as how to best plan for your future.

5. **Parenting plan tool:** The platform includes a tool to work collaboratively to develop a list of co-parenting agreements.

6. **Document repository:** The drag-and-drop document repository allows you and your team to organize all paperwork, making it accessible to everyone involved without the need to email endless PDFs.

These primary features, along with many others, such as the ability to comment, add notes, and develop settlement scenarios, make it easy for you to work proactively with your team. This ensures they have all the information they need, saving you time and money while giving you back control over decisions that you make today and for your future.

Storey Jones
Founder, dtour.life Divorce Managment Platform
New York, New York

Chapter 42
OurFamilyWizard
by Steven Bradley

Divorce Management Evolves with Technology

Traditionally, the divorce process has involved multiple face-to-face meetings, extensive paperwork, and lengthy court procedures. Those steps not only prolonged the process but also often exacerbated conflict and cost. However, with out-of-court processes like Amicable Divorce and digital tools and platforms, many aspects of divorce have become more accessible, more transparent, and less confrontational.

Technology has made the digitization of legal documents possible, allowing easier filing and retrieval. It has also improved communication among the spouses, legal professionals, and other stakeholders through various platforms. Technology used in divorce today reduces misunderstandings and promotes amicable resolutions.

A significant advance in divorce-related technology is the development of specialized online platforms like OurFamilyWizard. Such platforms cater to the needs of divorced or separated families, especially those with children.

Understanding OurFamilyWizard

OurFamilyWizard is designed to aid communication and coordination between co-parents. Launched in 2001, it has become a go-to resource for divorced and separated parents who need a reliable and neutral space to manage co-parenting responsibilities.

The platform offers a range of tools that help parents coordinate schedules, track expenses, share information, and communicate effectively without the emotional intensity that can occur with direct interactions. OurFamilyWizard can be particularly beneficial in high-conflict situations where direct communication may lead to tension and disputes and can be helpful to all parents looking to be organized, communicate effectively, and maintain all child-related communications in one place

Key Features

Shared calendar: One of the core features of OurFamilyWizard is its shared calendar. This allows both parents to input, update, and view important dates and events related to their children. The calendar can include school activities, medical appointments, holidays, and other events. The calendar helps prevent scheduling conflicts and ensures that both parents are always on the same page. (It also shows the date and time a parent adds an event, and the same for when the event is viewed.)

Expense tracking: Financial disagreements are a common source of conflict in divorce, especially when it comes to child-related expenses. OurFamilyWizard includes an expense-tracking feature that allows parents to log expenses, upload receipts, and request reimbursements. A transparent record of all financial transactions related to the children can be created, which can help reduce disputes.

Messaging system: The platform includes a secure messaging system that records all communication between the parents. It is particularly useful in high-conflict situations, as there is a written record to reference in case of a misunderstanding or a dispute. The tone meter, an additional tool within the messaging system, can even analyze the emotional tone of messages. The tone meter helps parents communicate effectively and reduces the risk of escalation.

Audio and voice calling: Real-time communication allows virtual visitation for long-distance or midweek connections. All calls are documented, listing details like duration and initiator. In that way, a reliable record is created for future reference. Boundaries are respected; communication is based on mutual consent, and calls are allowed only after both parents agree. Additionally, the feature maintains privacy by using internet-based calls without revealing phone numbers.

Information sharing: OurFamilyWizard allows parents to store and share important documents and information, such as medical records, school reports, and emergency contacts. Both parents have access to the same information, which is crucial for making informed decisions about their children's welfare.

Mobile accessibility: OurFamilyWizard can be used with either desktop or mobile devices, which lets parents manage their responsibilities on the go. The flexibility is particularly useful for busy parents who need to communicate and coordinate their schedules.

Benefits of Using OurFamilyWizard

Reducing conflict: One of the most significant benefits of OurFamilyWizard is its ability to reduce conflict between co-parents. By providing a neutral platform for communication and coordination, it minimizes the need for direct, potentially contentious interactions.

Enhancing communication: The platform's secure messaging system and tone meter help parents communicate more effectively. By providing a record of all communications, it reduces the chances of miscommunication and can improve the understanding of agreements and arrangements.

Improving organization: OurFamilyWizard's shared calendar and information-sharing features help parents keep track of important dates and documents. The likelihood of scheduling conflicts is reduced, and both parents will have access to the information they need.

Ensuring transparency: The expense-tracking feature provides a transparent record of all financial transactions related to the children. The feature can prevent disputes over money and helps ensure that both parents are meeting their financial obligations.

Supporting legal processes: OurFamilyWizard's features can also be used as evidence in court, providing clear and unbiased accounts of communication, scheduling, and financial arrangements. The platform can be particularly useful in cases where there are custody or support disputes or the parties fear there may be one in the future.

Reducing legal costs: By streamlining communication and reducing conflict, OurFamilyWizard can also help reduce legal costs of the divorce. It costs less when parents are able to resolve disputes and manage co-parenting responsibilities without involving lawyers.

Providing peace of mind: By using OurFamilyWizard, parents can feel confident that they are staying organized and meeting their responsibilities. Children will benefit from the reduced conflict and improved communication.

Steven Bradley
Safety and Technology Expert
OurFamilyWizard
Certified Amicable Divorce Professional
Dallas, Texas

Chapter 43
Using AI Tools
by Susan Guthrie

Divorce is often associated with stress, conflict, and uncertainty, but it doesn't have to be that way. Many couples aim to separate amicably, prioritizing effective communication, collaboration, and creative problem-solving. While navigating these challenges can feel overwhelming, emerging technologies, including artificial intelligence (AI), can provide invaluable support. AI tools such as ChatGPT, Gemini, and Claude are versatile and accessible, offering practical ways to improve communication, explore solutions, and prepare for challenging discussions. When used thoughtfully, these tools can help couples maintain a constructive approach and pave the way for a smoother resolution.

Here are three ways AI tools can support an amicable divorce:

1. **Refine co-parenting communication:** AI tools can help rewrite emotionally charged messages to ensure they are clear, neutral, and constructive. For example, you can input a draft message and ask the AI to rewrite it in a tone that aligns with Bill Eddy's BIFF (Brief, Informative, Friendly, Firm) method[3], reducing conflict and promoting collaboration.

2. **Generate creative solutions:** AI can help brainstorm options for resolving divorce challenges by reviewing relevant details and providing a curated list of potential options for consideration and review. For example, give the tool non-confidential information such as the home's estimated value, mortgage balance, and key considerations (e.g., one party wanting to stay). The AI can then suggest options like buyouts, selling and splitting the proceeds, and creative shared arrangements that perhaps the couple alone might not think of. This can help couples identify possible solutions tailored to their circumstances.

3. **Practice difficult conversations:** Use AI to role-play the challenging discussions that are common during divorce, such as negotiating financial terms or co-parenting logistics. Simulated scenarios can help you practice and refine your approach, thereby reducing anxiety and improving outcomes.

Best Practices for Using AI

While AI tools can be a helpful resource, it's essential to use them thoughtfully and with care. Here are some tips for ensuring data safety and confidentiality:

- **Protect privacy:** Avoid sharing sensitive or confidential information, such as financial or legal details, as AI tools are not secure platforms for such data.

---

3 Eddy, Bill, Annette Burns, and Kevin Chafin. *BIFF for Co-Parent Communication: Your Guide to Difficult Texts, Emails, and Social Media Posts.* Conflict Communication Series, 3. Paperback, November 3, 2020.

- **Preserve legal protections:** Do not upload attorney-client privileged materials into AI systems, which could inadvertently breach confidentiality.
- **Verify outputs:** AI-generated advice should never replace professional guidance. Always consult your attorney or mediator before acting on AI-generated suggestions.

By leveraging AI tools responsibly, divorcing couples can reduce friction, improve decision-making, and maintain focus on the future. These tools can't replace professional support, but they can serve as valuable aids in navigating the challenges of divorce with greater clarity and collaboration. In the end, a thoughtful and judicious use of AI tools can help couples move forward with dignity, setting the stage for a more peaceful and productive transition.

Susan Guthrie
Attorney and Mediator
Host, Divorce & Beyond Podcast and Make Money Mediating Podcast
No. 1 Bestselling Author
Chicago, Illinois

Chapter 44
Protecting Your Digital Privacy
by Holly Schymik

Modern life has added a new layer to manage during a divorce – your digital presence. From shared accounts and devices to sensitive data stored online, the technology you rely on can create vulnerabilities. Taking the right precautions helps secure your privacy, minimizes stress, and avoids unnecessary conflict.

There are practical steps you can take to protect your online life during a divorce. With a focus on personal devices, shared accounts, and digital assets, you'll learn how to safeguard your privacy and stay in control.

Step 1: Secure Your Accounts

Spouses often know each other's passwords, which can create risks if the couple is divorcing. Without precautions, your ex-partner could access email, finances, or cloud storage. Start by updating passwords for all accounts. Use strong, unique passwords and avoid anything that might be predictable, like birthdays or pet names. That advice applies to shared accounts as well as those that are in your name. Here are some key areas to address:

- **iCloud and family sharing** – Shared iCloud or family sharing accounts can reveal photos, purchases, and even real-time locations. Review and adjust your settings, disable features if needed, and secure any devices used by children.
- **Location tracking** – Apps like Google Maps and Find My iPhone can share your location. Disable such settings, and check your devices for any tracking software that may have been installed.
- **Smart home devices** – Shared home security systems, cameras, and smart locks may give your ex access to your home activity. Update logins for home devices or restrict access to them.
- **Shared devices** – Shared laptops and tablets often hold synced accounts and stored passwords. Avoid using shared devices for private tasks, and sign out of all personal accounts.
- **Browser syncing** – Browsers sync data like browsing history and saved passwords across devices. Turn off syncing on shared devices, and clear the stored data.

Step 2: Protect Your Devices

An essential part of protecting your privacy is securing your devices. Here is what you can do to secure them:

- **Update your passwords** – Even if you think your accounts are safe, change your passwords regularly. Use a password manager, like LastPass or 1Password, to stay organized.
- **Enable two-factor authentication (2FA)** – Add an extra security layer by requiring a second step, such as a code sent to your phone, to log in.
- **Adjust privacy settings** – Review privacy settings on apps, browsers, and devices. Ensure that sensitive data, like location or search history, stays private.

Step 3: Manage Shared Digital Assets

Dividing digital assets during divorce is just as important as dividing physical belongings. Here's how to proceed:
- **Update credentials for shared accounts** – For platforms like Netflix or Amazon, agree on who keeps access. Change login details to reflect who has access.
- **Secure cloud storage accounts** – If shared services like Google Drive or Dropbox hold personal data, transfer files in those platforms to private accounts and update login details.
- **Log out from shared devices** – Ensure that you're logged out of devices like smart TVs, gaming consoles, or desktops that your ex-partner can still access.
- **Clear stored passwords** – Remove any passwords saved on shared devices by using browser or app settings.

Step 4: Safeguard Important Documents

Keeping critical documents secure ensures that important details are private during the divorce. Here is how to do that:
- **Store digital copies safely** – Save financial records, legal documents, and tax forms on secure cloud platforms or an external hard drive.

- **Track financial transactions** – Keep detailed records of all financial activities during the divorce timeline. Apps like budgeting tools can simplify that process.
- **Audit your online profiles** – Evaluate your digital footprint – email addresses, social media, and online platforms – to confirm that all accounts are secure.
- **Protect metadata on files** – Metadata within photos or files can reveal details like locations or timestamps. Use editing tools to remove sensitive metadata before sharing any files.

Step 5: Exercise Caution on Social Media

Social media is an area where emotions and oversharing often cause problems during divorce. A cautious approach can help protect your privacy and reputation:

- **Avoid posting about the divorce** – Even innocent posts can be twisted and used in legal proceedings. Refrain from sharing frustrations, court details, or custody matters. Consider pausing your social media use.
- **Review privacy settings on old posts** – Adjust privacy settings for any older posts that could compromise your case. Speak to your lawyer before deleting any posts, as they may need to be preserved as evidence.
- **Restrict profile visibility** – Temporarily set your account to private and limit access to trusted connections. Exercise caution, though – information could still be shared unintentionally.

Step 6: Secure Communication Channels

Clear and safe communication is essential during a divorce, particularly when navigating sensitive topics or high tensions. You can take the following measures to protect your communication:

- **A new email account** – Use a separate email account that is specifically for divorce-related matters. Be sure that it has a strong password and two-factor authentication.

- **Foster respectful communication** – Aim for civility, even when emotions run high. Respectful exchanges can reduce conflict and speed up resolution.
- **Understand surveillance laws** – Avoid logging into your ex-partner's accounts without permission, even if you once had access. Such actions can lead to legal consequences.

Step 7: Preserve Evidence

Balancing privacy with legal compliance is critical during divorce proceedings. Be aware of legal guidelines governing digital data:
- **Know about data destruction laws** – Deleting or altering data needed in court may result in legal penalties. Retain evidence as required, and consult your lawyer for guidance.
- **Follow monitoring regulations** – Tempted to track your ex-spouse's activity? First, consult with a legal expert to avoid crossing any lines.

Your digital and personal lives are deeply intertwined, and a divorce can expose your privacy to new risks. By updating passwords, securing devices, and managing shared assets, you will take control of your digital safety, reduce stress, and give yourself greater peace of mind. Crafting a plan to protect your online world during divorce isn't just a proactive step – it's a necessary one.

Holly Schymik, JD
Board Certified Family Law
Texas Board of Legal Specialization
Dallas, Texas

STEP 2

ASSESS THE INFORMATION YOU HAVE GATHERED

Chapter 45
Understanding Alimony: Spousal Support
by Holly Schymik

Alimony, also referred to as spousal support, is a financial arrangement in which one spouse provides monetary assistance to the other during or after divorce proceedings. The primary purpose of alimony is to help the lower-earning – or non-earning – spouse maintain a standard of living similar to what they had in the marriage. Alimony therefore also helps the lower-earning spouse gain financial independence when the marriage ends.

Courts typically award alimony to address disparities in earning capacity or financial stability. Another goal is to ensure fairness in cases where one spouse may have sacrificed career opportunities to support the family or household.

Types of Alimony

Temporary alimony is granted during divorce proceedings to provide financial support to one spouse until the divorce is finalized. It ensures that immediate needs, such as housing and utilities, are met during that transitional phase.

Rehabilitative alimony is designed to help the receiving spouse become financially independent. Commonly, it covers education, job training, or certifications to increase employability. Courts may set conditions for the duration or purpose of the support in order to encourage self-sufficiency.

Permanent alimony is awarded when one spouse is unlikely to become financially independent due to age, health issues, or lack of work experience. This type of support typically lasts until the recipient remarries or one of the spouses passes away. However, permanent alimony is increasingly rare and usually only applies in long-term marriages.

Lump-sum alimony provides the entire financial support amount in a single payment instead of an arrangement of ongoing payments. The lump-sum option may appeal to couples who want a clean financial break.

Reimbursement alimony compensates a spouse for significant contributions to the other's education or career development during the marriage. For instance, it might be awarded when one spouse funded the other's medical or law school expenses.

Bridge-the-gap alimony is designed to help the recipient transition from married life to single life. Bridge-the-gap alimony addresses short-term financial needs, such as securing a new home or covering living expenses during the adjustment period.

Each type of alimony serves a specific purpose, and courts consider various factors when deciding the type, amount, and duration. The court will look at the length of the marriage, earning capacity of the spouses, and each spouse's financial needs.

Factors Influencing Alimony Amounts and Duration

The amount and duration of alimony awarded in a divorce case depend on various factors that courts assess to ensure fairness. Common factors considered by courts include:

- **Length of the marriage** – Longer marriages often result in higher and longer-lasting alimony awards. For instance, longer marriages may qualify for long-term or permanent support, whereas shorter marriages may result in temporary alimony to help with a spouse's transition to single life.
- **Income disparity** – The income and earning potential of both spouses is a consideration. If there is a significant gap, the lower-earning spouse may receive alimony to bridge the financial imbalance.
- **Contributions to the marriage** – A spouse's contributions to the marriage – financial and non-financial – can play a key role in determining

alimony. A spouse who stayed home to raise children, or supported the other's education or career, may receive alimony as compensation for those sacrifices.
- **Standard of living during the marriage** – In some states, alimony may be calculated to help the recipient maintain a lifestyle comparable to the one that was enjoyed during the marriage, to the extent possible.
- **Age and health of each spouse** – Older spouses or those with health issues may be more likely to receive alimony, particularly if they are unable to reenter the workforce or support themselves.
- **Ability of the paying spouse** – The court also considers whether the paying spouse has the financial ability to meet alimony obligations while maintaining their own standard of living.
- **Ability of the receiving spouse** – The ability of the receiving spouse to get employment, taking into consideration their work experience and education, will be weighed into the equation.
- **Access to assets** – The settlement of divorce assets, as well as the receiving spouse's access to separate funds, such as an inheritance, can be considered.

Variations in Factors Across States

While most states consider the following factors, the emphasis and interpretation can vary:
- **Fault in the divorce** – In some states, marital misconduct (for example, adultery) may impact alimony decisions. In others, fault is not considered.
- **Length-of-marriage thresholds** – States differ on what qualifies as a "long-term" marriage. For example, some states consider a marriage of 10 years significant, while others may require 20 years for longer alimony awards.
- **Income guidelines** – States such as Texas and Massachusetts use specific formulas or caps based on the paying spouse's income, while others leave the determination more open-ended.

Alimony Duration Across States

Guidelines for the duration of alimony awarded can vary across state lines:

- **States with time limits on alimony** – Many states, such as Texas, limit the duration of alimony; it's based on the length of the marriage. For example, if the marriage lasted less than 10 years, alimony is typically capped at five years. But for marriages lasting 10 to 20 years, alimony may last up to seven years.
- **States allowing permanent alimony** – Permanent alimony is rare. It is only available in certain states such as Florida or New Jersey for long-term marriages, or where one spouse is unable to become self-sufficient due to age or health.
- **Rehabilitative alimony focus** – States such as Tennessee and Illinois emphasize rehabilitative alimony. Payments are typically limited to a few years, allowing the recipient to gain skills or education to reenter the workforce.
- **Modifiable vs. non-modifiable alimony** – In some states, alimony duration and amounts can be modified if circumstances change, such as remarriage or if either spouse has a significant increase in income. Other states may enforce non-modifiable agreements.

Common Myths About Alimony

There are many common myths that people may have heard about alimony, often due to the variation in parameters among different states:

- **"Alimony laws are uniform nationwide"** – Many people assume that alimony rules are consistent across the US, but each state has its own approach. For example, Texas has strict caps on spousal maintenance, while states like California may grant longer-term or more substantial awards.
- **"Longer marriages automatically lead to alimony"** – In some states, the length of the marriage is a significant factor, but not in all. For

instance, a shorter marriage in a state like New Jersey might still result in alimony if one spouse demonstrates financial dependency.
- **"Fault in divorce always affects alimony"** – States differ on whether marital misconduct, like adultery, impacts alimony. For example, Texas considers fault, but it's not always decisive. On the other hand, California does not allow fault to play a role in determining spousal support.
- **"All states allow permanent alimony"** – Permanent alimony is becoming less common and is only available in a few states, such as Florida and New Jersey, under specific conditions. Many states, including Texas, primarily favor temporary or rehabilitative spousal support.
- **"All alimony is calculated the same way"** – Some states use formulas to determine alimony, while others rely on judicial discretion. Such differences can lead to widely varying outcomes, depending on where the divorce occurs.
- **"Alimony automatically ends if the recipient remarries"** – While most states terminate alimony upon remarriage, some require formal action to modify the alimony agreement. Failure to request a modification could result in unnecessary payments.
- **"The same income level will result in the same alimony everywhere"** – Even when spouses have similar incomes, state-specific caps, formulas, or judicial tendencies, the determination of alimony can have vastly different outcomes in different states. For example, Texas imposes a $5,000-per-month or 20 percent income cap, while other states might not have similar restrictions.

Why Legal Counsel Is Essential for Alimony

Given the significant differences in state laws, securing legal counsel ensures:
- **An accurate understanding of local laws** – Attorneys can clarify what is realistic, based on your state's rules.
- **Effective advocacy** – A lawyer can argue for a fair outcome by leveraging state-specific nuances.

- **Strategic planning** – Legal counsel helps identify the best jurisdiction where the divorce should be filed, especially if the case could apply to multiple states.
- **You will avoid surprises** – Attorneys help debunk alimony myths and will manage a client's expectations by providing tailored advice.

Holly Schymik, JD
Board Certified
Texas Board of Legal Specialization
Dallas, Texas

Chapter 46
Understanding Child Support
by Holly Schymik

Child support is money paid by one parent to the other to help cover the costs of raising a child after a divorce or separation. Child support ensures that the child's basic needs – like food, housing, healthcare, and education – are met, no matter where each parent lives.

Usually, the non-custodial parent (the one whom the child doesn't live with, most of the time) pays child support to the custodial parent. Both parents, however, remain financially responsible. And, child support often goes beyond the basics; it can be used for extras like sports, music lessons, medical expenses not covered by insurance, or other specific needs.

Child Support Amounts and Duration

Rules for the amount of child support depend on the jurisdiction, but there are two main ways that payments are calculated:

- **Income shares method** – Both parents' incomes are combined to figure out the total amount needed for the child. Then, the obligation is divided, based on each parent's share of the combined income.

- **Percentage of income model** – A set percentage of the non-custodial parent's income is used for child support. The percentage is adjusted, based on the number of children.

Child support usually lasts until the child turns 18. However, some states extend support payments if the child is still in high school after that age, has special needs, or is in college. Sometimes, agreements may include extra arrangements for tuition or other major expenses as the child grows. As part of their obligation to support a child, parents may be required to cover a child on health insurance, contribute to extracurricular or day care costs, or pay toward private school tuition. Every family's needs are unique, so it is essential to have a well-thought-out plan and an understanding of your jurisdiction's child support laws.

Jurisdiction Guidelines

Child support rules can vary significantly by jurisdiction. For example:
- In California and Georgia, the formula considers both parents' incomes, the time they each spend with the child, and tax factors.
- In Texas and the United Kingdom, there is a percentage-based system, tied solely to the non-custodial parent's income, without considering the custodial parent's earnings.

Because of such differences, it's always wise to speak with a family law attorney about child support. Small differences in policies, child support calculation, and other child expenses can greatly affect the amount owed, or how payments are enforced. Some areas take parenting time into account, and others do not. Often, in order to finalize a case, a judge must review the child support agreement and make sure that it complies with the applicable law.

Enforcement

Child support orders are legally binding, and states have ways to ensure that payments are made. Enforcement measures might include wage garnishment, the withholding of a tax refund, or the suspension of a license. There could even be jail time for severe non-compliance. And, due to federal laws, payments are enforceable across state lines. That means that financial responsibility cannot be evaded by simply moving far away. If you're owed support – or need to comply with an order – understanding your rights and options is crucial.

Changing Child Support Orders

Child support isn't set in stone. Modifications can be requested if major changes happen – such as the loss of a job, a big drop or increase in income, or a revision of custody arrangements. However, each state has its own process for filing child support change requests, and acting quickly is important. Courts rarely adjust past-due payments (arrears), so it's best to address any changes right away. A court-approved update ensures fairness and compliance with legal requirements.

Common Myths

There are many misconceptions about child support, like the following examples:

Myth	Reality
Custodial parents can use child support funds in whatever way they want.	The funds are meant to directly support the child, covering needs such as housing, food, education, and healthcare.
Child support automatically ends when the child turns 18.	Some states extend the support period for children in college, children with special needs, or children over 18 who are still in high school.
Shared 50-50 custody means that no child support is required.	Even with equal parenting time, child support may still apply – especially if one parent earns much more than the other. The goal is to maintain the child's standard of living in both homes.
A parent can avoid child support by quitting their job.	Courts often view this as "voluntary underemployment," and will calculate payments based on what the parent could earn, not their actual income.

PART 11: WHAT DO I NEED TO KNOW ABOUT ALIMONY AND CHILD SUPPORT?

Parents can agree to skip child support entirely.	While parents may initially agree not to set child support, courts always prioritize the child's best interests. A court can later require support payments if the child's needs aren't being met.
Custodial parents need to provide receipts or an accounting to the non-custodial parent.	Custodial parents are not required to provide receipts or any accounting of how child support was spent to the non-custodial parent, unless they are seeking reimbursement from the other parent. Courts do not want to turn child support into a continual source of conflict, and they trust the custodial parent to meet the child's needs. Child support is intended to contribute to the overall costs of raising a child, not to micromanage how the custodial parent spends the money. The law typically assumes that the custodial parent uses the funds for the child's benefit – including food, housing, clothing, utilities, transportation, education, and extracurricular activities.

Understanding the basics of child support can make the process less overwhelming. Whether you're paying or receiving support, knowing the rules can help you plan financially and protect your rights. Every situation is different; consulting an experienced family law attorney is the best way to ensure a fair outcome that meets the child's needs. With good planning and attention to detail, parents can create solid, lasting arrangements for their child's well-being.

Holly Schymik, JD
Board Certified Family Law
Texas Board of Legal Specialization
Dallas, Texas

PART 12

How Do We Divide Our Finances?

Chapter 47
Overview of Financial Divisions
237

Chapter 48
Create a Values-Based Divorce Strategy
242

Chapter 49
Achieve the Best Financial Results
247

Chapter 50
The Marital Balance Sheet
253

Chapter 51
Valuing a Small Business
256

Chapter 52
Complex Asset Valuation
262

Chapter 47
Overview of Financial Divisions
by Tracy Ann Moore-Grant

Dividing finances can be the most complicated aspect of a divorce. A mistake that divorcing parties often make is not taking the time to handle their finances properly. Often, people just want the fastest divorce possible, and they skip over the details of dealing with assets that could take a little more time and homework – like stock options, pensions, or small business issues. And often, the spouses are emotional about the funds because they have concerns about their ability to afford their future.

Certainly, both parties want to make sure they divide the finances and other assets appropriately in order to avoid tax consequences. The divorce process affords the couple the opportunity to gather information about their entire financial picture and to handle everything correctly.

When approaching asset and debt division, it is key to understand the standard for division. Most assume it would be a simple 50-50 split, but that may not be the case. Generally speaking, different jurisdictions have different standards for asset and debt division. It is important to know what the starting point is, so that you can negotiate from a realistic position. Being difficult and arguing about things that aren't legally possible or probable is a waste of time, effort, and money.

In the United States, states follow different legal standards for dividing property in divorce cases. The standards in the US primarily fall into two categories:

Equitable Distribution

Definition: Property is divided fairly, but not necessarily equally. The court considers various factors to determine what is fair for both parties.

States: All but nine states in the US follow the equitable distribution standard.

Factors considered:
- Each spouse's financial situation (ability to earn, any inheritances, premarital assets, etc.).
- Contributions to marital property (including non-monetary contributions, like homemaking).
- Length of the marriage.
- Health and age of each spouse.
- Future needs of each spouse (considering factors like earning capacity, future income).
- Cost basis: The cost basis – or the original price of obtaining the item – regarding the asset in question is considered.
- The debt of the marriage and monthly servicing costs.
- Circumstances of each case: for example, wasting marital assets.

Key point: The goal is fairness and what is "equitable," not strict equality; however, it is fair to say that 50-50 is a starting point.

Community Property Standard

Definition: Property acquired during the marriage is generally considered jointly owned, and is divided 50-50 upon divorce.

States: Nine states follow this standard: Arizona, California, Idaho, Louisiana, Nevada, New Mexico, Texas, Washington, and Wisconsin. Alaska allows couples to opt into a community property arrangement.

Community property includes:
- Income earned by either spouse during the marriage.
- Assets purchased with marital income.

Separate property: Property owned before the marriage – as well as gifts and inheritances – usually remain with the original owner, unless commingled.

United Kingdom Standard

The division of property in United Kingdom divorce cases operates under a principle of **"fairness,"** rather than strictly adhering to predefined rules like "community property" or "equitable distribution." The approach in the UK focuses on ensuring that the outcome is just and fair, tailored to the needs and circumstances of the divorcing couple.

Key Principles of Property Division in the UK

No fixed rules for division: There is no presumption of a 50-50 split or any strict formula. The division depends on the couple's circumstances, and what the court considers fair.

Matrimonial property and non-matrimonial property: Matrimonial property is usually shared and includes assets acquired during the marriage, such as the family home or joint savings.

Scotland's Distinction

Property division rules in **Scotland** differ slightly from those in England and Wales:

Scotland relies on the **Family Law (Scotland) Act 1985**, which defines **matrimonial property** as assets acquired during the marriage; typically, it is divided more equally.

Non-matrimonial property (in other words, pre-marital assets) is generally excluded, unless necessary to meet needs.

Special Considerations

Marital property vs. separate property: In both the United States and United Kingdom systems, property acquired before marriage, or through inheritance/gifts, is generally considered separate unless commingled with marital assets.

Prenuptial agreements: Such agreements can override state laws if valid and enforceable.

Retirement accounts and pensions: Retirement accounts are often divided using **qualified domestic relations orders (QDROs)**.

Clean break vs. ongoing payments: The court often aims for a **clean break**, where financial ties between the parties are severed, and each can move forward independently. A clean break approach would prioritize that the parties no longer carry a jointly titled mortgage, and would not allow for one party paying a debt in the other party's name.

Debts: Marital debts are typically divided in a similar manner to marital assets under each system.

When approaching your financial negotiations, it is important to make sure you have a full picture of the assets and debts. Each party should be working with the same list of items and their value. You should then understand the method of division in your jurisdiction, so you can assess the likely outcome.

As you begin the division of your finances, remember to separate your emotions from your finances. A common scenario seen during asset division is that one party will really want to stay in the marital home; however, financially it would be a huge burden on them. So, it is important to be realistic – although your financial future is certainly an emotional topic, try to approach decisions with a business-oriented mind. Be open to different options.

As always, use the correct professional for the job. And, seek advice from financial experts about the proper value and division of the assets and debts, as well as any possible long-term effects.

Health insurance and COBRA
by Andrew Hatherley

A major concern for people going through divorce is health insurance. Women, in particular, are:

- Less likely to have health insurance through their own jobs.
- More likely to be on policies as dependents.
- Much less likely to be offered employer-sponsored health plans if in part-time or in low-wage jobs than women with full-time or higher-wage jobs.

The Consolidated Omnibus Budget Reconciliation Act (COBRA) contains provisions that give certain former employees, retirees, spouses, and dependent children the right to a temporary continuation of health coverage at group rates. Many attorneys are aware that if an employee is covered under COBRA, an ex-spouse can opt to receive coverage at 102 percent of the actual employer's premium. Although it is expensive, it can allow 36 months of coverage that is not subject to pre-existing condition coverage.

Many attorneys are unaware that if an employer is not informed of the divorce (a life-changing event) within 60 days, **the non-employee spouse will lose his or her COBRA rights!** So, you will need to provide information about the entry of a final decree to the employer, so that their notice requirements are triggered. And, you will need to strictly adhere to the election process cited in any COBRA notice.

Chapter 48
Create a Values-Based Divorce Strategy
by Hirsch A. Serman

Creating your divorce strategy starts with self-care. Riding through that initial wave of emotions before deciding on anything is essential. It is a good idea to work through three steps: **prioritize, organize, and simplify.** This will help you stay focused, make the process easier, reduce stress levels, and help secure more of what you'd like. Remember, divorce is the first chapter in the rest of your life, not the last chapter in this part of your life.

Identify Your Priorities

Identify what you need and want during the divorce process – and after the divorce is final. What potential changes would you like in your life? Do not only think about your finances. Do you want to go back to school, or to change careers? Other desires could include aspects of your custody arrangement, the children's schooling, and your emotional well-being. You may want to keep the house or other assets. Learning new things and achieving successes – no matter how small – can create wonderful momentum.

Still, you may have to reality-test your decisions. For example, I had a client who insisted on 50-50 custody. The problem was, she traveled close to 60 percent of the time, making a 50-50 arrangement impossible.

Prioritizing may also reveal that you need to develop new skills, like managing your finances, or creating a budget, or learning to cook (my biggest fear was that I was going to starve my kids; I never cooked prior to my divorce). It is best to understand ahead of time what your specific goals are. Don't be discouraged by having to learn new skills.

When speaking with a financial professional in a divorce, you should clarify your priorities and what aligns with your values. (And priorities may change a little during the divorce process.) It is also a productive exercise for a client to pretend he/she is the client's spouse, to look at how the spouse's priorities match up. Doing that can reveal where difficult negotiations may occur and what spouses can "give up" to get more of what they want.

Keeping your priorities in mind helps you concentrate on what is truly important; there are many ways to get sidetracked. As you work on identifying what aligns with your priorities and values, it is equally important to identify the items that do *not* bring you joy. We often compromise to make a spouse happy. Cutting out these compromises – because they are no longer necessary – can lower your future expenses. Anything that is not a priority is clutter, and can possibly be used to negotiate a better outcome.

Organize for the Future

Create a game plan! The outcome of your divorce will effectively set up your life, going forward. Organizing for the future may take the support of a team, but you'll have skilled professionals to help. Hiring a team to assist you may sound counterintuitive in terms of cost; however, adding specific professionals can actually reduce costs, improve the outcome, and simplify your life.

You do not want to pay $500 to your attorney to be your therapist. Use the right professional for the right task. Have your team members interact with each other to work as a group rather than individually. You may be able to group some priorities and needs together. For instance, if you are struggling emotionally, you can bet that the children are too.

Simplify Your Life

You are going to want to simplify your life as much as possible. Divorce is complicated and it can make life feel like a whirlwind. Again, narrowing your focus to what is important and making a game plan will simplify your life.

A professional who is an expert in a specific area can help simplify the divorce process by creating a system to manage a task. In the area of personal finance, for example, a financial coach can set up a realistic budget so you can learn to manage your money and other assets.

Many divorcees are 50 years old or older and have never even paid a bill. I created a program called "Who Am I Financially?" specifically for women who need to understand their financial picture (net worth, bills, budget, and debt). Simplifying your life through proven systems and by working with the appropriate professionals can reduce your anxiety and make you more efficient.

Create Your Divorce Budget

Yes, you should have a budget; however, a budget often is not as effective as it should be. A traditional, basic budget is very limited: "money in, minus money out." But having a more comprehensive, workable budget gives you more control of your finances and the ability to plan for goals (such as vacations, college, or retirement). Working toward financial goals through a budget increases your likelihood of meeting your future needs.

The traditional budget model is:

Income

Less: Taxes

Less: Expenses

(Hope something is left over!)

This approach is okay; however, it leaves "money on the table" that should be in your pocket. Traditional budgets show your spending but do not identify or improve spending behaviors. It is crucial to understand your expenses – the essential expenses and "life enjoyment" expenses, as well as unnecessary spending.

Here is an improved way to structure a meaningful budget:

Step 1: Record essential expenses (nothing else!)

Step 2: Record nonessential expenses

Step 3: Know how much money is coming in

Step 4: Have a conversation

Step 5: Create healthy spending habits

Step 1: Record Your Essential Expenses

It is critical to categorize your expenses. The first category contains the essential expenses for survival. They include your rent or mortgage payments, grocery costs, electric bills, costs of basic transportation, etc. Essential expenses do not include cable TV or Netflix – you can survive without those! Your essential expenses are those that you absolutely must incur to cover your basic needs without putting your health, home, etc. in jeopardy (think Maslow's Hierarchy of Needs).

Step 2: Record Your Nonessential Expenses

Some expenses are nonessential. They include your "enjoy life" and unnecessary discretionary spending. It is fine to eat out; however, make it a treat instead of the norm. Yes, diligently recording your discretionary spending can be a pain; nevertheless, it is amazing how much you will learn. Realizing what you are spending money on will empower you to make educated spending choices.

A financial coach can keep you accountable until you are more comfortable and familiar with living within a budget. And when drafting your budget, highlight discretionary spending, so that those expenses stick out. It's useful to know exactly how many expenditures are discretionary; awareness creates a greater ability to take action.

Step 3: Know How Much Money Is Coming In

Many people equate their income with the amount they can spend out of what they earn. For most people, taxes and other deductions are taken out of one's paycheck. That means if you earn $100,000 before taxes and deductions, you do not have $100,000 to spend. If you are self-employed, you will need to figure on paying estimated taxes that relate to self-employment. Knowing the true amount of your take-home pay is vital.

Step 4: Have a Conversation

Be honest with yourself – or, even better, have a conversation with an objective third party who will keep you accountable. It is important for you to understand and evaluate which expenses are really necessary. And, any spending beyond what is necessary is discretionary spending, plain and simple. However, you do not need to eliminate *all* discretionary spending – that is not sustainable!

After you evaluate your discretionary spending, you will be able to make careful, objective, educated decisions. You'll be in a position to categorize the expenses you need to keep, the expenses you want to eliminate, and the expenses you want to scale back on.

Step 5: Create Healthy Spending Habits

Understanding your spending will make it easier to make adjustments. You will recognize your spending habits – healthy and not-so-healthy habits – and then can modify them as needed. Adjustments in spending during the divorce process will also facilitate permanent changes in spending after the divorce is final. You will become more aware of your habits; some basic skills can go a long way! Knowing and anticipating your upcoming expenses can reduce your stress, too.

Putting It All Together

After compiling a workable budget framework, you can create an overall strategy. List your priorities from most to least important. Keep your spouse's priorities in mind, too. After doing that, we can run through all the other items in your life and identify which ones to "trade" to get more on your list. Such items could include adjusting the split of retirement assets or non-retirement assets, evaluating available funds to buy the other spouse out (or funds to be bought out) of the marital home, making changes in the holiday schedule of the kids, or the timing of when to introduce a significant other to the kids. *The idea here is to get as creative as possible.*

PART 12: HOW DO WE DIVIDE OUR FINANCES?

It does not have to be a 50-50 split down the middle. Look at your larger picture; use a different lens. Our essential spending is a threshold we cannot go below, and our starting point is our "fully loaded" life. We need to shoot for as close to the fully loaded lifestyle as possible.

We are setting up a win-win situation without creating "buyer's remorse" (wishing you had asked for something different). Combining your priorities with your budget will drive your values-based financial strategy.

Hirsch A. Serman, MBA, CPA, CDFA
Divorce Financial Coach and Tax Professional
Certified Divorce Financial Analyst
Certified Public Accountant
Chicago, Illinois

Chapter 49
Achieve the Best Financial Results
by Andrew Hatherley

Your divorce settlement is the financial foundation for your new life after divorce. That's why it is so important that you get the divorce settlement right, particularly if your divorce is coming later in life. Adding to the challenge is that emotions may work to conspire against your financial future and could result in costly mistakes that may negatively impact your retirement – mistakes that could force you to work longer than you want.

I was unprepared for my divorce at age 52, even though I was a financial advisor with an MBA, lots of credentials, and 20 years of experience. So, after my divorce, I determined that the greatest value I could add as a financial advisor would be to share not only the mistakes that I had made but also some of the positives that came out of the divorce.

The single most important piece of advice that I give is to educate yourself about divorce – the sooner the better. In terms of financial preparation, here are seven financial keys to guide you:

1. **Make sure you have money available to you.** Divorce is very cash-hungry. There are filing fees, attorney fees and retainers, mediation fees, apartment rent, counseling costs, and many other expenses. Money that previously supported one household will now need to stretch to support two.

2. **Collect financial documents.** Preparing for divorce means that you collect all the relevant documents in your financial life. This means bank and brokerage statements, retirement accounts, pension, credit cards, mortgages, tax returns, car loans, etc. Once you've made copies, don't store these documents at home. Give them to a trusted friend or family member, or put them in a safe deposit box that only you can access.

Get a fresh credit report. Not only will you be able to keep tabs on your credit score but you may be able to tell if your spouse is wasting funds.[4]

3. **Don't overlook anything of value.** Consider everything. Even if you don't want an asset, its value can be exchanged for something that you do want.

Don't forget *smaller* assets. Some may not be as small as you think! Smaller assets include:
- Items in safe deposit boxes
- Frequent flyer points
- Deferred vacation and sick pay
- Businesses and side businesses – do they have value? If you and your spouse have a business that generates a substantial amount of revenue, you're going to want to have that business valued. But even side

---

4 You can only run a credit report on yourself. Legally, you cannot run a check on your spouse's credit without their approval. Consult with your attorney.

businesses that generate a small amount of income may have value, particularly if they have expensive equipment.
- Furnishings, vehicles, jewelry, hobby equipment.

4. **Consider the tax consequences!** Don't ignore the hidden tax costs of divorce in making decisions such as:
   - Should I take part of the retirement plan or the checking or brokerage account? Consider that a regular bank checking account is worth more in a divorce settlement on an after-tax basis than a Traditional IRA or a 401k. You're not taxed at your ordinary income tax rate when you take money out of your bank account. Roth IRAs and Roth 401ks are even better as earnings, and withdrawals are tax-free.[5]
   - Should I keep the house or sell it now? Married couples filing jointly may be eligible for the primary residence exclusion of up to $500,000 in capital gains if they meet the ownership and use requirements as established by IRS tax laws. That capital gains exclusion is $250,000 for a single person. To qualify, you must have owned the home for two years and lived in the home for two of the past five years.
   - It's important that the sale of the home be timed so that both spouses can maximize this exclusion. This is particularly important if you're the homeowner keeping the house after divorce. You may find that when you ultimately do sell the home, you end up paying more than you thought you would in taxes, and you don't get as much money out of the divorce as you thought you would in the settlement. If it's not obvious already, this can get a little complicated and I do suggest you speak to a tax professional if you are selling a home with substantial gains. And of course, these IRS tax rules change over time so you need to keep up to date.

---

5 Subject to IRS rules. Consult your financial or tax advisor.

5. **Consider your timing.**
   - Think about timing when it comes to the separation. Timing can be a key issue when it comes to work-related bonuses or legal settlements.
   - Think about Social Security. Timing is a key issue here as well. But this time it pays to wait. If you and your spouse have been married for 10 years or longer, when you reach Social Security age, you can collect benefits based on your earnings record, or his/her earnings record – whichever is higher.[6]
   - Another timing issue to consider is your tax filing status. It's important to know that your tax filing status for the year is determined by your marital status on December 31 of that year. So, it doesn't matter if you were married all year and got divorced on December 22. If your divorce is final before the end of the year, you cannot file jointly and enjoy the typically preferential tax rates of married filing jointly. In some cases, it might be worth waiting a few weeks and filing in January.

6. **Prepare a budget and a balance sheet.** A past budget review will help you figure out how much you spent on average annually and monthly. You can use these calculations to help you develop an accurate picture of what funds are required to maintain your standard of living. You must recognize that maintaining two households is more expensive than maintaining one, so you're unlikely to retain your marital standard of living, at least initially, after divorce.

7. **Get professional advice!** Even if you do the divorce yourself, which I don't recommend, or go through mediation, you should consult a good attorney somewhere along the way.[7] Hiring the right divorce

---

[6] I always recommend my clients schedule a personal consultation with the Social Security Administration to review their options. Check out this article on Social Security benefits and divorce. https://www.kiplinger.com/retirement/how-gray-divorce-affects-social-security-benefits

[7] https://www.transcendretirement.net/podcast/gray-divorce-podcast-episode-26-perils-diy-divorce-attorney-philip-spradling

professionals is key. Often, your first instinct will be to find an attorney. And you *will* need legal advice. But you also need a financial professional. Divorce *is* a legal process. But let's face it – it's really about **money**.

Why You Need a Divorce CFO

You need a caring, highly trained financial professional to help you avoid the financial landmines of divorce. I call that person a *Divorce chief financial officer* or *Divorce CFO*.[8]

Ideally, you would choose your Divorce CFO as early in the process as possible. That way, you and your financial professional can work with your attorney to structure a settlement that's not only fair but also sets a good financial foundation for the rest of your life. Your attorney may be great at family law, but he or she is not a financial planner who focuses on your financial health 20 to 30 years in the future.

Working with Your Divorce CFO Before or During the Divorce

A good Divorce CFO will work with your attorney as a core member of your divorce team. Here are some of the key areas where your Divorce CFO can help you work with your attorney to secure a settlement agreement that works for your financial future:

- Helping you gather essential documents and presenting them in a clear and comprehensive manner. The more you can help your attorney and financial advisor, the more they can help you. And the less it will cost you!
- Reviewing your current and post-divorce budgets.
  » Do you have the money necessary to get through the divorce process?
  » How much spousal support might you require after divorce?

---

[8] https://www.transcendretirement.net/podcast/gray-divorce-podcast-episode-56-why-you-need-divorce-cfo

- Creating a lifestyle analysis report may help to improve your case for spousal support.
- Highlighting financial issues such as marital settlement language that can help you with mortgage financing after divorce.
- Helping your attorney structure a tax-efficient settlement by analyzing how each asset will be taxed upon sale, which can result in you keeping more money for yourself and not giving it to Uncle Sam.
- Tracing separate property. Which of your marital assets are considered separate from the settlement conversation?
- Discovering undisclosed accounts. Is your spouse failing to disclose certain accounts?
- Help you understand how different types of retirement plans – 401k, 403(b), IRA, Roth IRA – are treated differently in divorce.
- Understanding retirement account distributions in divorce and how to avoid IRS penalties.
- Helping with complicated stock options issues.
- Reviewing whether future spousal support income streams are insured against the potential death of the payor.
- Helping the attorney navigate the complicated rules related to annuity division and divorce.
- Helping to understand the valuation and division of pensions.
- Explaining the implications of keeping or selling the primary family residence or investment real estate assets.

A good Divorce CFO will learn about your values, goals, and aspirations and care about your money (almost as much as you do!). It's important to trust him or her as you strive for a settlement that works toward your specific needs and goals: retirement, education funds for your children, more free time for your family, etc.

Your Divorce CFO will compile your financial team's advice and put together a plan that focuses on your long-term wealth and well-being. You remain your family's CEO, making the big decisions. Your Divorce CFO just helps you make the right financial ones.

It can be a challenge to find the right Divorce CFO for your situation. The most important person to look for is someone who relates to your values. It's also important to find someone who understands the nuances of divorce finances. Fortunately, there exists a specialist called a Certified Divorce Financial Analyst (CDFA). Ultimately, it's up to you to find a Divorce CFO with whom you are comfortable and can trust and who meets your needs. Divorce is about money! Taking an active role with your Divorce CFO during the process – the earlier the better – will serve you well after divorce as you lay the foundation for your personal and financial growth in your new life.

Andrew Hatherley CDFA®, CRPC®
Host, *The Gray Divorce Podcast*
Certified Amicable Divorce Professional
Las Vegas, Nevada
Greenville, South Carolina

Chapter 50
The Marital Balance Sheet
by Traci A. Weiss

The unknown can be the scariest part of divorce. Once you build a Marital Balance Sheet, the unknown becomes the known, and you are ready to start determining how to best allocate the assets and debts. Here is what you need to do to create the Marital Balance Sheet:

Gather the Necessary Financial Information
Here is what you need to gather:
- The most recent statement for each of the following:
  » checking and savings accounts
  » loans
  » money market, brokerage, investment, and retirement accounts including all IRAs, 401ks, and pension accounts

- » credit card accounts
- Record which accounts are in your name and which are joint accounts.
- You will also need to list all assets and debts including houses, cars, personal loans and car payments, boats, motorcycles, and cash.

Most of this can be easily downloaded online. A good rule of thumb is to download up to 12 months of statements for each. Put them all into an electronic folder. You may need to print them out as well.

You will give all of this information to your attorneys or a Certified Divorce Financial Analyst (CDFA), who will then share it with your spouse. Your spouse will do the same. The goal of a Marital Balance Sheet is that this one document is a clear picture of all assets and debts for either party or the parties jointly. You will then have a clear picture of all of the assets and debts that will need to be divided as part of your divorce.

Share the Information Voluntarily

If you share information openly, your spouse is less likely to think you are hiding things than if you make them jump through hoops for the information they already have a legal right to see. Many try to play games when they delay to provide information or do not give everything asked of them. This is really just a waste of time and money. Each spouse is entitled to a full financial picture of the marital finances and anything in their spouse's name. There is no benefit to delaying your response, or not providing thorough, honest information. Also, exchanging that information by agreement will save you a lot of money on legal fees that will incur if you insist on a formal discovery process.

Prepare for the Balancing Act

Once you have the necessary information to build your comprehensive balance sheet, it is helpful to include information that will determine which items will go to each spouse. Include the last four digits of each account number, to be clear which account it is. Also, identify whose name(s) is on each account.

People often end up keeping the accounts that are in their own names, and make transfers to balance out the net value that each party will keep in the end.

Prepare to Update

If you, or someone on your team, is doing a Marital Balance Sheet in a program like Excel, it is important to know that all values will be as of the date you and your spouse provide the information. So if you pull documents and balances for November 1, the values are only good as of that date. If you are attending mediation on December 1, it is a good idea to pull all balances the day of mediation or the day before so the spreadsheet can be updated. It is also wise to ask your spouse to do the same – or the parties agree on a particular valuation date for their accounts. If one party has balances on November 1 and the other October 1, then they are not negotiating with the same information.

Traci A. Weiss
Family Law Attorney
Guardian ad Litem
Certified Amicable Divorce Professional

If you are using dtour.life you will see that the Marital Balance Sheet is called the Net Worth Report, but is the same as a Marital Balance Sheet. If you sync your accounts with dtour.life, then the Net Worth Report will update each account balance every day. For items that don't sync, like a house or a car, you can create a "card" for each item and include any documentation with that item, like an appraisal. The assigned value will pull over to the Net Worth Report. If you are syncing accounts with dtour.life, the system will also pull a minimum of 18 months of a transaction history for each account. This will alleviate the need for you to download statements; but always check with those on your team to see their preferred method of information collection.

Chapter 51
Valuing a Small Business
by Dan Branch

When a divorcing couple owns an interest in a privately held business, a business valuation should be performed to determine the value of the business. It's important to understand some of the fundamentals of business valuations. While grasping valuation basics may not make you an expert, you'll understand the essentials – and, therefore, you'll be more confident when determining the total marital assets to divide. Simply put, a business valuation is a financial analysis of a company; it provides a value of that company at a point in time.

When considering hiring a professional to assist with business valuations, you should consider the professional's credentials and experience in family law matters. Business valuation credentials are typically held by forensic accountants; local attorneys in your area may be able to point you to some. Otherwise, each of the three organizations listed below have online databases of credentialed professionals. Specific business valuation credentials (and the associated acronyms) to look for include:

- **Accredited in Business Valuation (ABV)** through the American Institute of Certified Public Accountants (AICPA)

- **Accredited Senior Appraiser (ASA) in business valuation** from the American Society of Appraisers (ASA)

- **Certified Valuation Analyst (CVA)** from the National Association of Certified Valuators and Analysts (NACVA)

Business valuations use commonly accepted financial approaches and methodologies. Although those approaches and methodologies can be complicated, they follow some standard practices. Although your case may be handled outside the court system, that doesn't mean that you should forgo the standard steps for valuing assets. Parties seeking an Amicable Divorce should still take the time to have a small business valued so they can negotiate a settlement with the best information possible. Often in an amicable divorce, the parties agree to use one business valuation expert who works as a neutral to get information and documentation from both sides, and share results equally and transparently, to efficiently provide a valuation to the parties.

Standard of Value

Sometimes called the *basis of value*, a simple way to think about *standard of value* is that it is essential to establish the basis of "value" that is being determined. Keeping the standard of value in mind helps ensure that the two parties are looking at the business on the same level (i.e., apples to apples). If the standard of value is different between the two parties, then they are *not* talking about the same business value level (i.e., apples to oranges), and that can hinder negotiations or a settlement.

The most common standard of value in family law is *fair market value*. However, each state decides which standard of value will be applied in that state, so make sure you check with the applicable state's guidelines. Also, an Amicable Divorce Network family law attorney can help guide you in determining your state's standard of value.

Let's focus on using the *fair market value* as the baseline for discussing valuation, since fair market value is the most accepted standard of value.

Fair market value is the price at which a property under consideration would change hands in an arm's-length transaction between a willing buyer and a willing seller, neither being under a compulsion to buy or sell and both having reasonable knowledge of relevant facts.[9]

---

9 Section 20.2031-1(b) of the Estate Tax Regulations.

This concept of fair market value is established by regulations and guidelines published by the Internal Revenue Service (not surprisingly, the tax man has established *most* of the fundamentals on which business valuations are based).

Valuation Approaches

Typical approaches used by business valuation experts include an asset-based approach, a market-based approach, and an income-based approach.

Asset-Based Approach

The asset-based approach adjusts a company's assets and liabilities from book value to fair market value. Adjustments include such factors as the recognition of market-based values (for example, real estate, inventories, fixed assets, and liabilities) and the value of non-operating items (like a personal motorboat that is titled to the company). After the assets and liabilities have been adjusted, fair market value of the equity interest *equals* the fair market value of the assets, *less* the fair market value of the liabilities.

About the asset approach:

- This approach may be best suited for asset-intensive businesses (for example., real estate holding companies, manufacturing, etc.), and less suited for service-oriented businesses (e.g., dental practice, restaurant, etc.).
- This approach may not reflect the fair market value of intangible assets in the business (for example, name/brand recognition, patents, customer lists, etc.), which can be significant.

Market Approach

A market approach is a way of determining the value of a business using one or more market-based methods. Those methods compare the subject business to similar businesses that have either been sold in "arm's-length transactions" (a deal in which the buyer and seller act independently, without one party pressuring or influencing the other), or are traded on publicly traded markets (like stock exchanges). The market-based approach implicitly assumes that the comparative companies and their transactions share characteristics with the subject company, and are similarly valued. A market approach generally focuses on a multiple of earnings, cash flow, or revenues observed in the comparative companies and transactions, and then applies that multiple in the valuation of the subject company.

A critical step in the market-based approach is the selection of comparative companies and/or transactions. It is often difficult to find publicly traded companies or acquired companies that are exactly similar to the company under analysis. In fact, it can be rare that a perfect comparative company exists. Nevertheless, the market approach can generate a useful range of value.

About the market approach:
- Business valuation experts have access to databases with information about companies that have been sold.

Income Approach

The income approach to valuation generally determines the value of a business using various methods to convert anticipated economic benefits into a single value. The approach is based on the premise that the value of a business entity is a direct function of both *the cash flow that the business expects to generate* and *the risk involved with the cash flow*. Typically, two methods can be employed in an income approach: a historical methodology (which looks at past records and determines a single cash flow to assess) or a future methodology (which looks forward in time and predicts a series of future cash flows). In theory, the two methodologies will provide similar values. But typically, in family law matters involving a privately held business, looking *only* at the historical methodology is common practice.

About the income approach:
- There are often many subjective assumptions that go into an income approach; a business valuation professional can best identify them.

Control and Marketability Issues

In the valuation of privately held companies, consideration should be given to the size of the interest being valued (5 percent? 49 percent? 100 percent?) and its *marketability,* which can be reflected in discounts related to *lack of control* and *lack of marketability.*

Control is commonly defined as the "power or authority to guide or manage." A shareholder owning a majority interest (greater than 50 percent) typically has effective control over a business. Conversely, shareholders owning a minority interest (less than 50 percent) typically lack the authority to influence how the business is run.

As such, business valuation experts typically apply a discount related to that *lack of control* to minority interest owners who do not have characteristics of *control.*

All things being equal, investors have a preference for assets that can be easily traded, such as stocks of publicly traded companies (these are considered *very liquid*), and will typically pay less for investments that are *not liquid.* Business valuation experts typically apply a discount related to that *lack of marketability* when interests are *not liquid.*

There are numerous studies used by business valuation experts to help determine the appropriate discount.

About discounts related to control and marketability issues:
- Experienced business valuation experts will be able to effectively communicate the *control* and *marketability* issues specific to the business in question (and how those factors affected the concluded value) to a court or jury.

Personal Goodwill

While determining the value of a business, a business valuation expert must consider *goodwill* in the analysis. This can be especially true in family law when the asset in question (ownership in a privately held business) needs to be divided.

What is goodwill? As defined by the American Society of Appraisers, goodwill is "that intangible asset arising as a result of elements such as name, reputation, customer loyalty, location, products, and related factors not separately identified and quantified."[10]

In the state of Georgia, particularly, goodwill is recognized as "property" in family law cases; and therefore, it (or some portion thereof) may be subject to equitable division. Are some of those goodwill elements (such as the name, reputation, or customer loyalty) a result of the specific actions of the business owner (in other words, more of a *personal goodwill* nature)? Or, are they a function of the business in general and would likely transfer to a buyer of the business (in other words, more of an *enterprise goodwill* nature)? Business valuation experts may use terms like *personal goodwill* or *individual goodwill* when referring to those elements directly tied to the owner; and *business goodwill*, or *institutional* or *enterprise goodwill*, when referring to those elements that relate more to the business.

If *personal goodwill* is identified, it may be treated as separate property of the business-owning spouse for purposes of building the marital estate on the marital balance sheet. Personal goodwill is a complicated issue to address and determine. If you are presented with a situation where personal goodwill could be a factor (or if it is a factor that the opposing party focuses on), again, it would benefit you to involve a business valuation expert with

---

10 This is the guiding standard for American Society of Appraisers (ASA) credential holders. Goodwill is similarly defined by NACVA (for CVA credential holders) and AICPA (for ABV credential holders).

a deep understanding of valuation guidelines, comprehension of relevant court case law, and experience in testifying.

In conclusion, there are many factors to consider when putting together a business valuation of a privately held business in a divorce. Having a qualified, experienced business valuation expert is important, if not essential, as he or she can help you navigate all the steps involved. The valuation expert can also help present your view of the matter to the court.

Dan Branch, CPA, ABV, ASA, MBA
Partner, IAG Forensics & Valuation
Certified Amicable Divorce Professional
Atlanta, Georgia

Chapter 52
Complex Asset Valuation
by Laurie Dyke

Some of the most complicated assets to divide in a divorce are pensions, stock options, and restricted stock units that stem from one spouse's employment. The extent of those assets may not even be known by the non-employee spouse.

Dividing the assets is complex because the value is based on unpredictable future events, and transferability may be restricted. It is important to understand exactly what the assets are, how to get information about them, the ways to value them, and their implications for divorce settlements.

What Are the Assets?

Pensions are defined-benefit retirement plans. They are different from defined-contribution retirement assets like IRA and 401k plans, which can be valued using a statement. Pension plans are more difficult to value, because payments are made over a period of time in the future.

A *stock option* is the right to purchase shares of stock of a company for a defined price ("grant" or "strike" price) and to sell the stock at its market value, once earned. Stock options are granted to employees as compensation earned during a period of time called the vesting period. Once an option is vested, the stock may be purchased and sold (usually simultaneously) like any other share of the same stock.

A *restricted stock unit* (RSU) is a unit of stock that is owned by an employee but is not able to be sold for a period of time. When RSUs are vested (meaning that restrictions are lifted), the shares of stock may be held or sold, like any other share of stock. RSUs may be acquired in various ways. They may be purchased through an employee stock purchase plan, awarded as part of a company-wide performance plan, or awarded individually. Together, we refer to stock options and RSUs as *employer equity*.

How to Identify Assets

The primary source for general information about a spouse's pension and employer equity is usually a summary plan description (SPD) provided by the employer. The SPD describes the benefits that the employee is entitled to receive. It's important to ask for the SPD that applies to the employee spouse's specific job classification, because different levels of benefits may be offered to different levels of employees. Additional information may be obtained through statements provided to the employee, employment offer letters, and equity award letters. Year-end pay stubs often provide a wealth of information, in addition to W-2 forms. Year-end pay stubs should always be requested in situations where pensions and employer equity may exist.

Determining Value

The goal in deciding the value of a pension is to determine the present value of a future income stream. That requires making estimates and assumptions about when the employee is likely to retire, how long the employee is likely to live, and what the monthly payments will be at the date of retirement (including cost-of-living adjustments, if applicable, and an appropriate discount/interest rate).

The present value of a pension is the amount that could be invested today, subject to earnings based on the determined interest rate, with withdrawals over time equal to the expected pension payment and timing (ending on the death of the employee). Pension valuations are always wrong, because nobody ever lives exactly as long as the mortality tables estimate – and other assumptions are just that, assumptions.

The *intrinsic value* of a stock option is the value today if the option were to be exercised. It is calculated as the market value of the stock, less the strike price. For RSUs, the current value is simply the value of the stock. Stock options and RSUs are current assets with a marital component that must be considered in a divorce, but the *intrinsic* value may not be the best indicator of the actual market value. The actual market value also includes *extrinsic* components, such as the time to vest and exercise the equity, price volatility, and dividends.

Mathematical models may be used to estimate the true market value of employer equity. However, it's often more practical to transfer a percentage of the options or shares to the non-employee spouse when they are received by the employee spouse.

What Belongs to the Marital Estate?

In a divorce, it must be determined how much of the pension or employer equity asset belongs to the marital estate. It is also important to decide if any portion is to be excluded from the marital estate and remain the sole property of one of the parties. Marital assets are defined by the laws of each state; but, in general, assets acquired during the marriage from the efforts of both parties are considered to be marital assets.

The earnings period for pensions is typically the time from the date of entry into the plan to termination of employment (which may be retirement). The earnings period for stock options and RSUs is typically from the grant date to the vest date. If the earnings period is entirely during the marriage, the asset will probably be considered marital.

A common method of determining the marital portion of a pension or employer equity when the earnings period started before the marriage or will end after the divorce is to use a *coverture fraction*. The denominator of the coverture fraction is the total earnings period. The numerator is the portion that was earned during the marriage. If the earnings period started before the marriage, the marital time period is from the marriage date to the vest date, or to the termination-of-employment date or divorce date (whichever is earlier). If the earnings period started during the marriage, the numerator is the start date to the date of the divorce.

Implications

Some benefits may be subject to regulation by ERISA (the Employment Retirement Income and Security Act of 1974) and some may not be, especially for high-level executives and partners in large consulting and accounting firms. ERISA-regulated plans are *qualified* plans that typically can be transferred during a divorce, subject to a qualified domestic relations order (QDRO). Nonqualified plans are not subject to QDROs.

Teacher and municipal pension plans are often not transferable to the non-employee spouse. If a pension or equity cannot be directly transferred to a spouse, it may be able to be "traded" with another asset. In such cases, a discount may be applied to account for the uncertainty and risk in pension and equity assets. Or, it may be appropriate to transfer a portion of the asset (when received) to mitigate the risk for both parties.

Pension payments are typically taxable as ordinary income. Taxability of employer equity depends on the type of equity – for example, whether RSUs are purchased or granted, and whether stock options are classified as incentive stock options or nonqualified stock options. It's important to understand the tax implications of each asset when considering how to divide it.

The language in divorce agreements regarding pensions and employer equity needs to be comprehensive, specifically addressing each issue. The following aspects should be covered:

- Exactly what is going to be transferred, and when (often expressed as a percentage).
- How it is going to be transferred.

- Who will be responsible for the taxes, and how they will be paid and reconciled.
- The employee spouse's responsibility to protect the non-employee spouse if assets cannot be transferred immediately.
- The right of the non-employee spouse to exercise stock options, and the procedures for doing so.
- What will happen if the employee spouse's employment is terminated.

Laurie Dyke, CPA/CFF, CFE
Founding Partner, IAG Forensics & Valuation
Complex Asset Valuation

PART 13

What Do We Do with the Marital Home?

Chapter 53
Selling the Marital Home
269

Chapter 54
Appraising the Marital Home
272

Chapter 55
Post-Divorce Housing
276

Chapter 56
Real Estate Collaboration Specialists
283

Chapter 53
Selling the Marital Home
by Lauren Loper

The Story of the Marital Home

"John, I've been thinking," Sarah began, her voice soft as she sipped her tea. "About the house."

John, engrossed in the evening news, looked over at her, a question in his eyes. "What about the house?"

Sarah hesitated, the weight of their situation heavy on her shoulders. "Well, you know, with the divorce... We need to figure out what to do with it."

John sighed. The news on the TV faded into the background. "I know. It's a lot to think about."

"I was thinking...we could sell it," Sarah suggested, her voice barely a whisper. "It would be a clean break, a fresh start."

John nodded slowly, a thoughtful expression on his face. "I suppose that's one option. But what about the kids? They love this place."

Sarah's heart ached. "I know. It's tough. Maybe we could rent it out for a while? Give us some time to adjust?"

John considered her suggestion. "That might work. But we'd need to find a good property management company to handle everything"

"And what about the financial implications?" Sarah asked, her voice filled with concern. "How will we divide the proceeds?"

"We'll need to discuss that with our lawyers," John replied. "They'll help us figure out the best way to handle it."

Sarah nodded, her mind racing. "I just want to make sure we do what's best for everyone involved. For us, for the children…"

John reached across the table and took her hand. "I know. We'll get through this together."

As they sat in silence, the weight of their decision hung heavy in the air. The future of their marital home was uncertain, but they would face it together, step by step.

Can You Sell Your Home During a Divorce?

The characters in the above scenario engaged in a very common dialogue that most divorcing couples have. The short answer is: Yes, you can sell your home during a divorce. In fact, selling the marital home is a common strategy to divide assets and generate funds. However, it's important to approach the decision with careful consideration and legal counsel.

Key Factors to Consider:

1. **Legal implications:**
- **Joint ownership:** If you and your spouse jointly own the home, both parties typically need to agree to the sale.
- **Division of property:** The sale may be part of your overall property division settlement, which can be complex and often requires court approval.
- **Consult an attorney:** Seek legal advice to understand your rights and obligations regarding the sale.

2. **Financial considerations:**
- **Net proceeds:** Determine how the net proceeds from the sale will be divided between you and your spouse.
- **Mortgage payoff:** Ensure that the mortgage is paid off in full from the sale proceeds.
- **Closing costs:** Factor in closing costs, such as real estate agent commissions, property taxes, and legal fees.

3. **Timing and market conditions:**
- **Divorce process:** The timing of the sale may depend on the overall divorce process and any settlement agreements.
- **Market conditions:** Consider the current real estate market to determine the best time to sell.

4. **Preparing your home for sale:**
- **Staging:** Present your home in its best light to attract potential buyers. Consider getting a real estate home staging consultation to get an outside opinion of what would help sell your home faster and for more money.
- **Repairs and updates:** Address any necessary repairs or updates to increase the home's value. Hiring a home inspector to accurately reveal the home's condition will help pinpoint areas that need to be addressed.
- **Professional help:** To alleviate the stress of selling the house, consider hiring a real estate agent to assist with the process. A Realtor with a designation as a real estate collaboration specialist experienced in divorce can help gather all the house-related documents and manage the sales process from start to finish.

5. **Emotional considerations:**
- **Attachment:** An emotional attachment to the marital home can make the selling process difficult.
- **Support system:** Seek support from friends, family members, or a therapist to help you cope with the emotional challenges.

Alternative Options:

- **Rent the property:** If you're not ready to sell, consider renting out the home as a temporary solution.
- **Buyout:** One spouse may buy out the other's share of the home.

Seeking a real estate expert with a special designation for divorce is a great resource to have when considering all factors in the situation. If the agent has the RCS-D™ designation (Real Estate Collaboration Specialist in Divorce), they can help gather all the home documents and can refer couples to a team of professionals for each area of concern. By carefully considering all options and seeking professional advice, you can navigate the sale of your marital home during a divorce with confidence and peace of mind.

Lauren Loper
Real Estate Collaboration Specialist – Divorce
Certified Amicable Divorce Professional with Financial Expert Special Designation
Certified Probate Real Estate Specialist
Pricing Strategy Advisor
Atlanta, Georgia

Chapter 54
Appraising the Marital Home
by Mike Congemi

In our lives, we make many decisions – some of which are emotionally charged and have significant financial implications. One such decision is buying or selling a house, an action that becomes even more complex during a divorce. With emotions running high and financial stakes considerable, determining the accurate value of real estate assets during a divorce – such as the marital home – is crucial. Various resources can help in such a valuation, including online tools, tax records, real estate agents, and certified appraisers. There are a few options that a homeowner might consider in valuing the marital home.

Online Valuations

Online valuation services may initially appear appealing, because they provide a quick, cost-free estimate on a property. However, such services often have significant biases and limitations. Many online services allow the owner to go online and add features to the property. Changes could create a bias if the added information is not true, and could influence what the online service uses as comparable sales. Online valuation services are typically involved in buying and selling properties or offering mortgages, which can influence their valuations.

Moreover, online valuation tools rely heavily on public records, which are frequently outdated or inaccurate. These tools also cannot assess the interior condition of a property, leading to potential inaccuracies. For instance, a homeowner might manipulate data on the platforms to make their property seem more valuable than it is. For example, an owner might include a basement in the square footage of the living area without considering that basements are valued differently.

iBuyer Services

iBuyer (instant buyer) services are another option that one might consider. Companies that offer those services promise quick sales by providing an initial online offer. However, their business model is to buy low and sell high, meaning that the final offer after an in-person inspection is often significantly lower than the initial one. Such valuations are inherently biased toward the company's goal of purchasing properties at the lowest possible price.

Tax Records

Tax records are another common resource used to value a home, because they are easily accessible and perceived as authoritative. However, tax assessments are conducted using mass appraisal techniques that analyze sales prices and home sizes within a defined tax neighborhood. Mass appraisals are based on the principle of uniformity. These assessments are often based on outdated data and do not account for current market values or the condition of a property's interior. Moreover, tax assessors hold different licenses and qualifications than fee appraisers, leading to potential discrepancies in valuation.

Previous Appraisals

A previous appraisal, such as one conducted for a mortgage refinance, might seem like a reliable resource. However, these appraisals are specifically intended for mortgage transactions and may not accurately reflect the current market value. They are often dated and do not consider recent market changes, making them less reliable for current needs. Mortgage-related appraisals are for the benefit of the lender, to help them evaluate the collateral's risk when they make the loan. There are several instances within a mortgage appraisal that state that the report is for mortgage purposes only. Any party involved in a divorce is not the intended user of such an appraisal.

Real Estate Agents

Real estate agents can provide a comparative market analysis (CMA) or a broker price opinion (BPO). While these professionals have valuable market insights, their valuations can be biased – they represent the interests of the buyer or seller. Additionally, CMAs and BPOs often rely on the same public records used by online tools, leading to similar potential inaccuracies. Typically, a CMA or a BPO is completed with the expectation of getting a listing. Remember that the real estate agent has a fiduciary responsibility to maximize the price of the subject property.

Benefits of a Certified Appraisal

Certified appraisers provide an unbiased opinion of the property's value. That objectivity is particularly crucial in scenarios like divorce, where an unbiased valuation is often required in court or mediation. Unlike providers of online valuations, certified appraisers will conduct a detailed observation of both the interior and exterior of the property. The process allows the appraiser to consider the overall condition, updates, and any deferred maintenance.

An appraisal report will outline the methodology and the adjustments made, providing a transparent and understandable valuation. For instance, the sales comparison approach used in appraisals is particularly reliable for divorce cases. This approach compares the property to similar recently sold properties, accounting for differences in features and condition. This method ensures a fair market value that reflects the property's true worth.

Certified appraisers have professional credentials and often undergo specialized training, such as the Real Estate Collaboration Specialist-Divorce (RCS-D) certification. Such expertise is essential in complex analyses where an accurate valuation is critical. Appraisers with the RCS-D certification understand the nuances of a divorce-related valuation, ensuring a more credible report. Additionally, certified appraisers are required to adhere to strict professional standards and ethics, ensuring the integrity and reliability of their valuations. Adherence to professional standards is particularly important in legal contexts, where an accurate, credible, and unbiased appraisal can significantly affect the outcome of mediation or court proceedings.

While there are various methods to determine the value of real estate, hiring a certified appraiser offers the most reliable and unbiased outcome. Mediators and attorneys prefer the neutral and reliable services of a certified appraiser – the appraiser's expertise can help resolve a case in a timely manner. Moreover, using a certified appraiser can reassure clients that the marital home is accurately valued. The benefits of professional expertise, detailed observations, and comprehensive methodologies in emotionally and financially charged decisions – especially in legal contexts like divorce – are invaluable. By choosing a certified appraiser, those involved in divorce can ensure a fair and objective valuation. That expert valuation will strengthen a client's position in negotiations or court proceedings.

Mike Congemi
Principal, Appraisal Workx, LLC
Associate Member, Appraisal Institute, and RCS-D certified
Atlanta, Georgia and Missouri

Chapter 55
Post-Divorce Housing
by Tami Wollensak and Jennifer Brown

For most couples, the marital home is the largest asset, carrying not only significant financial value but also emotional weight. Decisions surrounding the home can often be complex, especially if you or your spouse wishes to keep it. Unfortunately, without a structured and proactive approach, financial and emotional decisions about the house can quickly lead to roadblocks.

Divorce mortgage planning is a specialized approach to help you make informed decisions about your home – choices that align with both your immediate and long-term goals. Your options may include:
- Selling the home and then buying or renting a new home
- Buying out your spouse and retaining the home
- Assuming the current mortgage and retaining the home

Divorce mortgage planning involves analyzing the financial and legal implications of all real estate decisions. It's more than just figuring out who stays in the home, or who gets which assets. It's about ensuring that you can achieve your financial goals, like the ability to buy your next home, while minimizing risk. It is important when you are dealing with a mortgage and a divorce that you select a mortgage professional who has experience and expertise in divorce mortgage planning. These professionals specialize in knowing how to handle child support and alimony with a mortgage, how to suggest language for a settlement agreement, and how to give everyone involved a realistic picture of mortgage options and divorce. It is always recommended that you meet with a divorce mortgage planning professional as soon as you can in the divorce process. They will assist with what financial options you have regarding a mortgage. Mortgage guidelines are very different from your legal options, and your selected legal professional is not knowledgeable about mortgage guidelines. To be successful in deciding what is best for you and knowing your options, let's talk about what you need to take into consideration.

Understanding Property Title and Ownership

One of the first issues to address is the title of the property. Many people assume that if they are awarded the home in the divorce, they automatically own it outright, but that's not necessarily the case. Holding the title and having mortgage responsibility are two separate things. Even if the court awards the home to you, you and your ex-spouse both may remain financially tied to it if both of your names remain on the mortgage.

Divorce mortgage planning helps ensure that title and ownership are correctly addressed to prevent future disputes or liability issues. If you are awarded the home, it is likely that that you will need to refinance the mortgage in your name to release your spouse from responsibility. Whether or not you are currently on the title (and if so, for how long) will affect your refinance options. A critical factor in refinancing will be your ability to qualify for a new mortgage.

Qualifying for a New Mortgage

Qualifying for a mortgage after a divorce can be more challenging than expected, especially if assets have been split or if you are transitioning back into the workforce. Through divorce mortgage planning, you will learn about your options when it comes to qualifying for a new mortgage – whether you are buying a new home or refinancing the existing one.

Mortgage lenders will consider various factors in the qualification process, including credit score, debt-to-income (DTI) ratio, income consistency and stability, and existing liabilities. Divorce often has an effect on such factors, which means they should be addressed early on. For example, if you are awarded support income, such as alimony or child support, that income may be used to help you qualify for a new mortgage. However, lenders typically require a history of consistent payment (often six months to a year) before considering support income as qualifying income. The waiting period means that proactive planning is essential to make sure you can successfully qualify for a new loan when needed.

Support Income and Impact on Mortgage Qualification

When determining a mortgage qualification post-divorce, support income such as alimony or child support can play a significant role, particularly if you are dependent on those payments. However, as mentioned, lenders have specific guidelines for counting support income as qualifying income. In addition to requiring evidence that support income is consistent and reliable, lenders also often look for an assurance that the income will continue for at least three years.

Without advance planning, you might not be immediately able to secure a mortgage if you're relying on support income to qualify. For example, if you receive support but lack the required payment history, you may be forced to delay purchasing or refinancing. That delay could possibly leave you in an uncertain housing situation. Divorce mortgage planning is a proactive step to ensure that you understand all requirements. Part of your preparation might involve negotiating temporary housing arrangements, or setting up a payment schedule that will support qualifying for a mortgage in the future.

Returning to the Workforce

Many couples decide during their marriage that one spouse will leave the workforce to raise their children. After a divorce, if you decide to return to the workforce, the lender may designate a waiting period before your income is considered consistent and stable. While some mortgage loan programs have very definitive guidelines on timelines for qualifying income, others do not. If you are re-entering the workforce, divorce mortgage planning will help you set a realistic time frame for qualifying for a new mortgage. Some factors that will affect your ability to qualify are:
- How are you compensated? Hourly wages, bonuses, commissions, and self-employment are calculated differently than salaried positions.
- What is your previous work history? Were you employed two consecutive years previously?

- Are you returning to the workforce in a field in which you have prior experience?
- Did you earn a degree or certification that applies to your field while out of the workforce?

Contingent Liabilities and Debt Obligations

Another critical element in divorce mortgage planning is addressing contingent liabilities. Contingent liabilities are financial obligations that are assigned by court order. While contingent liabilities are not included in your debt-to-income ratio and would not have an impact on your ability to purchase a new home, you are responsible if the other party fails to pay. Additionally, your credit score will be adversely affected if timely payments are not made. In the context of divorce, this situation most commonly arises when you are both on the mortgage, one of you intends to keep the home, and you would like to preserve your financing terms.

Agreeing to remain liable for the repayment of debt requires a high level of trust. Your settlement agreement should contain language protecting you if you agree to the liability. Some key points to consider including in the agreement are:

- Names remain on the home title until they are released from the liability
- Notification when a payment is posted or is late
- Notification when property taxes and homeowner's insurance premiums have been paid (or are late)
- Notification of any changes to the monthly payment

Addressing potential contingent liabilities early in the divorce process helps you understand the pros and cons – as well as the risk involved – when agreeing to remain liable on debt.

Mortgage Assumptions and Complexities

What does it mean to assume a mortgage, and is it an option for you? When you assume a mortgage, the original terms of the mortgage remain the same. In a qualified mortgage assumption, your spouse is fully released from liability. Therefore, that type of mortgage assumption requires you to fully qualify. However, if you are required to make an equity equalization payment, and you need to finance the buyout using your home as collateral (in other words, a refinance or home equity line of credit), an assumption is not an option.

When assuming a mortgage, your principal balance cannot increase, and most assumptions do not allow secondary liens on the home.

The first step in assuming a mortgage is securing a legal agreement that awards the home to you. Your mortgage servicer will not allow a request for an assumption before your marital settlement agreement is finalized, executed, and recorded. The agreement should state that you are required to assume the mortgage and are responsible for future payments.

The second step is contacting the servicer of your mortgage to inquire about applying for an assumption. If you have an FHA, a VA, a USDA, or a conventional adjustable-rate mortgage (ARM), your mortgage is eligible for assumption if you qualify. Conventional fixed-rate mortgages do not have an assumption component. However, because of the circumstances of divorce, your mortgage may be assumable at the servicer's discretion. Here are some things you should consider:

- You must adhere to applicable income and credit guidelines – which will vary, depending on the type of mortgage.
- Additional requirements may include, but may not be limited to:
  » The loan is secured by a primary residence.
  » The loan is current and remains current throughout the process.
  » All liens except the first mortgage, including second mortgages and home equity lines of credit, may be required to be paid in full and closed.
- Additional exclusions may include, but may not be limited to:

- » Previously modified loans may be ineligible for assumption.
- » Second mortgages and home equity lines of credit may be ineligible.
- » LLCs or trusts may be ineligible.
- » Loans with mortgage insurance may be ineligible.
- » Loans with a non-occupant co-borrower may be ineligible.

- Your mortgage servicer may require that you provide evidence that you made the mortgage payment for a specified period – for example, for the most recent six months – from a solely owned account directly to the servicer.
- Fees and costs associated with an assumption are determined by the servicer. Reasons for fees and costs may include, but are not limited to: a title search, title insurance, a credit report, a specified percentage of the unpaid principal balance, a processing fee, a closing agent, notary services, recording fees, mailing costs, and transfer taxes. Such fees cannot be financed, so you will need to be prepared to pay them out of pocket when the assumption documents are completed.
- Timelines vary, and are determined by the servicer.

Remember, if you have a conventional fixed-rate mortgage, you should always have a backup plan. Your servicer is under no obligation to approve a mortgage assumption, even if you qualify. Work with your divorce mortgage planning specialist to be sure you know what the refinancing terms would be, that the payment is within your budget, and that you qualify in the event the assumption is not approved.

Planning for Long-Term Financial Impact

Divorce mortgage planning also provides a structured way to assess the long-term financial effects of real estate decisions. Often, divorcing couples focus only on immediate needs – such as deciding who will keep the home or how assets will be split – without fully considering financial implications down the road.

For example, you may wish to keep the home to provide stability for your children – but without proper planning, that decision could lead to financial strain later if you can't afford mortgage payments on a single income. Alternatively, you might agree to relinquish your share of the home's equity without fully understanding how that will factor into your ability to buy a new home in the future.

By working with a divorce mortgage planning specialist, you will gain a clearer picture of how today's decisions will affect your financial well-being down the line. Consultation would include assessing affordability, potential tax implications, and the broader financial landscape you will face, post-divorce.

Conclusion: Making Informed Choices for a Stable Future

Making well-informed choices now can lead to greater stability and security in the years to come. Divorce mortgage planning at the beginning of the divorce process will allow time for thoughtful analysis. You will gain a solid understanding of your options, your obligations, and potential outcomes of various choices you might make. You will also have time to make necessary financial adjustments, such as building credit or establishing a payment history for support income, which will aid in qualifying for a new mortgage.

The biggest takeaway here is: Divorce mortgage planning should always be addressed before your settlement agreement is finalized. Decisions about the home and mortgage are some of the most financially impactful choices made during a divorce. Don't wait until the last minute to think about mortgage planning – take control of your financial future by prioritizing that critical step.

Tami Wollensak
Divorce Mortgage Specialist
Certified Divorce Lending Professional
NMLS #1963450
Chicago, Illinois

Jennifer Brown
Mortgage Loan Originator
Certified Divorce Lending Professional
Certified Veterans Lending Specialist
NMLS #207017
Certified Amicable Divorce Professional
Atlanta, Georgia

Chapter 56
Real Estate Collaboration Specialists
by Lauren Loper

The sun beat down mercilessly on the seemingly peaceful suburban street. Inside a small, tidy house, Sarah and David sat across from each other – the tension palpable. Their once-loving marriage had crumbled, leaving behind a trail of hurt and resentment.

Their looming divorce was a daunting task, made even more complicated by the tangled web of shared assets. A particular concern was their beloved family home. Just the thought of dividing their possessions made them feel emotionally overwhelmed. They knew they needed help. But where to start?

A glimmer of hope appeared when Sarah stumbled upon an article about real estate collaboration specialists who are certified for divorce situations and carry a Real Estate Collaboration Specialist – Divorce™ (RCS-D™) designation. Intrigued, she delved deeper, discovering that these professionals help couples navigate the complex real estate issues that are typical in divorce.

With renewed determination, Sarah and David sought the guidance of an RCS-D. Their chosen expert, a knowledgeable yet compassionate individual, immediately put them at ease. The RCS-D patiently listened to their concerns with an understanding of their emotional turmoil.

Together, they embarked on a journey to untangle the complexities of their situation. The RCS-D helped them assess each area of their home ownership to get them to the right professionals to help answer their questions, exploring options. They discussed selling the home and talked about the possibility of one person keeping it. They guided Sarah and David through the process of gathering the documents that would help minimize conflict surrounding the marital home and other properties they owned. The goal was to maximize their chances of a smooth transition if they decided to sell the properties. The documents, part of a legal package, were to be shared with the attorney, judge, and/or mediator.

As the weeks passed, Sarah and David began to see a light at the end of the tunnel. The specialist's expertise and support had empowered them to make informed decisions and to move forward with confidence. They were no longer overwhelmed by the daunting task of dividing their property; instead, they felt informed and empowered.

The real estate specialist's role extended beyond the gathering of house-related documents. The specialist guided the couple to knowledgeable professionals who would be able to provide the necessary practical advice, data, and documents to move forward. Sarah and David would be able to get themselves in the strongest position in the market, and would be able to prioritize next steps, even if one of them ultimately would stay in the home. Most importantly, the couple became better equipped to cope with the emotional roller coaster of divorce. The specialist, the RCS-D, had helped make a challenging experience more manageable and less stressful.

In the end, they emerged from the divorce process with a sense of closure and hope for the future. The real estate specialist had played a pivotal role in helping them navigate the complex real estate aspects of their situation.

When it comes to buying, selling, or renting a property, there's no better person than a professional Realtor to help make the process smooth and desirable. While properties can be profitable investments, they are also one of the most common assets responsible for personal disputes.

Whether the circumstances involve the death of a family member, a divorce, or another daunting scenario, it's challenging to deal with any real estate process during a time of upheaval. That's when you need an RCS-D, a real estate specialist with a special designation. It takes specific training and education to become a Real Estate Collaboration Specialist – Divorce.

What Is an RCS-D?

More often than not, many couples in the process of divorce do not seek professional help when making decisions about their property. An RCS-D – a real estate collaboration specialist with a "divorce" designation – is a title achieved by a Realtor after becoming qualified in divorce-related real estate sales through detailed coursework and a successful examination. The RCS-D course is offered through Divorce This House, a consultant firm that trains financial professionals, mortgage professionals, and real estate brokers and agents regarding divorce situations.

A Realtor with the RCS-D designation can work directly with family lawyers and financial professionals to help you solve disputes over property.

Benefits of Having a Realtor with the RCS-D Designation

As the title implies, an RCS-D Realtor mainly deals with couples going through a divorce. A couple often needs guidance in making informed decisions on whether to keep or sell the jointly owned marital home (or other properties owned by the couple).

While such assistance may sound utterly simple, such cases can be highly complex. Each half of a divorcing couple may have opposite demands. Sometimes, one person will want to keep the marital home, but it simply isn't practical or feasible. In the course of a divorce and the probate process, many homes could require major necessary repairs or have insurance or lien issues that the involved parties are unaware of. It can be hard to find a middle ground for a family in transition.

The following is a quick breakdown of the benefits of having a Realtor with an RCS-D designation:

1) You Can Make Informed Decisions

Without a doubt, a marital home is often the largest asset for any couple going through a divorce, and deciding whether to keep the house can be a real challenge without the help of a professional RCS-D.

With accurate knowledge, comprehensive research, and detailed understanding, an RCS-D can act as a project manager to gather the house documents. Being able to carefully review all of the documents can help clients make informed decisions. Having all the information is critical to avoid potentially extreme consequences and any further pain to those involved.

2) You'll Learn the Basics of Property Division

Since property division is a vast topic to cover, it's important to find a real estate agent with expertise in this area. A real estate divorce specialist can discuss property division, and make it easier for you to arrive at unbiased decisions that don't cause conflict. The RCS-D will also be able to refer you to financial and legal professionals who will help you fully comprehend the fundamentals of property division and any possible consequences.

3) You'll Understand the Legalities

When it comes to the divorce-related real estate niche, you can't neglect the importance of understanding the legal matters involved in order to avoid any hassles. For that reason, look for an RCS-D who works with a team of experts to discuss each area pertaining to the house. Such experts might include a certified financial analyst, an insurance agent, a mortgage lender, an inspector, and an appraiser. The RCS-D Realtor will guide you through the nitty-gritty of divorce-related real estate, focusing on issues such as contracts, transactions, approvals, and closings.

If all factors are not thoroughly discussed, costly mistakes could cause severe and possibly permanent ramifications. Specifically, mistakes could also mean financial losses and unsatisfactory decisions – decisions that often cause couples to blame each other.

The Bottom Line

Never underestimate the importance of having a professional RCS-D who remains with you throughout the process of your sensitive real estate matters.

Lauren Loper
Real Estate Collaboration Specialist – Divorce
Certified Amicable Divorce Professional with Financial Expert Special Designation
Certified Probate Real Estate Specialist
Pricing Strategy Advisor
Atlanta, Georgia

# STEP 3

RESOLUTION: DIVIDING, RESOLVING, AND MAKING AGREEMENTS

PART 14

How Is Our Case Resolved?

Chapter 57
Overview of Settlement Options
291

Chapter 58
Alternative Dispute Resolution
292

Chapter 59
The Mediation Mindset
303

Chapter 60
Types of Divorce Mediation
308

Chapter 61
Resolving Impasses in Negotiation
313

Chapter 57
Overview of Settlement Options
by Tracy Ann Moore-Grant

Everyone's goal in an amicable divorce is to resolve all issues so that the case is settled and no issues go to court. To reach a settlement, many different methods, or a combination, may get your case to the finish line.

1. **Direct settlement negotiations** – Often called a "kitchen table agreement," this is where parties talk to one another directly to make agreements.

2. **Early dispute resolution** – Once lawyers are engaged, they speak and memorialize any issues the parties have resolved and focus in the future on unresolved issues.

3. **Settlement offers** – Lawyers can send to each other offers to discuss with their clients to attempt to settle the case.

4. **Alternate dispute resolution** – Parties can engage in mediation, parent coordination, or arbitration to resolve issues. If these processes don't work, parties are encouraged to attend an arbitration before going to court.

With over 90 percent of family law cases resolving themselves without the need of a court hearing, it is important to be ready to explore all of the different ways your case can be resolved out of court. This section of the book explores the different ways a case gets resolved.

Chapter 58
Alternative Dispute Resolution
by Kathy J. Bloom

What Is Alternative Dispute Resolution?

Alternative Dispute Resolution (ADR) is an umbrella term used to describe methods of resolving disputes outside of court. The idea is that the primary way to resolve a dispute is with a judge as the factfinder whereas ADR provides alternative methods. These main methods are: Early Dispute Resolution (EDR), mediation, arbitration, and parenting coordination.

What Is Litigation Like?

Alternative Dispute Resolution (ADR) is different from litigation because the processes do not depend on the court system and the judge is not the decision maker. When a matter is litigated through the court system, the parties, usually through their lawyers, speak to the court in documents called *pleadings* and *the process is adversarial.* The process continues with various *pleadings,* which could be in the form of petitions or motions, and the other side then has the opportunity to answer those *pleadings* and file counterclaims. Both sides get information from the other side by *propounding* discovery requests, which translates to formal requests for information.

There are four basic forms of formal discovery:
- **Interrogatories**, which are written questions that one side asks of the other person who must answer in writing under oath.
- **Requests for the production of documents**, which are exactly what they sound like: requests for specific documents such as years' worth of bank statements, or proof of income.
- **Requests for admissions**, where one side states a premise and asks the other side to admit that it is true (or deny it).

- **Depositions**, where the lawyer for one party questions the other party under oath, and a court reporter records the questions and answers.

That is just the gathering of information that is described as Phase 1 in the Amicable Process. You can see when compared to a litigation, or "in court" case, how exhaustive the gathering of information can be in a litigated case. When petitions are filed, court hearings and/or conferences are scheduled by the court, and the parties and attorneys must show up in court. The court doesn't really care if you have something else to do or if you have work or childcare issues. While they might "continue" a hearing for good cause, if everyone agrees, there are times the order to appear states that the hearing will not be continued.

A hearing is a formal proceeding in which the judge sits on the bench and the parties sit at tables on each side of the courtroom just like you have seen on TV and in the movies. Witnesses are called to the witness stand as lawyers present their case. Witnesses are sworn in and must answer the questions the attorneys ask. Then the other side gets to ask questions or "cross examine" the witness. Lawyers can object to the questions and/or the answers, and the judge can then sustain or overrule the objection. A court reporter records the process in a transcript.

A conference is less formal than a hearing or a trial. The judge may talk to the attorneys in the courtroom, or call the attorneys back to the judge's chambers to discuss the case and see if she or he can work it out with the lawyers, or whether a hearing is needed. Most of the time, the parties do not get any input during the conferences. The attorneys may come out and ask if the parties agree to what is discussed. If both parties do not agree to what is proposed, then a hearing is held, either at that time or scheduled for another time in the future.

This process goes on and on until the case is resolved. If a case involves divorce, custody, and support, each of those issues are dealt with separately and involve the same processes of filing a complaint, petition, motion, answer, counterclaim, and then going through the process that the jurisdiction has in place to deal with that part of the matter.

After all of the evidence is gathered, the courts have specific processes to resolve the division of assets. Some courts have you meet with a master or hearing officer, who is the first stop before appearing before a judge. You might have several appearances before the hearing officer, and it might resolve at that point. On the other hand, if it does not, the next step is to go before the judge. That could be one hearing, or it could be a series of hearings.

If your case involves custody, it is the same process of gathering information before you move forward. Since different jurisdictions handle cases differently, the process can be handled differently from one county to the next within the same state. Some jurisdictions send you to an intermediary before seeing a judge in a custody matter. That person is usually an attorney known as a custody conciliator, a hearing officer, or a custody master. The conciliator gets the basic information about the case and tries to get the parties to come to an agreement. In more contested cases, a guardian ad litem is a different professional who investigates the best interests of a child and reports back to the court. The prevailing view is that parties are in the best position to make custody decisions. One judge once told the parents during a custody trial to go out on the street and find a stranger to make the decision for them since that is what it is like for a judge to make those decisions.

Alternative dispute resolution processes are much different than what is described above. Instead of strangers making decisions for you, you are making the decisions yourself with the help of specially trained professionals who get to know you and your situation. The court is not part of the procedure except to process and approve the paperwork – and have a judge approve the resolution and issue an order or decree after the parties have come to an agreement.

What Are the Goals of Alternative Dispute Resolution?

There are many goals of ADR. One of the main goals is to give you a voice in your process. People often come to me and tell me they want their day in court. When I ask them what that means, they inevitably tell me they want to tell the judge their story. I explain that if they go to court, they will probably never get a chance to do that. The loudest voices in court are the lawyers, with the judge directing traffic. If you want to tell your story, the best way is to stay out of court and use any of the available forms of ADR. Those of us involved in it are active listeners and genuinely believe in helping and guiding you to tell your story.

We focus on your goals and interests, not positions. When we look at your goals, we get a clearer picture of what you really need. When people take positions, it is like drawing a line in the sand and saying you will not cross it, even when it might be in your best interest to do so. Both parties might take positions that seem diametrically opposed; but when we ask what each of your goals are, they might be totally aligned. Using ADR methods, we help you communicate your goals and figure out the best way to reach them.

ADR gives the power to the parties, not the court. It saves time, money, and the embarrassment of airing your dirty laundry in court, and it puts the children first when there are issues involving children. We make sure that you are "driving the bus," and we, as professionals, are just riding along to help you navigate the road when and if it gets bumpy.

What Professionals Are Used in Alternative Dispute Resolution (ADR)?

You can choose from several different types of ADR processes, and with those processes come different dispute resolution professionals. The obvious professionals are attorneys who choose to keep their clients out of court and encourage their clients to seek alternative methods to resolve their matters rather than slugging it out in court. Litigious attorneys make everyone miserable. ADR attorneys are the good guys and are the difference between a miserable experience and a civilized and collaborative process. While attorneys are involved in the ADR process, they are still your advocate.

a. Neutral Professionals Used in Alternative Dispute Resolution

Mediators, parenting coordinators, and arbitrators are all neutral professionals who play important roles in similar but different methods of ADR.

All of those professionals and processes will be discussed in more detail below.

In addition to mediators, parenting coordinators, and arbitrators, we often use other neutral professionals in ADR to help resolve cases. When finances are complicated, we look to financial professionals known as certified divorce financial analysts (CDFA) to help us with financial matters. Mental health professionals help us with communications and help to keep everyone, including the lawyers, on an "even keel." Children might have special needs; so we look to child specialists to help with those special needs as well as other parenting issues. If we need to value the marital home, we bring in a neutral appraiser. Realtors, mortgage brokers, and other neutrals can play an important role to help resolve real estate matters, too.

b. Professional Advocates Used in Alternative Dispute Resolution

Parties involved in ADR still need professional advocates as well as professional neutrals. Clearly, attorneys who choose to keep their clients out of court and encourage them to seek alternative methods to resolve their matters rather than in the courts are first and foremost advocates for their clients. Just because your attorney is encouraging you to use out-of-court processes does not mean they do not have your back. They do!

Some people may want a mental health professional in their corner, or a financial advisor to help them plan for the future. ADR allows for both advocates and neutral professionals to help resolve your case.

What Are the Advantages of Alternative Dispute Resolution (ADR)?

ADR is private and more personal, and more importantly it allows you to participate in the process more actively, taking control of the decision-making. You are not at the mercy of the court to appear at a hearing or conference that interferes with your job or during a time that is impossible for you to get there. Also, you do not have to pay for your attorney to sit around outside the courtroom for your case to be called. For that reason and others, it is more cost effective and is usually far less expensive than litigation. You also control the timing and pacing. You can ask to speed up the process or slow it down depending on the circumstances.

What Is Mediation?

Mediation is a process that uses the services of a neutral party called a mediator. The mediator is specially trained to help the parties talk to each other to try to resolve their issues. People often confuse mediation with arbitration. They are not the same. The mediator helps the parties have productive conversations, helping them work through their issues, whereas the arbitrator hears the issues in the case and makes a binding decision like a judge.

Some mediators will schedule the mediation for a full day, or as long as it takes to try to resolve the issues. Other mediators schedule a series of mediations in two-hour increments. Mediations can take place with or without attorneys present, usually depending on the type of mediation. Mediations can be in-person or even online. As technologies advance, mediation advances as well.

How Can a Mediator Help You?

Mediators have special training to help parties talk to each other in constructive ways. Sometimes people who are at odds with each other do not hear what the other person is saying. A mediator tries to listen very carefully to hear what each person is trying to communicate and then "reflects" that message in nonthreatening simple terms for the other person. It is amazing how this method can make a conversation more productive. At certain points, the mediator summarizes the main points in an inclusive and productive way to make sure everyone is on the same page and has the same understanding.

The mediator also "checks in" on the process to see what direction the parties want to take and whether to stay with a topic or move in another direction. Sometimes, the mediator sits back and lets the parties talk directly to each other if they are in the same room. Mediators can also evaluate the facts and circumstances and propose ideas on a common ground or reasonable resolution. The mediator uses all of those tools to help the parties try to reach an agreement. With a mediation, the parties have control over the agreement and the terms. The mediator is a neutral professional guiding them to an agreement.

What Does Mediation Cost?

Mediation costs vary depending on the location, experience, and skill of the mediator. Attorney mediators usually charge by the hour, and the rates are usually the same as their regular rate. Some mediators charge a flat fee per mediation session, which includes the preparation of a memorandum reflecting the agreements between the parties. Mediators can also be mental health professionals or financial professionals. In some jurisdictions, no educational level is required – simply the taking of a mediation course. For all mediators, their rates are dependent on their location and level of experience. When in doubt about the cost, just ask. Generally, resolving your matter using a mediator is an efficient and economical way to resolve legal issues, especially in family law matters.

What Is Arbitration and How Is It Different from Mediation?

Arbitration is another way to resolve a legal matter without going to court. You can think of an arbitrator as a private judge, and arbitration as a private process.

So often people confuse mediation and arbitration, but they are very different. A mediator works with the parties to help them determine their own outcome. Whether the mediator is transformative or evaluative, the end result is an agreement between the parties, if an agreement can be reached. There is no guarantee, however, that an agreement will be reached in a mediation process.

On the other hand, the arbitrator is the one making the decision as to the outcome when a case is arbitrated. Unlike arbitration there will be a determination, and an award or directive issued.

How Does Arbitration Work?

Arbitration can take different forms from simply each side drafting documents called pleadings that are submitted to the arbitrator, from which he or she makes a decision, to a full-blown evidentiary hearing with a court reporter. Even with a hearing, this is still done in a far less formal setting than court.

The first step is to choose an arbitrator and negotiate an arbitration agreement. The arbitration agreement spells out exactly the type of process that is going to take place (i.e., an arbitration based on just the pleadings, a full-blown evidentiary hearing, or something in between). The scope of the issue or issues is addressed in the arbitration agreement. Deadlines for each part of the process are determined. Of course, how much the arbitrator will be paid is also negotiated and made part of the agreement.

In cases that are decided on the pleadings, each party submits their case to the arbitrator, in writing, spelling out the details of the case and why they think they should prevail and what type of award they should receive. The arbitrator makes a decision based on those pleadings. He or she may need more information and then goes back to the parties and asks for clarification. A decision is made, and an award is issued according to the deadline addressed in the agreement to arbitrate.

Sometimes, especially for complex issues, more complicated proceedings take place. It can be similar to litigation without the intervention of the courts. Interim issues can be addressed by both sides, addressing those issues with the arbitrator. Both sides can communicate with the arbitrator, but must also include the other side in those communications. This avoids what is known as *ex parte* (one-sided) communications, so the arbitrator retains neutrality.

The arbitrator listens to the issues presented from both sides, in pleadings, conferences, and actual hearings, if that is what is agreed upon. Both sides can present evidence and call witnesses to testify under oath. The parties can choose to have a court reporter there to transcribe the proceeding.

Once both sides are satisfied that all available evidence has been presented to the arbitrator, the arbitrator then makes a decision regarding the case. The arbitrator then awards whatever he or she deems appropriate based on the evidence presented and substantive law. The arbitrator puts the award in writing.

What Powers Does an Arbitrator Have and Is It Binding?

An arbitrator has broad powers, but there are limitations to those powers. Please note that these vary by state and county, so please ask your selected legal professional about your jurisdiction to learn more. Generally, an arbitrator does not have the ability to (1) grant a divorce or annulment, (2) terminate parental rights, (3) grant an adoption or guardianship of a child or incapacitated individual, or (4) determine that a child is delinquent in dependency court. Only a judge can make those determinations.

Once an award is made by the arbitrator, it is binding, which resolves the issue and removes it from the court system.

How Much Does Arbitration Cost?

Arbitrators generally charge by the hour, and their hourly rate is based on the typical rates in their geographic area – and also on their credentials and experience. It becomes cost effective because it is an efficient process, and no one is wasting time in court waiting for their case to be heard or appearing for a status conference at which nothing is accomplished. The contact with the arbitrator is focused and meaningful, which makes the process expeditious and, therefore, cost effective.

What Is Parent Coordination?

Parent coordination is a process that uses a neutral professional to help parents make decisions about parenting issues when they do not or cannot agree with each other. Parent coordination is used in a divorce to help the parties take time to develop a Parenting Plan. In high-conflict custody cases it can also be used by parents who want to remain on good terms with each other, but sometimes disagree on the other's parenting style or what to do in certain circumstances.

Parent coordinators do not provide therapy or counseling to parents or children. It should not be confused with co-parent counseling, which is generally done by a mental health professional. This professional helps parents learn to co-parent when they are often angry, especially after a nasty breakup.

What Does a Parent Coordinator Do?

A parent coordinator (PC) is a neutral party who acts as a decision maker after hearing both sides of the story from parents who cannot agree on child-related issues. The parent coordinator will work like a mediator to get the issue resolved. If that does not work, the PC is often vested with arbitration authority to make a decision so the parties can move forward. The parent coordinator's decision is based on what is in the best interests of the child. PCs are either agreed upon by the parties or appointed by the court for parents involved in repeated litigation involving parenting matters. PCs have limited powers that are always subject to review by the court.

Parent coordination can also be used by parents who want to remain in agreement when it comes to parenting, and want to give their children the best experience when the family is no longer intact. The parties can bounce their ideas off the PC to get another perspective. PCs can also help parents in the process of divorce to work through parenting plans and other issues that arise during the process.

Who Can Be a Parent Coordinator?

Different jurisdictions require different qualifications to be a PC. Most require a PC to be an experienced licensed attorney or mental health professional, with additional training such as mediation training and specialized psychological knowledge or training. In certain jurisdictions, domestic violence training is also required.

A PC works with parents regarding day-to-day custody issues that are often too minor to litigate or need a timely resolution. Those issues might include custody exchanges, school issues (other than school selection), issues involving extracurricular activities, use of electronic devices and social media, vacations, clothing and personal possessions, and coordination of court-ordered services for the children.

What Are the Limits of Authority for a Parenting Coordinator?

PCs cannot make decisions about the following issues:
- A change in legal custody
- A change in primary physical custody
- A custody change that reduces or expands one party's time with the child(ren)
- Allocation of responsibility for financial issues other than payment of the PC
- Relocation issues (change in the residence of the (child(ren))
- Major decisions affecting the health, education, or religion of the child(ren); and
- Any other issues limited by the court

How Much Does Parent Coordination Cost?

Parent coordination is an effective cost-saving measure especially for parents who have used the courts to resolve their parenting issues. It eliminates the need to consult and pay individual attorneys, there are no court filing fees, and there is no need to take time off from work to attend court hearings or conferences.

Rates for PCs vary by geography and profession. PCs usually have a retainer and charge by the hour, and those fees are split between the parties in whatever ratio is negotiated between them.

Why Should You Use a Parent Coordinator?

PCs, like most other forms of alternative dispute resolution, offer the benefits of saving time, money, and keeping your matter private. Since the focus is always on what is in the best interests of the child(ren), the children also reap the benefits of their parents working through the issues quickly and without going to court.

Kathy J. Bloom
Attorney, Mediator, Arbitrator, Parenting Coordinator
Certified Amicable Divorce Professional
Philadelphia, Pennsylvania

Chapter 59
The Mediation Mindset
by Chloe Ouditz

Mediation is a powerful and successful tool to resolve disputes in divorce without the need for drawn-out court proceedings. However, preparing for mediation requires careful planning, a strategic mindset, and emotional awareness. In this chapter, we'll cover the essential steps to prepare for mediation, and ensure it bears positive results. If mediation is approached with a focus on compromise and collaboration, you can achieve resolutions collaboratively that set a positive foundation for your future.

Shifting Your Mindset: Negotiation, Not Battle

One of the most significant challenges when you approach mediation is to shift your mindset, and see divorce as a negotiation rather than a battle. Many people enter mediation still fueled with anger, frustration, and a desire to *win*. But divorce, by its very nature, involves two parties with shared history, responsibilities, and, often, children. Viewing it as a zero-sum game can sabotage the process and prevent meaningful resolutions.

In mediation, success is not about defeating your spouse. Rather, it's about working together to find mutually acceptable solutions that reflect each party's needs. Think of mediation as a negotiation where both sides must think creatively in order to resolve the situation. Compromise doesn't mean settling for less; it means focusing on what truly matters, and prioritizing long-term well-being over short-term satisfaction. This shift in perspective can transform mediation from a confrontation into a constructive dialogue.

Accepting that conflict is inevitable is also crucial. Divorce inherently involves disagreements, but they don't need to escalate into full-blown disputes. Instead of avoiding conflict, focus on managing it constructively. Mediation provides a structured environment where both parties can express their needs and concerns while a neutral third party helps facilitate the conversation. If you embrace this mindset, the door is open to more collaborative solutions and will minimize unnecessary emotional distress.

In this context, it is important to understand that the mediator is not a judge. They are a neutral third party who is there to help you negotiate effectively. This means the mediator will not take sides, nor will they render a judgment. The agreements reached in mediation are nonbinding until they are signed off by the court – this is not a mock trial.

Defining Success: Clarifying Your Goals

Before you walk into mediation, it's essential to take the time to clearly define what success looks like for you. Without clear goals, you will get sidetracked by emotions or the small details. Ask yourself, *What are my priorities? What are the non-negotiables? Where am I willing to compromise?* Write these items down. As mediation can get stressful and upsetting; it is important to be able to center yourself by looking back at your written goals.

Consider your long-term vision. For instance, if you have children, think about what kind of co-parenting relationship you want to have with your former spouse in the years to come. If financial security is a key concern, make sure you're focusing on practical arrangements that ensure a stable future. Your goals should reflect both your immediate needs and your broader vision for life post-divorce. These goals will form the basis for a set of criteria upon which you'll agree with your spouse in order to meet your needs. Criteria might include, for example: *we should both be able to live close to each other so the children don't have to travel far between the two homes; we should both be able to afford to buy a property after the divorce; we should ensure the children's routine is not disrupted.* Any potential settlement you discuss will be reviewed according to these criteria to help you stay focused and avoid making decisions based solely on emotions in the heat of the moment.

When defining success, it's helpful to create a list of the issues you'll be negotiating, such as child custody, asset division, spousal support, and future living arrangements. For each issue, outline your ideal outcome, your acceptable range of outcomes, and your bottom line. Do not enter the negotiation with an expected outcome. The idea is to brainstorm solutions together. It is unlikely your predefined position will be the end result, and it will stifle your willingness to be open-minded.

Gathering Facts: Organizing Your Financial Information

Solid preparation is key to a successful mediation – and a crucial part of that is gathering all the necessary documents. In any mediation, but especially one involving finances, facts matter. Before the mediation process begins, ensure you have a full understanding of your financial situation.

Start by collecting all relevant financial documents, such as bank statements, tax returns, pay stubs, property deeds, pension valuations, and investment accounts. In many cases, you will also need to obtain independent valuations for shared assets like real estate or businesses. Transparency is essential; withholding information or failing to disclose assets will not only derail mediation but also may have legal repercussions later on. If using dtour.life, these documents can be collected and placed in your portal and shared with your lawyer, your mediator, or even your spouse.

Additionally, it's a good idea to create a detailed budget that outlines your monthly expenses, future financial needs, and any child-related costs. This gives you a clear sense of what you will need moving forward, and will help to inform your negotiation strategy. The more informed you are, the more confident you'll feel during mediation, and the more likely you are to reach fair agreements.

If using dtour.life, please sync your banking, investment, and retirement accounts and credit cards with the system (if sync is available for your area). In doing this, dtour.life will pull out data from these records and autocategorize the information in the "expenses" section. Review this information and see if anything needs to be renamed as the system makes its best guess. Then go into "Spending Plans." You will see that all expenses have been pulled into this tab. You can go down the spending plan to create both your present and future budget. You can categorize current expenses and also predict and budget for items you might have in the future.

Learning How to Negotiate Strategically: Focusing on Interests, Not Positions

At the heart of effective mediation is interest-based negotiation. Unlike positional bargaining, where each party takes a stance and haggles until one side gives in, interest-based negotiation focuses on understanding the underlying needs and concerns that drive each party's position. This approach encourages both parties to explore a range of options that can satisfy their interests, often resulting in more creative and lasting solutions. You are effectively sitting down together to resolve a joint issue: that of disentangling your lives. In that respect, you share a common goal, and this should remain your primary focus.

For example, instead of arguing over who gets the house, explore why you or your spouse wants the house. Is it because of emotional attachment? Financial stability? Proximity to children's schools? By identifying the interests behind the positions, you may uncover solutions that address both parties' needs more effectively, such as one partner keeping the house in exchange for other assets, or selling the house and splitting the proceeds.

To prepare, consider your own interests and try to anticipate your spouse's as well. What are your underlying concerns regarding finances, parenting, or living arrangements? If you don't know what your spouse's point of view is, start the mediation by letting them explain their own objectives. Knowing these will help you stay flexible and generate multiple options that address both parties' concerns.

Managing emotions is equally important when negotiating. Divorce is an emotional process – emotional outbursts or defensiveness can derail productive conversations. Learn to stay calm, take breaks when needed, and approach the discussions with a problem-solving mindset. Your mediator can also create an environment that encourages constructive communication and minimizes emotional triggers.

Communicating Effectively: Clear, Respectful, and Open Dialogue

Effective communication is the backbone of a successful mediation. It is often said that negotiation is nothing more than communication with results. Poor communication, such as using inflammatory language, sarcasm, contempt, or blame, can quickly derail a productive session. Instead, focus on the CIC rule: be concise, informative, and civil in how you express your needs and concerns.

When speaking, use "I" statements to convey your perspective without assigning blame. For example, say, "I need stability in my financial future," instead of, "You're ruining my chances at a secure life." This minimizes defensiveness and keeps the conversation focused on finding solutions.

Nonverbal communication is just as important as what you say. Maintain positive body language, such as making eye contact and sitting in an open posture, which signals you are engaged and willing to collaborate. Tone of voice also plays a crucial role. A calm, neutral tone helps de-escalate tension, while an aggressive or sarcastic tone can create unnecessary conflict.

A consideration that should drive your behavior throughout the negotiation is to use a future-focused conversation. Mediation is not the opportunity to revisit past feuds or to assign responsibility for the end of the marriage. This is an attempt to build a plan for your future after the divorce. Always try to keep the conversation about the path ahead, rather than the previous chapter.

Lastly, remember that listening is just as important as speaking. Truly hearing your spouse's concerns, rather than waiting for your turn to talk, shows that you're committed to finding solutions that work for both of you. Active listening can foster trust and give you invaluable insights into what type of proposals your spouse might accept.

Conclusion

Preparing for family mediation involves more than gathering documents and knowing what you want. It is about approaching the process with the right mindset, understanding your goals, and mastering both negotiation and communication techniques. With thoughtful preparation, you can turn mediation into an opportunity to resolve disputes peacefully, and set strong foundations for the next chapter of your life.

Chloe Oudiz
Certified Divorce Coach (CDC)
The Divorce and Separation Coach
London, England

Chapter 60
Types of Divorce Mediation
by Tracy Ann Moore-Grant

In a family law matter, mediation is a process where a neutral third party, called a mediator, helps a couple negotiate and reach agreements on key issues. Those issues could involve disagreements over items like child custody, property division, and spousal support. The mediator would assist the couple with any topics in their case, allowing the spouses to resolve their divorce without going to court.

Employing a mediator means that the parties are making decisions on their own terms instead of having a judge decide for them; the goal is to facilitate communication and find common ground. The ultimate goal of the mediator is to assist the spouses in reaching agreements on all disputed issues and avoid court.

What a mediation looks like varies greatly from country to country, from state to state, and even from jurisdiction to jurisdiction.

Who Is at the Mediation?

Of course, the parties to the case are at the mediation; and sometimes, mediators meet separately with each party beforehand. However, there is no standard rule on whether lawyers accompany their clients to a mediation. In some jurisdictions, like Georgia, lawyers almost always accompany clients to mediation, so the client has immediate access to legal advice. An attorney's presence also makes the mediation binding. In other geographic areas, lawyers may not attend, but may prepare their clients or be available by phone if an issue arises.

Are the Parties Together?

Although both parties are part of the mediation, they may or may not be in the same room. If the parties are in separate rooms (either in person, or in online breakout rooms) the mediation is called **caucus** or **shuttle mediation**.

Benefits of Utilizing Shuttle Mediation

There are benefits to using separate rooms at a mediation, including **reduced emotional tension**. The separation allows the spouses to express themselves openly without anxiety. They can explain concerns and priorities candidly, without feeling pressured or intimidated by the other person. The separate-room approach is especially beneficial in cases with potential high conflict or hostility.

Separate rooms during mediation provide **a safe, private space**. Some individuals may feel unsafe or uncomfortable being in the same room with the other party, particularly in high-emotion cases, such as those involving domestic violence.

Many times, a spouse simply does not wish to discuss concerns in front of the other spouse; also, they may want to be able to express themselves without fear of retaliation. Shuttle mediation can lead to **better communication** because there is more openness and honesty. The individuals can freely express their needs and concerns. If lawyers are present, a client can ask legal questions and receive advice privately. Parties and professionals can each propose multiple scenarios for resolution, without each party hearing all the available options and choices.

Separate spaces in mediation can **mitigate an imbalance** in situations where one party has significantly more power than the other. Separation can help level the playing field.

Shuttle mediation is a tailored approach that can be used to address specific disputed issues when direct communication is difficult. Parties can always try being in the same room at first, and then ask to be separated if need be.

Cons of Shuttle Mediation

One drawback to shuttle mediation is the **potential for miscommunication**. The mediator must accurately convey information between parties; if communication is not accurate, it could lead to misunderstandings. Mediators must determine how to convey offers and information to the other party.

Having separation during mediation can result in **a lengthier process**. Shuttle mediation can take longer than traditional mediation due to the back-and-forth communication between the mediator and each party.

Shuttle mediation has **less direct interaction**. It may not deliver the same level of understanding of the dynamics between the spouses as in a face-to-face mediation.

It may not be suitable in all cases. When the parties are willing and able to communicate directly with each other, shuttle mediation is probably not appropriate. Keeping parties separate could create tension where it did not exist before.

When the parties are separated, the situation **relies heavily on the mediator's skills**. Shuttle mediation requires an expert mediator to effectively navigate the communication between parties and facilitate a productive resolution.

> **If there are any concerns about safety** and the case is going to mediation, the mediator should be immediately made aware of the safety concern so they can proceed appropriately. Cases should be screened before mediation for a domestic violence background and/or safety concerns, so everyone can proceed carefully – if at all.

Is the Mediation Binding?

The ultimate goal of any mediation is for the parties to resolve one or more issues and move forward with an agreement. It is important to note, however, that not all mediations are binding at the mediation itself. The binding nature of the mediation is often governed by local or jurisdictional rules; it's something that the spouses will be notified of before the mediation.

If you are attending a binding mediation, it is important to make sure you understand – and are prepared to follow – all of the terms of the agreement. If the mediation is not binding, you should find out how your agreement can become binding. You do not want to spend a lot of time and effort on mediation that does not lead to a conclusion. If you are going into a mediation, and if it is not clear whether it is binding, hit the pause button. Ask the mediator and your lawyer about the nature of the mediation before proceeding.

Is the Mediation Confidential?

A mediation's confidentiality can be determined in different ways. If the mediation's confidentiality status is unclear before the start of mediation, you should ask for clarification. If the parties are in the same room, it is unlikely that the mediation would be confidential, because the parties would be speaking candidly in front of one another. However, there may be a court rule mandating that even if parties are in the same room, mediation discussions – and potentially even offers – are confidential. If the mediation is conducted in caucus or via shuttle, it is more likely that all – or part – of the mediation is confidential.

Pros of a Confidential Mediation

In a confidential mediation, you can speak candidly about your issues, concerns, and priorities without fear that the information will be shared, or testified to, in court. You would also be able to make your best offer to avoid the cost, conflict, and uncertainty of court. If your best offer isn't accepted, no one will know what it was if your case goes to a court hearing or trial.

Cons of a Confidential Mediation

You may want to be able to share the unreasonableness of the other party, or their offers, with the court. That would not be possible if the mediation was confidential.

Confidentiality is a big part of mediation. Before your mediation, make sure that you are entirely clear on what is – and what is not – confidential and private.

How Many Sessions Are in a Mediation?

The straightforward answer to a question about the number of mediation sessions in a case is: "It depends." It depends on the parties, on their professional teams, and on jurisdiction rules and standards.

In some areas, just one mediation is required by local rules or is ordered by a judge. When that happens, the spouses and the professionals involved will feel that they have just one bite at the mediation apple. That will result in one long "marathon" mediation, which can last as long as everyone is willing to keep going (and yes, that can mean until 1 a.m.!).

It is important to note, however, that many jurisdictions have no mediation requirement; nor do they specify the mediation's duration or number of sessions. The parties could mediate as many times as they need to, and could also customize the duration of each session. If just a few hours is ideal due to the stress of negotiation, or because the spouses want to divide sessions up by topic, those factors should be considered. Long mediation sessions may get the job done, but they also leave the spouses and professionals mentally and physically fatigued.

In the Amicable Divorce Process, mediation can be customized for the parties. It is important to review the different forms of mediation, and also the factors in your case that may apply. Let your lawyer know what type of mediation that you think is best for you.

In many locations, there are no rules regarding duration, the number of sessions, who is required to be at the mediation, and whether the mediation has the parties together or in caucus. If there is a factor or form that holds priority for you, feel free to express that, so the mediation can be designed for success.

Chapter 61
Resolving Impasses in Negotiation
by Dara L. Marias

One of the reasons I love amicable divorce is because people make decisions for themselves. While judges use a hatchet to split things in half, amicable divorce employs a scalpel to carve out the best solutions. In my experience, divorcing couples are surprisingly in agreement about most issues. When they disagree, however, each can get pretty entrenched in their position. This chapter will teach you how to resolve these impasses by focusing on the underlying needs instead of the options on the table.[11]

---

[11] The approaches discussed here are based, in part, on the information provided in the Relationships Course taught by Oren Jay Sofer on the Happier Meditation app. Sofer, O. J., Harris, D., & Happier Inc. (2022). Happier Inc. (6.9.2) [Meditation Courses on Relationships]. Readers are encouraged to purchase a subscription to the Happier Mediation app to access the Relationships course for comprehensive information on communication techniques.

Needs Versus Strategies

Human behavior is driven by our desire to meet our *needs*. Needs are fundamental as well as universal. They include **physiological needs** (e.g., eating, sleeping), **psychological needs** (e.g., connecting, sharing, intimacy, safety, fulfillment, agency), **intellectual needs** (e.g., learning, creative expression), and **financial needs** (clothed, fed, sheltered, experiences), etc. *Needs* are different from *strategies*. *Strategies* are how we try to satisfy our needs. To illustrate the difference, consider this simple example:

Mr. Smith sells insurance to earn money for his family.

Why does money matter to Mr. Smith? Because Mr. Smith has an underlying *need* for his family to be financially secure. Selling insurance is his *strategy* to get money. **Financial security is his need.**

When conflict arises, it is usually because people are focused on defending their strategy instead of considering what they want to accomplish (i.e., satisfying the need). This is key. **When you can distinguish between the two, you can hold on to your need and let go of your strategy.** There are often many strategies that meet a need. Resolving an impasse requires a mutually acceptable strategy that meets everyone's needs.

Figuring Out Your Needs

The first step in an impasse is to figure out what *you* need in a situation. Then, you can approach conversations prepared to consider different strategies. You must explore what matters to you and why. The following exercise can help you practice identifying your needs:

What Are Your Needs?

1. Think about something that happened last week where someone did something that you didn't like. (Don't pick an overwhelming thing.)
2. Get clear on what happened. What did this person say or do?

3. Think about what it is that you *wanted* to have happen. Is there something they could have said or done that you would have enjoyed more?
4. Whatever it is you want, ask yourself, "Why does that matter to me? What's important about this to me? If I had that, then what would I have?"
5. Keep asking this until you arrive at a place where you feel you are at the core of what matters to you. (This is your need.)

Figuring Out the Other Person's Needs – Flex Your Empathy Muscle

Once you are very clear about *your* core needs in a situation, it is time to figure out the *other person's* core needs. Empathy can help you do this. Empathy lets you connect to someone else's experience and listen for what matters to them. As an added benefit, when you empathize with someone, they start to consider you an ally.

Connecting to Another's Needs

1. **Abandon your own ideas about what should be happening.**
   Stop trying to convince the other person that they should or should not feel a certain way. What we really need is to talk with them so we can understand and acknowledge what concerns and matters to them.

2. **Connect to the person's emotional experience.**
   Next, consider what you know about this person and use this information to connect to their emotions. When people feel that their emotions are understood and validated, they lower their defenses and are more likely to let you in.

3. **Ask yourself, "Why does this matter to them?"**
   In the same way you dug around in your own thoughts to figure out why something matters to you, take what they have said and what you know, and ask yourself why this might really matter to the other person. Use what you know to dig deeper.

4. **Use "sounds like" or "I imagine" statements to gain understanding and confirm information.**

The key part of understanding is making sure you get the information right. You can do this with facts and feelings. For example: "It sounds like it's really important for you to get the credit card debt paid off, which is why you want to sell the house, right?" In this real-life scenario, Husband wanted Wife to stay in the house so their child would have only one new home to live in; but Wife wanted to use her half of the house equity proceeds to pay off her credit card debt. Husband knew Wife had at times overspent, and that she wanted to start fresh with a clean financial slate after the divorce.

Brainstorming Mutual Strategies

You know your needs. You're pretty sure you know their needs. Now it's time to brainstorm. Let's return to the above scenario to see their solution. Husband ended up using separate property funds to pay off Wife's debt. In return, Wife agreed to delay selling their family home for a year. Both were extremely happy with this approach. Husband's need to provide a stable home environment for their daughter, and Wife's need for financial stability, were both satisfied by a novel solution customized to their individual needs. To be clear, no court would have ordered this, but through careful analysis of their underlying needs, the parties designed their perfect solution!

Let's take another example:

Scenario

Husband has worked throughout marriage. Husband has always had a 401k. Wife was a teacher's aide, but quit when they had children. Wife oversaw the home and family. The parties' marriage deteriorated, and Wife was unfaithful. They decided to divorce.

Impasse

They are on fairly good terms, but Husband's 401k became an issue. Wife wants half. Husband wants it all because he feels like it represents his hard work. He is willing to compensate the difference with other assets. Wife insists on equally dividing all assets and wants 50 percent of the 401k balance. They are at an impasse.

Wife's Thought Process

Question: Why does half of the 401k matter?
Answer:

- This money accumulated while I was doing unpaid and unthanked work raising our kids. I want something from this time to show for my efforts.
- I'm 52 and scared I won't have the finances to ever retire.
- I want to become a teacher to support myself, and I need to finish college. I'm doing this for financial security.

Husband's Thought Process

Question: Why does keeping the full 401k matter?
Answer:

- I never got to see my kids. I worked all the time. She has a closer relationship with them now because of it. I need something to show for giving up this time with my kids.
- She cheated on me with her trainer that I paid for. She doesn't deserve any part of my 401k.

Analysis

The trick here is to reframe what is going on in terms of *needs*. Wife has needs for financial stability and self-worth for her time as a homemaker. Husband has needs to feel that his efforts mattered, accountability for the infidelity (possibly), and a need to connect more with their children.

Armed with this information, the parties can think about ways to address these needs creatively. There is no one right solution. There are many right solutions. If the parties stick to their strategies, there will be no movement.

But if the parties take time to understand what really matters to each of them, they have a way through the impasse.

Validating Needs

A lot of progress can happen when both people pick at least one or two needs of the other person and validate them.

Examples of Need Recognition

Husband: You are a fantastic mother. I know how hard you worked to volunteer in school and to take care of their activities and projects. There is no way our kids would be as great as they are without you.

Wife: I just want to say I am so sorry for my conduct. That is not the person I want to be, and that was not the person you deserved. You never let our family down. You worked hard. That company was so challenging sometimes, but you always stuck it out. Our kids are super lucky you are their dad.

[Guards come down. Emotions settle. Each person opens to options.]

Creative Options

Husband: What if I kept 70 percent of the 401k, and you used 30 percent to create an IRA right now; and I gave you more equity in the house, which you could sell and invest some of the proceeds in your IRA?

Wife: That might work, but I don't know how to invest money; and I don't want to sell the house until the kids are through college.

Husband: Mikie is done with college in three years. What if I pay you half of the 401k appreciation every year until you can sell the house – and we find a financial planner you trust? Then you aren't missing out on the appreciation.

Wife: That could work.

Examining and validating needs helps people move through impasses. If you are negotiating and the process is stuck, ask yourself, "Why does this matter to me?" Then, honestly consider what matters to the other person. What need are they trying to satisfy? Stop defending your ideas, and instead brainstorm solutions that meet everyone's needs.

Dara L. Marias, JD, MSW
AV Preeminent Attorney
A.P.F.M. Certified Advanced Practitioner
Certified Amicable Divorce Professional
Las Vegas, Nevada

PART 15

What Makes a Good Settlement Agreement?

Chapter 62
Components of a
Good Settlement Agreement
323

Chapter 63
Qualified Domestic Relations Orders
329

Chapter 64
The Tax Consequences of Divorce
335

Chapter 62
Components of a Good Settlement Agreement
by Kathryn Harry

A *Settlement Agreement*, sometimes referred to as a *Marital Settlement Agreement* or *Divorce Settlement Agreement*, is a legally binding contract between divorcing spouses that outlines the terms of their separation and the division of their marital estate – and specifically is a document that addresses financial matters. While some couples reach this agreement easily and informally, ultimately, it must be a written document, signed by both parties, and, in many cases, approved by the court to become legally enforceable. A Settlement Agreement is usually incorporated into the final divorce decree and becomes an enforceable court order.

A good Settlement Agreement is drafted with the intention of preventing future disputes, and clearly states each party's rights and obligations. The most effective agreements eliminate ambiguity and provide clear, concise directives, and enable both individuals to proceed with certainty following the divorce. When crafted properly, it can maintain the amicable tone of the divorce, reduce the risk of misunderstandings, and promote long-term cooperation. In short, if a stranger to your situation reads this agreement they should understand how all assets and debts of the marriage were divided.

Components of a Settlement Agreement

While each Settlement Agreement will be unique and tailored to the couple's specific needs and circumstances, there are several common elements that are usually included. Detailed attention to each of these components will ensure that the final document is equitable, clear, and enforceable.

1. **Property Division**

   Marriage often involves the accumulation of shared assets, such as real estate, personal belongings, vehicles, bank accounts, retirement plans, and investments. The Settlement Agreement should describe all marital assets and non-marital assets (also referred to as separate property such as an inheritance) sufficiently, specifying which asset will become the property of which party as a result of the divorce. It should delineate whether the parties' assets are considered marital or separate property, and detail any procedures necessary for transferring titles, deeds, or account ownership along with deadlines for doing so. Unambiguously describing the division of assets and liabilities allows both parties to avoid conflicts later while understanding their financial obligations as they move into life after divorce.

   It is not recommended that the parties continue to jointly own assets after a divorce is finalized because such joint ownership is often nightmarish, especially if important details are left out of the settlement agreement. At times, however, such a situation may be unavoidable. For example, the children may need to stay in a particular school district, or selling the property at the time of the divorce is not financially prudent. If you find yourself in a situation where you are going to be jointly owning an asset with your spouse following the entry of your divorce decree, the Settlement Agreement should include very specific details about who is responsible for the expenses associated with the asset after the divorce, and how the equity accrued before the divorce and that accrued after the divorce will be divided when the asset is sold. A complete settlement agreement will also provide for terms and conditions on how the property should be treated if the death of a party occurs post-decree while the parties jointly own the asset.

2. **Debt Apportionment**

   In addition to dividing assets, divorcing spouses must also decide how to allocate responsibility for joint and/or individual debts, such as credit card balances, mortgages, student loans, and car loans. Unsure what debts are in your name? Pull a credit report to make sure everything is included. The Settlement Agreement should, at a minimum, state who will take responsibility for each obligation. Clear language is critical here. If one spouse agrees to take a particular debt, the agreement should indicate how and when they will pay it. If both spouses share a responsibility, the agreement should outline the cost-sharing mechanism, including how the debt will be paid by each party and when. The agreement should also contain a hold-harmless clause, such as "Wife shall hold Husband harmless from said debt(s) and agrees to indemnify Husband for any liability incurred as a result of Wife's failure to pay, including attorney's fees." Addressing debt explicitly helps minimize future disputes over who owes what and reduces the possibility of negative financial consequences if one party fails to pay.

3. **Child Support**

   In some jurisdictions, settlement agreements will also include provisions surrounding the payment of child support. If child support is ordinarily included in the settlement agreement in your jurisdiction, it should specify the amount of child support to be paid, how often it will be paid, and when it may be subject to review or modification. It should also cover which parent is responsible for health insurance costs, educational expenses, extracurricular activities, uncovered medical expenses, and other child-related costs. Clearly written provisions regarding child support reduce misunderstandings and help to make collecting it easier. Consult the requirements in your jurisdiction to ensure you are calculating support correctly – or in the alternative, if you are permitted to waive the payment of child support by one parent or the other. Child support is more thoroughly addressed in another chapter.

4. **Spousal Support (Alimony or Spousal Maintenance)**

   In some divorces, one spouse may be entitled to receive spousal support. A well-thought-out Settlement Agreement will outline whether any alimony will be paid, and if so, in what amount, for how long, and by whom. If the couple decides that no alimony is going to be paid by either spouse, that decision should also be reflected in the agreement in the form of a waiver. Consult conditions in your jurisdiction as some states require specific language for a waiver of alimony to be valid and enforceable. Additionally, the agreement should specify the terms and conditions under which alimony might be modified or terminated, such as the recipient spouse's remarriage or the residing with a paramour, as well as the ramifications of a significant change in either party's financial circumstances. Any alimony arrangement must be specific in terms and amounts to prevent future disputes and to protect both parties' interests in the long run. Spousal support is addressed more thoroughly in another chapter.

5. **Tax Considerations**

   Divorce can have significant tax implications. Therefore, you should specify in your settlement agreement how the parties will handle tax filings in the future, including who will claim any dependents and how tax-related benefits will be allocated between the parties in the future. The agreement may also cover potential tax liabilities on the sale of property or the transfer of assets. It is also a good idea to address the expected actions of each party if one of them is notified of an audit or a correction of a previously filed joint tax return.

   Don't forget to assess whether each party has timely and properly filed tax returns during the marriage, and whether any old tax debt remains unpaid. Making provisions for the payment of an old tax liability incurred by either party during the marriage is a critical component of any settlement agreement.

Including real and possible tax implications in your agreement at the time of the divorce will help you mitigate the likelihood of costly surprises down the road. It is important to note that some tax rules are governed by the Internal Revenue Service (IRS), which are federal-level laws and regulations, and they cannot be changed or negotiated in a state divorce agreement. If you have tax questions or concerns, please meet with a tax professional prior to signing any Settlement Agreement.

6. **Enforcement and Modification Terms**

   Your Settlement Agreement may include the conditions under which its terms may be modified. Life circumstances do change. For example, children grow older, financial situations shift, and living arrangements evolve. Including language in your agreement that outlines how and when modifications may occur ensures that the agreement remains relevant and adaptable over time. Note that in many jurisdictions, the allocation of the property between the parties is not modifiable. However, alimony and child support payments are often modifiable.

   Enforcement of an agreement is typically done by seeking court involvement, and it is called a contempt or enforcement action. State or jurisdiction laws will describe the mechanism in which its terms and conditions may be enforced by either party. Laws may require the parties to mediate or arbitrate the dispute first before seeking court intervention; but even if not required in your area, it is always good to try to resolve issues this way as it may save incredible time and money. You also might include a provision requiring the party seeking enforcement to first notify the other party in writing, stating the claim alleged and giving the offending party a timeline in which to remedy the situation before resorting to filing motions in court, unless there is an emergency.

Negotiating a Settlement Agreement

Reaching a fair and workable Settlement Agreement typically involves negotiation, cooperation, and sometimes compromise. Even if both spouses share a common goal of an amicable divorce, they may have different perspectives or priorities when it comes to what is fair, dividing property and establishing their financial independence from one another. The negotiation process is your only opportunity to ensure that your rights, interests, and future are protected in the final settlement agreement.

The Importance of Legal Representation

While some couples may be tempted to draft their own Settlement Agreement to save costs, the guidance of an experienced attorney will prove invaluable. Over the years, I have encountered many couples who have spent more money on attorney's fees retaining a lawyer to *fix* the settlement agreement after the divorce is finalized than they saved when doing it themselves. The old adage "you don't know what you don't know" applies to creating a Settlement Agreement. There are many nuances that the average person who is divorcing for the first or even second time does not know. Save yourself some real money and have a lawyer prepare your Settlement Agreement document. An attorney will ensure that the document is both comprehensive and enforceable. Their expertise can:

1. Clarify Legal Rights and Obligations
2. Prevent Ambiguity
3. Protect Your Rights and Interests
4. Ensure Enforceability in Court
5. Streamline the Process

Securing Your Future

A Settlement Agreement is much more than just a set of papers to sign. Rather, it is the key to establishing a stable financial future after your divorce. By carefully defining property division, debt responsibilities, and support obligations, the Settlement Agreement forms a working framework so both you and your former spouse may move forward with clarity and confidence.

Negotiating a Settlement Agreement can be challenging, but staying focused on preparation, maintaining respectful communication, and embracing a solution-oriented approach can yield a beneficial outcome for both parties. Most importantly, working with a knowledgeable family law attorney ensures that the final agreement is complete and enforceable, and it protects your rights and interests. This professional guidance provides the peace of mind you need as you begin a new chapter of your life.

In the end, a well-crafted Settlement Agreement embodies the spirit of an amicable divorce because it sets the stage for resolution, stability, and cooperation, minimizing surprises and disputes down the road. With the right tools and support, you can create an agreement that truly serves as your roadmap to a secure and peaceful future.

Kathryn Harry
Family Law Attorney
Georgia and Illinois

Chapter 63
Qualified Domestic Relations Orders
by Kathryn Harry

Dividing retirement accounts during a divorce can be one of the most complex and important tasks. Retirement funds often represent a significant portion of a couple's assets. However, dividing these accounts is not as simple as splitting bank balances, for example. In many cases, a special legal document called a Qualified Domestic Relations Order (QDRO, pronounced *kwa-droh*) is necessary to ensure that each party receives their share of these retirement accounts or benefits, and avoids IRS penalties often associated with early withdrawal from retirement accounts.

A QDRO is a court order separate from your divorce decree and is used to divide *private* employer-sponsored, qualified retirement plans such as 401ks, pensions, and other qualified plans after the divorce. The divorce itself allows parties to take advantage of this tax-neutral division event. These types of accounts are not automatically divided by the divorce decree or Settlement Agreement alone even though those documents may include the general details of how those accounts will be divided as a result of your divorce. Rather, a QDRO is required to instruct the retirement plan administrator (manager of the plan) as to how to split the retirement assets between the former spouses, including how to manage survivor benefits, whether a separate interest is created for each party, how Cost of Living Adjustments will be shared between the parties, and the like. It is easy to imagine how an improperly drafted QDRO or failing to implement one at all could spell financial disaster for either party.

It is crucial to note that QDROs are only required for **employer-sponsored** retirement plans, which are plans that meet certain standards set by the federal government. These include pensions and 401k accounts. For other types of retirement accounts, such as IRAs, the division can be handled within divorce decree without the need for a separate order like a QDRO. When in doubt, please contact the plan administrator for the plan and they can tell you their rules of division.

When and How Should a QDRO Be Used?

Why divide the retirement accounts or benefits at all? Why not just offset a party's share with other marital assets? For example, Spouse A has a 401k account valued at the time of the divorce at $250,000. The parties own a marital home with $250,000 in equity due to the continually rising property values in the area. The parties have agreed to divide these marital assets 50-50. Some might suggest it would be easier or appropriate for Spouse A to keep their 401k account, and, as an offset, Spouse B should be awarded the entire ownership of the marital home. $250,000 in retirement funds in exchange for $250,000 in the form of home equity sounds fair, right? WRONG.

The value of these assets is not equal. Stated quite simply, the retirement account is worth less than the house. Why? Taxes. 401k accounts, along with many other types of retirement accounts, are funded with pre-tax dollars.[12] This means that the owner of the account did not pay income taxes on the funds when they placed the funds into the 401k so they must pay taxes on those funds when they withdraw them in retirement. The house, on the other hand, was purchased with after-tax dollars. In this example, the parties scrimped and saved their money until they had a sizable down payment to use when they purchased the home. From where did those funds originate? From their income from employment or gains made in the stock market or a gift from Grandmother, on which income taxes were already paid. Throughout the marriage, the mortgage payment was made using the party's earnings from employment (on which income tax had been paid). When Spouse B sells the house, Spouse B is not required to pay income tax on the equity.[13]

Because retirement plans are so complex, it is prudent to become very familiar with the retirement plan and all that it offers to the plan participant or the spouse by obtaining and consulting the plan's Summary Plan Description. This should be done in advance of the drafting and signing of the Settlement Agreement. The Summary Plan Description contains a description of the benefits and "rules" of the retirement plan, if you will. A QDRO must be drafted in accordance with these rules because a QDRO cannot direct the plan administrator to do something that is not otherwise permitted by the plan.

Once you have chosen to divide the retirement plan as part of your settlement agreement, seek the advice of a competent attorney to put the right words in your Settlement Agreement before signing it. Once the divorce

---

12 The exception is a Roth IRA or a Roth component of a 401k that is nontaxable.
13 Tax rules are subject to change.

decree is entered and your Settlement Agreement is incorporated, it's too late to start investigating the terms and conditions of the retirement plan. It is much easier to get the QDRO right the first time than it is to go back and attempt to correct something in your divorce paperwork.

A QDRO should be obtained **contemporaneously** with the divorce decree or as soon as possible afterward. The process involves several key steps:

1. **Agree on the division of assets:** Before a QDRO can be drafted, the couple must agree on how to divide the retirement assets. This agreement is typically reflected in the divorce settlement. It may look something like this: *Spouse A's 401k at Employer X shall be divided by QDRO. Spouse B's share shall equal 50 percent of the marital share of Spouse A's account and shall include gains and losses on Spouse B's share prior to distribution. Until final distribution of Spouse B's share, Spouse B shall have survivor rights against the plan.*

2. **QDRO drafting:** Once the division of the retirement asset is agreed upon and the Settlement Agreement is prepared and signed by both parties, an attorney or a QDRO specialist can draft the QDRO. The QDRO shall specify how much of the retirement account the non-participant spouse will receive and mirror the benefits referred to in the Settlement Agreement. (*Hint:* This is why it is important to obtain and review the Summary Plan Description prior to drafting or signing the proposed Settlement Agreement.)

3. **Approval of plan administrator:** A smart attorney or QDRO specialist will submit the agreed-upon proposed QDRO to the plan administrator for review and quasi-approval as to the language prior to submitting it to the judge for a signature. The plan administrator may have suggestions about the terms used in the QDRO. Remember, a QDRO cannot force a plan administrator to do something he is not already authorized to do under the Summary Plan Description. If a plan administrator refuses to implement the order and divide the assets according to your agreement, it is much less costly and time consuming for the parties to revise a proposed QDRO *before* it is

signed by a judge than to vacate a QDRO that has already been signed by the judge and made part of your court file.

4. **Court approval:** After the QDRO is approved by the plan administrator, it must be submitted to the court for the judge's signature.

5. **Submission to the retirement plan administrator:** Once the QDRO is signed by the judge, a Certified Copy of the QDRO must be tendered to the retirement plan administrator. (This is the organization that manages the retirement account, such as the company that sponsors a 401k or a financial group like Fidelity.) The administrator will implement the order and divide the account accordingly. The plan administrator will communicate with both parties and provide instructions on how to transfer the share to the other spouse. You must read all instructions carefully and follow them exactly to avoid any unpleasant and unexpected income tax consequences.

The Risks of Delaying a QDRO

One of the biggest mistakes you can make is to delay entering a QDRO. If a QDRO is not processed promptly, there are risks such as:

- **Lost opportunity for a fair division:** Without a QDRO, the retirement funds will not be divided according to the divorce decree. Even if the divorce decree specifically orders a division of assets, the retirement plan will not recognize the division until a QDRO is properly submitted and implemented by the plan administrator. If enough time goes by, you risk that your spouse may have left their employer and taken their 401k with them or liquidated it for their own use, including your share.
- **Negative financial impact:** Delaying the QDRO could also result in the loss of interest or growth on the portion of the retirement account that belongs to you depending on how your Settlement Agreement incorporated into your divorce decree was written. Over time, this could negatively affect the value of your share significantly while enriching your former spouse.

- **Delayed retirement income:** If the QDRO is not implemented soon after the divorce, you may encounter difficulties when you or your ex-spouse retire. It could delay the ability of either party to access their portion of the retirement funds when the time comes.

Why You Should Work with an Attorney to Draft and Submit a QDRO

While it might seem tempting to save money and attempt the QDRO process on your own, doing so may not be in your best interests. A QDRO is a legal document that must meet specific requirements and be worded *precisely* to ensure it is enforceable. A small mistake in the drafting and implementation of a QDRO could lead to delays in receiving your money, the failure to properly divide the retirement asset, or an unexpected tax liability.

Working with an attorney who has experience in drafting QDROs is crucial for the following reasons:

- **Legal Expertise**
- **Customization**
- **Timeliness**
- **Ongoing Support**

Delaying the QDRO can lead to financial losses and legal complications that could impact you far into the future.

The process of drafting and submitting a QDRO is not something that should be handled without professional help. Retaining an experienced attorney will ensure that the QDRO is done correctly and in a timely manner, protecting your rights and ensuring that your share of the retirement funds is secured. By taking these steps, you can avoid the stress and uncertainty that comes with trying to divide retirement assets without the right help or advice.

Kathryn Harry
Family Law Attorney
Georgia and Illinois

Chapter 64
The Tax Consequences of Divorce
by Jason Wiggam

Divorce is a significant life event; it brings emotional and financial challenges. Among those challenges, navigating the tax implications of a divorce is often overlooked. However, considering those effects on your taxes is essential for safeguarding your financial future. Divorce can greatly affect taxes, through factors like alimony, child support, property transfers, and filing statuses.

Alimony and Child Support

When one spouse provides financial support to the other during or after a divorce, it is crucial to understand the tax consequences of those payments. Alimony has seen changes in its tax status in recent years. For divorces finalized on or before December 31, 2018, alimony payments are tax-deductible for the paying spouse and are taxable income for the recipient. However, divorces finalized on or after January 1, 2019 are subject to a new tax rule, implemented by the Tax Cuts and Jobs Act. Under that rule, alimony payments are neither deductible for the payer nor taxable income for the recipient. This shift eliminates the tax benefit previously associated with alimony payments, and may influence how divorces are negotiated.

In contrast to alimony, child support payments have always had straightforward tax treatment. Child support is neither deductible for the paying parent nor considered taxable income for the recipient. This tax treatment ensures that the focus remains on meeting the child's financial needs, without creating additional tax burdens for either parent.

Property Transfers

Dividing property during a divorce can have significant tax implications, but transfers made as part of a divorce agreement are generally nontaxable.

That means that if one spouse transfers ownership of a home, car, or other assets to the other as part of the divorce, there is no immediate tax liability from that transfer. Such transfers are treated as gifts for tax purposes, provided that they are made incident to the divorce – and within one year of the divorce being finalized.

While the transfer itself may not trigger taxes, the recipient must be mindful of the property's original tax basis (the cost) and the holding period, which are carried over during the transfer. The basis is essentially the original purchase price of the property, adjusted for improvements or other factors.

The basis becomes important if the recipient decides to sell the property later. For example, if you receive a home with an original purchase price of $200,000, and later sell it for $300,000, you may owe capital gains tax on the $100,000 increase in value. If the property was held for less than a year, it would be considered a short-term capital gain, subject to ordinary income taxes. Properties held for more than a year are subject to capital gains tax rates, which are lower than ordinary income tax rates. Understanding the tax basis and holding period can help you plan for future sales and avoid unexpected tax liabilities.

To prepare for potential future tax obligations, it is essential to maintain detailed records of the property's original purchase price, any significant improvements, and documents related to the transfer. Such records will be invaluable when calculating potential gains or losses if the property is sold. You should keep those records for at least three years after you file the tax return that reports the sale.

Filing Income Tax During and After Divorce

Your tax filing status can change during the divorce process and after it is finalized, and the timing of the changes can affect your overall tax liability. If your divorce is not finalized by December 31 of the tax year, the IRS considers you married for that tax year. In that case, you can choose between filing as "married filing jointly" or "married filing separately." Filing jointly often results in lower tax rates, but it also makes both spouses jointly responsible for any taxes owed. Filing separately allows each spouse to be responsible only for their own taxes, although that option typically results in higher overall tax rates.

Once the divorce is finalized, your filing status changes. You may file as "single" if you do not have qualifying dependents, or as "head of household" if you have a qualifying dependent and meet other requirements. The "head of household" status offers more favorable tax rates compared to filing as "single" or "married filing separately," making it a valuable option for eligible taxpayers.

A key issue for divorcing parents is determining who will claim the children as dependents for tax purposes. Generally, the custodial parent – the parent with whom the child lives for the majority of the year – has the right to claim the child as a dependent. However, that right can be transferred to the non-custodial parent if the custodial parent signs a waiver, using IRS Form 8332. Divorcing couples often negotiate the issue as part of their settlement agreement, allowing for a more predictable tax outcome for both parties.

Additional Tax Considerations

Divorce often involves dividing retirement accounts, which requires careful handling to avoid unexpected taxes or penalties. If retirement assets are split, the transfer must be completed under a qualified domestic relations order (QDRO) to ensure compliance with tax laws. Failure to follow rules can result in immediate income taxes and, in some cases, early withdrawal penalties.

Another potential issue arises when one or both spouses have unpaid taxes or tax liens. If the IRS has filed a tax lien, it may complicate property division, particularly if one spouse is awarded an asset – such as a home – subject to the lien. While the lien typically attaches to the property rather than the individual, resolving lien-related issues often requires negotiation and careful planning to ensure a smooth transfer of assets.

Understanding the tax implications of divorce is crucial for making informed decisions during a challenging time. Whether you are navigating alimony, child support, property transfers, or changes to your tax filing status, being aware of the tax rules can help you avoid unexpected tax burdens and ensure a stable financial future. For complex tax situations or additional guidance, consult a tax professional or attorney who can provide tailored advice based on your unique circumstances.

Jason Wiggam, JD, LLM
Wiggam Law
Atlanta, Georgia

PART 16

How Do We Make a Good Parenting Plan?

Chapter 65
Legal vs. Physical Custody
341

Chapter 66
Create a Parenting Plan
345

Chapter 67
Holiday Schedules
349

Chapter 68
Long-Distance Parenting
354

Chapter 69
Keeping Schools in the Loop
360

Chapter 65
Legal vs. Physical Custody
by Neena Saxena

"We both love our children, and we both want what is best for them. This should be the one area of divorce where we can agree."

This is what most parents tell themselves as they begin the divorce process, and even though the sentiment holds true, as the divorce proceedings start to unfold, it can become painfully clear that there *will* be a fight for custody. But what does custody mean? In the context of divorce, custody refers to the legal and physical responsibility a parent has for a child after the parents separate or divorce. This involves two main aspects: legal custody and physical custody.

Legal Custody

Legal custody refers to the rights and responsibilities to make important decisions about the child's life. This includes decisions about education, healthcare, religion, extracurricular activities, and the general upbringing of the child. Legal custody can be shared between both parents (joint legal custody) or awarded to one parent (sole legal custody). When one parent has sole custody, that parent has the right to make decisions about the child's upbringing. Sole custody may be awarded when a parent is unfit due to substance abuse, mental illness, domestic abuse, incarceration, relocation, etc.

When parents have joint legal custody, the parents should maintain a co-parenting relationship where they are expected to consult with one another and reach mutual decisions as to the best interest of the child. However, if the parents are not able to reach a mutual decision, then one parent will be designated as the *final decision maker* when it comes to the particular area.

Physical Custody

Physical custody pertains to the living arrangements of the child after a divorce. It focuses on where the child spends their time and with which parent they reside. Physical custody can be arranged in a variety of ways depending on the parents' situation and what is in the best interests of the child. The most common types of physical custody arrangements are: joint, primary physical, sole, split, and bird's nest custody. However, each of these types carries its own legal and practical considerations and, of course, challenges.

In a joint physical custody arrangement, the children spend equal time living with both parents. While the exact division of time may vary, typically it involves equal or close-to-equal distribution of time between both parents. Joint physical custody is often seen as favorable because it allows both parents to maintain an active role in the child's life, and the courts may favor joint physical custody when both parents live in reasonable proximity to each other and can communicate effectively about the child's needs. There are many joint, or 50-50, parenting schedules. If you are interested in reviewing these, please visit the DivorceAmicably.com website to learn more.

Practically speaking, joint physical custody works best when both parents are capable of cooperating and willing to maintain consistent routines, communicate effectively, live close to one another, and make decisions collaboratively, as opposed to unilaterally. Challenges may arise with the back-and-forth nature of the arrangement, especially if the parents live far apart from one another, if there is high conflict between the parents, or when one parent is unwilling to cooperate with the other parent and the child's best interest.

Primary physical custody refers to the situation where the child's primary residence is with one parent, but the other parent (the non-custodial parent without primary custody) is still actively involved. Primary physical custody suggests that.

Primary physical custody is often awarded when one parent is considered better suited to meet the child's daily needs, either due to proximity, financial stability, or a more established caregiving role.

Courts may also award primary custody when there are concerns about the other parent's ability to provide for the child's welfare, which could include a history of abuse, substance issues, mental health challenges, or neglect. This arrangement provides more stability for the child and can be particularly important for young children who benefit from consistent routines and attachments. The non-custodial parent typically has scheduled time with the child, often including weekends, holidays, and/or vacations. This arrangement allows the non-custodial parent to maintain a relationship with the child. One of the significant challenges of primary physical custody is the emotional impact on the non-custodial parent, who may feel alienated from day-to-day parenting, which can affect their relationship with the child.

While the term "primary physical custody" is sometimes used interchangeably with "sole physical custody," they are not identical. In sole custody, the child lives with one parent all of the time, while the other parent has no substantial visitation with the child. Sole custody is typically awarded when it is in the child's best interest, such as when one parent has a history of abuse, neglect, or substance issues, or if one parent is absent or uninvolved.

In a split custody arrangement, siblings are separated, and each parent takes physical custody of at least one child. This arrangement is relatively rare and is typically used when there is a significant difference in the needs or preferences of the children. Courts generally prefer to keep siblings together, but the court will prioritize the child's best interests. The major challenges and concern is the emotional strain on the children as they are separated from their siblings, and that may lead to feelings of isolation or abandonment.

Bird's nest custody is a unique arrangement in which the children remain in the family home, and the parents alternate moving in and out based on their scheduled time with the children. This arrangement can minimize disruption for the child by allowing them to stay in the same home, although it can create logistical and financial challenges. Bird's nest custody is less common and is generally seen as a temporary arrangement during the divorce process, rather than a long-term solution.

How Is Custody Determined?

Ultimately, any custody arrangement must be based on the best interests of the child. Factors to consider include: the child's age, emotional needs, and relationship with each parent; the parents' ability to communicate, cooperate, and make joint decisions; and the children's preferences. Children thrive on stability and consistency in their daily routines – including where they live, where they go to school, and where their friends are. Custody plans should strive to minimize disruption in the child's life. Clear communication, flexibility, and the ability to put aside personal conflict for the sake of the child is key to making any custody arrangement work. Remember that the ultimate goal is to create a stable and supportive environment that allows the child to thrive emotionally, physically, and socially.

Neena Saxena, Esq.
Attorney, Patterson Moore Butler
Certified Mediator with the Georgia Office of Dispute Resolution
Certified Guardian ad Litem
Certified Amicable Divorce Professional
Atlanta, Georgia
Boston, Massachusetts

Chapter 66
Create a Parenting Plan
by Neena Saxena

It's not about winning or losing. It's about creating something that works – something that feels fair to both of us and, most importantly, gives our children the stability and security they need.

When parents divorce or separate, one of the most crucial steps in ensuring the well-being of their children is developing a clear and comprehensive parenting plan. A parenting plan is a written agreement that serves as a roadmap for parenting responsibilities and schedules, ensuring that the child's needs are met consistently despite changes in family dynamics. While the specific terms of a parenting plan will vary from family to family, the goal is always the same: to create a framework that supports the child's physical and emotional needs in a stable and predictable environment.

The primary purpose of a parenting plan is to provide structure and stability for the child. It helps to minimize confusion and conflict by setting clear expectations for both parents. A well-thought-out parenting plan ensures that children experience continuity in their daily routines, which is crucial for their emotional well-being during what can be a difficult transition. For parents, the plan offers a clear roadmap for how to handle child-rearing responsibilities and co-parenting obligations, reducing potential disputes and misunderstandings. It is intended to ensure that both parties are working toward the same goals for their child's future.

Parenting plans are often formalized in legal terms, particularly in family court proceedings, and many jurisdictions require parenting plans to ensure that both parents remain actively involved in their child's life and that their responsibilities are clearly defined.

A comprehensive parenting plan typically includes several key components to ensure that all aspects of child-rearing are addressed. These elements work together to create a balanced and cooperative arrangement that focuses on the child's well-being.

Custody Arrangements

There are two types of custody. One is legal custody, which pertains to decision-making authority and access to information about the child. The second is physical custody, which determines where the child will reside, and the time spent with each parent; in short, where the child physically is.

Visitation Schedules/Parenting Time

This is one of the most critical aspects of a parenting plan. It outlines how often the parents will see the child. It helps ensure the child has regular and meaningful contact with both parents, fostering emotional bonds and a sense of security.

The schedule should address:
- Frequency of visits (e.g., weekends, holidays, vacations).
- Duration of visits (e.g., overnight, full weekends; exact starting and ending times must be included).
- Holiday and vacation time: Special arrangements for holidays and school vacations ensure both parents have time with the child on important occasions. Make sure you include all holidays and school breaks that are important to your family. This can be customized for your religious and cultural celebrations or family traditions.
- Conflicts between the regular schedule, holiday and vacation – which one prevails over the other.
- Transportation: Who will pick up the child at the start and end of the parenting time? Will the parties exchange the children through school. Will the parties meet at a certain location?

Decision-Making Responsibilities

In addition to the division of parenting time, the parenting plan should outline how major decisions regarding the child's life will be made, which

is often called "legal custody." Not every jurisdiction articulates or has legal custody, and some have differing topics, so it is important to consult with your legal professional about what is required in your case. Legal custody topics may include:
- Medical care: Will both parents share responsibility for medical decisions, or will one parent have the final say?
- Education: Who will choose the child's school and manage educational decisions?
- Extracurricular activities: Who will choose the activities? How many activities per year/season/month?
- Religious upbringing: If relevant, how will religious practices be handled?

The plan may provide for joint decision-making and designate one parent as the final decision-maker in specific areas if a mutual decision cannot be reached. Clarity on these responsibilities is essential for minimizing conflict and ensuring that both parents are informed and involved in their child's upbringing. It is unlikely a court will get involved in these types of decisions in the future, or that they will do so in a timely manner. So determining these issues during the initial divorce can save time and money in the future.

Communication Guidelines

A parenting plan should outline how parents will communicate about the child's needs and activities and also when the parent who is not with the child will be able to contact the child. This may include:
- Method of communication: Will parents use email, text messages, phone calls, or co-parenting apps to communicate; e.g., OurFamilyWizard? How will the parent contact the child?
- Co-parenting tools: Shared calendars or co-parenting apps like OurFamilyWizard can be helpful for tracking visitation schedules, medical appointments, school events, and other important details.
- Frequency of communication: How often will parents communicate and what type of information should be shared about the child (e.g.,

medical updates, school progress, or extracurricular activities)? How often, and for how long, will the parents contact the child? What if the child has their own cell phone?

Other Considerations

Access to records and information: How will parents access and share this information? Passports and important documents?

Travel: How will parents share information about travel the child will take? If the child has a passport, who will hold the passport when not in use?

Morality clause: Is there a need to include a clause regarding romantic partners, including overnight stays with romantic partners?

Conduct of the parties: Establish clear expectations regarding the behavior of both parents toward each other and their children.

A thoughtfully crafted parenting plan offers numerous benefits to both parents and children. It is a tool that helps reduce stress and conflict, providing a foundation for positive co-parenting relationships. When parents have a clear plan in place, it reduces the likelihood of misunderstandings or disputes over custody and visitation. A written agreement makes it easier to resolve disagreements because the terms are laid out ahead of time.

Challenges to Creating a Parenting Plan

While creating a parenting plan offers many advantages, it is not without challenges. Parents may have strong emotional reactions to the separation, which can make it difficult to work collaboratively. Differing parenting styles, unresolved conflict, or lingering resentment can create barriers to effective communication and agreement.

As children grow and circumstances change, the parenting plan may need to be adjusted. For instance, a visitation schedule that works well when children are young may become impractical as they grow older and develop their own social activities or school schedules.

A parenting plan provides clarity and structure, benefiting both the child and the parents. By addressing key components and anticipating challenges, parents can create a plan that supports their child's well-being and fosters effective co-parenting. Ultimately, a thoughtful and detailed parenting plan can make a significant difference in how children adjust to the changes in their family dynamic, offering them the security of knowing both parents are committed to their well-being, even as their family structure evolves.

Neena Saxena, Esq.
Attorney, Patterson Moore Butler
Certified Mediator with the Georgia Office of Dispute Resolution
Certified Guardian ad Litem
Certified Amicable Divorce Professional
Atlanta, Georgia
Boston, Massachusetts

Chapter 67
Holiday Schedules
by Morgan Given

Holiday schedules take priority over the normal parenting schedule. These lay out the specific dates and times that each parent has the children during holidays and school breaks. Your holiday schedule can be customized to meet your family's needs and traditions. It helps to start with a template and then work from there, making changes that meet your individual family needs.

A holiday schedule template noting many possible holidays is included below:

Holiday	Mother	Father
New Year's Day (from January 1 at 12:00 p.m. until January 2 at 12:00 p.m.)	Even Years	Odd Years

Holiday	Mother	Father
Easter Sunday (from 9:00 a.m. until 7:00 p.m.)	Odd Years	Even Years
Spring Break (from 9:00 a.m. Monday until 9:00 a.m. on Friday)	Odd Years	Even Years
Mother's Day (from 9:00 a.m. until delivery to school on Monday)	Every Year	N/A
Memorial Day Weekend (from Friday after school until Monday at 8:00 p.m.)	Odd Years	Even Years
Father's Day (from 9:00 a.m. until Monday at 9:00 a.m.)	N/A	Every Year
July 4 (9:00 a.m. through July at 9:00 a.m.)	Odd Years	Even Years
Labor Day Weekend (from Friday after school until Monday at 8:00 p.m.)	Even Years	Odd Years
Halloween (from 3:00 p.m. through 9:00 p.m.)	Odd Years	Even Years
Thanksgiving (from Thursday at 9:00 a.m. until Friday at 9:00 a.m.)	Even Years	Odd Years
Winter Break Week One*	Odd Years	Even Years
Winter Break Week Two*	Even Years	Odd Years
Christmas Eve (December 24 at 12:00 p.m. through December 25 at 12:00 p.m.)	Odd Years	Even Years

Holiday	Mother	Father
Christmas Day (December 25 at 12:00 p.m. through December 26 at 12:00 p.m.)	Even Years	Odd Years
New Year's Eve (from 12:00 p.m. through January 1 at 12:00 p.m.)	Even Years	Odd Years
Birthdays The parties shall celebrate their birthdays and the children's birthdays during their respective regular parenting time.		
*Winter Break shall be defined as pickup from school on the last day of school preceding Winter Break until return to school on the first day of school following Winter Break. The exchange halfway through Winter Break shall occur at 12:00 p.m., unless such halfway point occurs on Christmas Eve or Day, in which case the parties shall exchange the minor children at 10:00 a.m. on December 26. If Winter Break has an odd number of nights, the parent with the first half of Winter Break shall have the minor children for the extra night.		

The above template can be customized in many ways. If your family does not celebrate certain holidays, you can simply remove them from the schedule. Different school systems also have different holidays. For example, Fall Break, like a Spring Break, is popular in some states; and in some areas Winter Break is actually in February while the December/Christmas break is called Holiday Break. Easter can often fall during Spring Break. Before developing a schedule, look at the online calendar for your child's school system. Likewise, if there are other days that your family does celebrate, such as religious holidays or important birthdays, those can be added in.

The times can also be adjusted. For example, Thanksgiving could be defined as:

1. Thursday from 9:00 a.m. to 9:00 p.m.

2. Pickup at school on the last day before Thanksgiving Break until return to school after Thanksgiving

3. Thursday from 9:00 a.m. until Friday at 9:00 am.

4. One parent has 9:00 a.m. to 3:00 p.m.; the other parent has 3:00 p.m. to 9:00 p.m.

If you typically take extended trips over Spring and Winter Break, consider fashioning the schedule to provide for longer stretches of time with each parent during those breaks. For example, during Winter Break you could delete New Year's Eve and New Year's Day from the schedule, so that the parent who gets the second half of Winter Break will have a nine-day uninterrupted period during which they can travel with the children. Some families even choose to alternate the entire Winter Break period so that they can travel abroad for the holidays.

In addition to the holidays listed on the template above, there are several days throughout the year that children have no school, such as Indigenous Peoples' Day, Veterans Day, teacher's institute days, and the like. Instead of separately allocating these holidays, you can include a provision that provides that the parent who has the weekend abutting the non-school day shall have the school day off added to their weekend. This will prevent the children from having to undergo multiple back-and-forth exchanges between households. See the sample language for this provision below:

All holidays or school days off not otherwise specifically addressed herein that fall on a Friday or Monday, including, but not limited to, Presidents' Day, Martin Luther King Day, Columbus/Indigenous Peoples' Day, Veterans Day (observed), teacher institute days, etc., will be allocated to the parent who has parenting time the weekend attached to the holiday/day off (e.g., if the holiday/day off falls on a Friday, then the weekend following, or if the holiday/day off falls on a Monday, then the weekend preceding the holiday). If the holiday or day off falls on a Friday, the parenting time will commence at 9:00 a.m. If the holiday or day off falls on a Monday, the parenting time will end at 5:00 p.m.

You may be wondering if the normal schedule "resets" after a parent exercises a holiday weekend, such as Memorial or Labor Day. For example, if Mom has parenting time Weekend A, and Weekend B is Mom's Memorial Day weekend, would Mom still get Weekend C, which is her normally scheduled weekend? One way to address this is to include the following language:

PART 16: HOW DO WE MAKE A GOOD PARENTING PLAN?

It is the intention of the parties that neither party shall have parenting time with the minor child three weekends in a row. By way of example, if either party is exercising parenting time during a holiday weekend, and the weekend would not otherwise have been his or her weekend in the normal rotation, the party who gave up their parenting time during the holiday weekend shall have parenting time the weekend after the holiday weekend, and the alternating weekend schedule shall continue thereafter.

However, it is best to not have to do a reset as this can become confusing. A way to avoid a three-weekend-in-a-row situation with holidays is to articulate that holidays like Spring Break are "the Monday through Friday the child is released from school." This way, everyone keeps their regularly scheduled weekend and adds the five-day holiday to it, still getting a full week of vacation time.

Another common question is: What if I need to make modifications to the holiday schedule? Co-parents can always make changes to the parenting schedule by agreement. If you believe you need to make an adjustment to the holiday schedule, contact your co-parent well in advance to propose the change. If they are in agreement, firm up the agreement in writing either via text message, email, or a co-parenting communication app such as OurFamilyWizard. You, your ex, and your children will benefit if the parents are flexible with each other when it comes to accommodating reasonable requests to modify the schedule. What goes around comes around. If you say "yes" to your ex's request now, hopefully they will be more likely to accommodate a request from you when you need to make a change.

Think about a schedule from the child's perspective. If you include Halloween and it is a Wednesday, is this stressful for the child with school the day of and the next day? Will a child go in a car from one house to another on a major holiday?

While your divorce is still pending, you can also enter a temporary holiday schedule. Start talking with your ex, or ask your ex to contact their attorney, well in advance of any upcoming important holidays so that you can figure out how to divide those days. Once you have an agreement, you can enter an agreed-upon order setting forth the temporary holiday schedule, which will remain in place until the final divorce decree is entered.

Judges are notorious for denying "emergency" motions regarding holidays. If you wait until the last minute to appear before the judge, and ask the court to set a temporary holiday schedule, the judge might refuse to hear that request on an emergency or expedited basis. The court's rationale for this is typically that it was known to all parties that the holidays were coming up, and waiting until the final days before a holiday to attempt to resolve the issue is not appropriate.

The most important thing to consider when drafting your holiday schedule is that you want it to be clear and easy to reference. If your holiday schedule is detailed and unambiguous, you will prevent future disagreements with your ex after the divorce.

Morgan Given
Family Law Attorney and Mediator
Chicago, Illinois

Chapter 68
Long-Distance Parenting
by Chloe Ouditz

Whether local or long distance, parenting plans are the best way to ensure you and your former spouse agree on how you will work together going forward. It's common for people to feel put off by the idea of having a formal written agreement that feels inflexible. However, relying on informal discussions or assuming that arrangements will be easily handled on a case-by-case basis can lead to misunderstandings, conflicts, and unnecessary stress for both parents and the child. A better way of thinking about it is that documenting your agreements ahead of time ensures that you have a baseline agreement on how you want to co-parent. It does not mean that you cannot ever flex this plan, or even amend it if circumstances change. What it does mean, however, is that you have a plan A on which you can both rely if you can't reach an agreement in a specific situation. It avoids constantly renegotiating every aspect of your arrangement because you don't agree or you made different assumptions.

Co-parenting is challenging in any situation, but when distance separates the parents, the complexities multiply. Whether you've relocated due to work, family, or personal reasons, maintaining a strong relationship with your child while living far from their other parent requires careful planning and commitment. A well-structured, long-distance co-parenting plan not only ensures better co-parenting between the parents, but also fosters a meaningful relationship between the child and both parents, no matter the miles between them. Here's how to craft a plan that works for everyone involved.

Unlike co-parenting in the same city or neighborhood, the logistics of travel, communication, and shared decision-making become more complex. Most of the common templates available on the internet do not reflect these complexities that arise during long-distance co-parenting. This is why it is important to use appropriate frameworks for your situation and to consult specialized professionals

Getting Specialist Advice

When creating a long-distance parenting plan, it's a good idea to consult with specialists, such as family lawyers, divorce coaches, or mediators with experience in long-distance cases. Their expertise can help ensure that all legal requirements are met and that the plan addresses potential pitfalls. Professionals can guide you through specific areas you may not have considered, such as international travel logistics, important decision-making, or communication between the child and the parent living abroad.

Additionally, if you're dealing with an international move, it's important to stay aware of both countries' legal systems and how they affect custody, child maintenance amounts, visitation rights, and parental responsibilities.

The Devil Is in the Details

The success of a co-parenting plan often comes down to the small details. Parents naturally focus on major points like school holidays. But other issues, such as who handles the cost of a child's travel, or what happens when there is a medical emergency, can lead to significant conflict if not clearly outlined in the plan.

Planning for these elements in advance ensures that both parents have considered every aspect of co-parenting in this context. Here are some key elements to reflect on when building a co-parenting plan for long-distance parents:

1. Travel Arrangements

One of the most important aspects of a long-distance, co-parenting plan is how the child will travel between their parents. This includes:

Travel Logistics

Will the child fly, take the train, or use another form of transport? You need to decide how the child will get from one parent's home to the other, and whether one or both parents (or someone else) will accompany them on trips. Other related topics include which parent will keep the children's passports and how these will be provided and returned by the other parent before and after travel. Who oversees renewing the passports and securing travel visas? There are a multitude of scenarios to think through to be clear on roles and responsibilities, including the time and location of the handovers.

Age Considerations for Independent Travel

At what age will the child be allowed to travel alone? What happens when they learn to drive? Many airlines have specific rules for unaccompanied minors, and parents need to agree on the minimum age for independent travel. Determining how that travel will happen once the child has reached a certain age will help. Think about which modes of transport they can take alone, the length of the trip, and who will collect from the airport.

Financial Responsibility

Paying for travel is often a big area of disagreement because travel costs can add up quickly – especially if the child is flying or taking long trips regularly. Determine who is responsible for covering the travel expenses (or how they will be shared), including transportation, accommodation for the accompanying parent, and any passport renewal or visa costs, if applicable.

What Happens if Plans Change

Parents should consider the rules for when plans need to be amended. How will this be handled if this is due to the child's schedule (attending camp or having a sports game at that time, for example) versus if it is a request from one of the parents? Will the visiting time simply be moved to another time or is it lost? Who covers any potential expenses relating to this change of travel plans? How long ahead of time do these plans need to be confirmed? The more you can anticipate potential issues and agree on how they will be addressed, the less likely you are to find yourself arguing over these points later down the line, at a time where emotions are running high.

2. Regular Contact Outside of In-Person Visits

Maintaining a strong bond with both parents is essential for the child's well-being, and this requires regular communication when the child is with the other parent. Consider the following:

Devices and Technology

From what age will the child be allowed to have a phone, tablet, or computer to communicate directly with the far-away parent? Discuss the devices the child will use and how these will be managed.

Frequency and Method of Communication

How often will the child have scheduled phone calls or video chats with the far-away parent? Agree on a realistic frequency that supports the child's emotional needs without interfering with the time they spend with the other parent. This is a point on which you must accept that it will evolve over time as your child matures and favors certain times or forms of contact.

Special Occasions

How will the child celebrate birthdays, holidays, or other special events with the far-away parent? Virtual celebrations, surprise gift packages, or pre-planned visits can all help the child feel connected to both parents on these important days.

Needless to say, a consistent and predictable communication schedule helps the child feel secure, and allows the far-away parent to stay actively involved in their life.

3. Include the Far-Away Parent in the Day-to-Day Parenting

Just because one parent lives far away doesn't mean they should be excluded from important decisions or day-to-day events. The co-parenting plan should outline how the distant parent will stay informed and involved in the child's life, including:

Medical Appointments

How will the far-away parent be involved in medical appointments? While routine check-ups may not require both parents' involvement, decisions about significant medical treatments or emergencies should involve both parties. Will the distant parent be notified about every appointment or just those of major importance?

School Events and Parent-Teacher Meetings

How will the distant parent participate in school-related events? With technology, it's easier than ever to attend parent-teacher conferences remotely or to receive updates on the child's academic progress. Discuss whether the far-away parent will join meetings virtually or if they will stay in the loop via emails or reports. Ensure both parents' email addresses are listed with the school so they both receive communications, and that the far-away parent also has access to any homework- management application the child is using.

Maintaining Both Parents' Cultures

If the parents come from different countries, speak different languages, or have different religions, consider how the culture of the far-away parent will be maintained in the child's life. Will they attend a weekend school to continue to learn their second language? Will you read books or celebrate holidays that pertain to the far-away parent's culture? Remember that growing up within a bi-cultural environment is a huge asset for your child, and that it is usually in their best interest to maintain the cultural influence of both of their parents.

Emergencies

How will emergencies be handled? Outline how urgent decisions will be made, particularly when the distant parent isn't immediately available to provide input. How will the other parent be informed and within what timeline? Make sure both parents know their roles in these situations.

4. Common Mistakes to Avoid

Lack of clarity: A co-parenting plan must be detailed and specific to avoid confusion. Vague agreements can lead to disagreements, especially when interpreting terms like *reasonable contact* or *regular visits*.

Ignoring the child's needs: Remember that a co-parenting plan should prioritize the child's well-being. Overloading the child with travel or too many virtual check-ins can be overwhelming. Consider jetlag when deciding on travel dates before returning to school. The objective here is to strike a balance that works for both parents and the child.

Not planning for change: Children grow and circumstances change. A co-parenting plan that works for a toddler may not suit a teenager. Also, think ahead to what will happen when one of the parents meets someone new. How and when will that person be introduced into the child's life? Because you cannot predict every scenario, make sure you build flexibility into the plan and agree to revisit and adjust it periodically as the child's needs evolve.

Failing to communicate: Communication between parents is key to making a long-distance arrangement work. Both parents need to commit to ongoing dialogue about the plan's effectiveness, and to any issues that arise.

Conclusion

Building a strong co-parenting plan for long-distance parents takes careful consideration and collaboration. By addressing key elements like travel, communication, and detailed day-to-day involvement, parents can create a plan that fosters a healthy relationship with their child, regardless of the distance. Remember to seek specialist advice, prioritize the child's needs, and plan for the future to ensure that your long-distance, co-parenting arrangement works smoothly for everyone.

Chloe Oudiz
Certified Divorce Coach (CDC)
The Divorce and Separation Coach
London, England

Chapter 69
Keeping Schools in the Loop
by Stephanie Robins

Divorce is tough – and when you have children, it's even more important to make sure they are supported. While figuring out the details of your new life, one of the most important steps is to involve your child's school. Their teachers, counselors, and school staff can be great allies to help your child navigate this significant change – but they need to know what's going on to offer the right kind of support.

In this chapter, you will learn how to share your divorce details with the school, provide the necessary documents, help educators understand any custody or decision-making arrangements, and get the emotional support your child may need.

Why You Should Tell the School About Your Divorce

Your child spends a considerable chunk of their day at school, so it's essential that the people they see regularly – like their teachers and the school counselor – know about significant life changes, such as divorce. If your child is struggling emotionally or academically, the school staff can step in; but they can only help if they know what's happening at home.

By informing the school, you tell them your child might need extra attention or support. Many schools also offer resources like counseling or peer support groups specifically for kids going through tough family transitions.

Sharing Custody Agreements and Important Documents

Once your divorce is in process or finalized, ensure the school has the correct documents about who's responsible for your child and the custody arrangements. This is important because it clarifies who can make decisions for your child, who can pick them up, and who to call in an emergency.

Here's what you need to do:

1. **Provide a copy of the divorce decree:** Give the school a copy of your divorce decree. This should include any specific instructions about who can pick up your child or if there are any restrictions.
2. **Upload documents to the school portal:** If your school uses an online portal, see if you can upload your custody documents there. This will make them easy for the school staff to access when needed.
3. **Clarify custody terms:** Sometimes schools aren't familiar with legal terms like *joint custody* or *legal custody*. You might need to explain what your arrangement means in practice, especially if it affects who makes decisions about your child's education or well-being.
4. **Schedule a meeting if necessary:** If your situation is complicated, it might be a good idea to meet with your child's teacher or the school administration. This way, you can clarify any details, like if only one

parent has legal custody or if there's a specific schedule for who picks up your child.

5. **Provide emergency contact information:** Ensure the school has up-to-date contact information for parents and anyone else authorized to pick up your child. The school must know who to call first in case of an emergency.

Understanding Tie-Breaking Authority Over Education

In some custody agreements, one parent might have *tie-breaking authority over education*. If you and your ex can't agree on an important decision about your child's education, the parent with tie-breaking authority gets the final say.

This can come up in a few different ways:
- **School choice:** If you and your ex can't agree on what school your child should attend, the parent with tie-breaking authority makes the final decision. This could be about switching schools, deciding between public and private schools, or choosing a school after a move.
- **Special education services:** If there's a disagreement about whether your child needs special education services or testing, the parent with tie-breaking authority decides what happens next.
- **Class placement:** Sometimes, parents have differing views about whether a child should be placed in an honors class or advanced placement or stay in a regular classroom. If this happens, the parent with tie-breaking authority can decide.
- **Extracurricular activities:** Parents with tie-breaking authority can also settle disagreements about whether their child should participate in particular sports or activities, especially if they affect schoolwork.
- **School discipline:** If there's a severe disciplinary issue, like a suspension or detention, the parent with tie-breaking authority decides how to handle it.

Make sure the school knows if one parent has this authority in order to avoid confusion, and who to contact when these important situations arise.

Accessing School Counseling and Divorce Support Groups

One of the best ways to help your child through the divorce is to take advantage of school counseling services. Many schools offer individual counseling for students, and some even have peer support groups for kids whose parents are going through a divorce.

Here's how to make sure your child gets the support they need:

1. **Ask about divorce support groups:** Some schools have group counseling sessions where kids can meet others in similar situations. These groups are an excellent way for your child to feel less alone, and to learn coping strategies from peers and counselors.

2. **Meet with the school counselor:** Schedule a meeting with the school counselor to discuss your child's emotional needs. The counselor can keep an eye on your child's well-being, offer one-on-one support, and help with resources that might benefit your child such as referrals to outside counseling services.

3. **Explain the divorce situation:** Be open with the counselor about how your child copes with the divorce. If you've noticed any changes in their behavior – like withdrawal, anxiety, or anger – let the counselor know so they can be aware of potential issues.

4. **Check in regularly:** Stay in touch with the counselor throughout the school year. Regular check-ins ensure you're current on how your child is behaving, and allows you to address any concerns early on.

5. **Ask about additional resources:** Many school counselors can point you to community resources, such as support groups for kids or families dealing with divorce. Don't be afraid to ask what's available for you and your child.

Helping Your Child's Teacher Support Them

Your child's teacher is involved in their day-to-day school experience, so keeping them informed can make a huge difference.

Here are some ways to make sure your child's teacher is set up to support them:
- **Make sure both parents are added to school communication:** If you're co-parenting, ask the teacher to add both parents to all school communication platforms so you both get important updates about homework, events, and school activities.
- **Share your child's visitation schedule:** If your child moves between households during the week, give the teacher a copy of the visitation schedule. This helps the teacher know which parent picks up on which days and prevents mix-ups.
- **Share how your Child is coping:** If you feel comfortable, let your child's teacher know how they are handling the divorce. Teachers can be a great source of support, especially if they know what to look out for regarding changes in behavior or performance.

Conclusion

Divorce is never easy, but keeping your child's school in the loop can help them maintain stability during this challenging time. Make sure the school has the information they need, from legal documents to your child's emotional needs, and use the resources available to support your child as they adjust. With open communication and the proper support, you can help your child continue to thrive at school, even as your family navigates big changes.

Stephanie Robins, LCSW, CADP
Alpharetta Family Therapy
Certified Amicable Divorce Professional
Alpharetta, Georgia

STEP 4

MOVING, FORWARD INTO YOUR FUTURE

PART 17
How Do We Go from Partners to Co-Parents?

Chapter 70
Co-Parenting 101: Nurturing Children Through Divorce
369

Chapter 71
Relationship Between Children and Parents
374

Chapter 72
Dealing with a Challenging Co-Parent
378

Chapter 70
Co-Parenting 101: Nurturing Children Through Divorce
by Dara L. Marius

People are not born with coping resources. They develop as we move through life. Challenges, like divorce, can be fertilizer for a child's personal growth. In fact, children can develop useful coping skills in the aftermath of divorce that will more effectively prepare them to navigate future life trials. The key is to create a co-parenting environment that encourages children to flourish. Effective co-parenting requires:

1. Transitioning to a business relationship
2. Implementing "Co-parenting CPR"
3. Nurturing emotional expression
4. Conducting yourself in a way that values your child's well-being.

Keep in mind that a strong co-parenting relationship does not develop overnight. The first year can be stressful while navigating holidays, vacations, and parenting timeshares. Moreover, the vestiges of anger and sadness from the divorce itself may linger longer for one parent, making them less focused on the child and more absorbed with their own pain. Be patient. Remember, the simple act of *one* parent consistently modeling good co-parenting behavior can positively shape your child's life experience and your own.

#1: Reframe Your Relationship: From Spouses to Co-Parents

Co-parenting, at its core, is a **respectful business relationship** where people work together to raise healthy, happy, well-adjusted children. The hallmarks of any business relationship include:

1. No assumptions about the other person
2. No unspoken or unwritten expectations
3. More formal interactions
4. Low emotional intensity and personal involvement
5. High personal privacy and low personal disclosure
6. Effective emotion management

No doubt, this transition will feel strange at first. You are both used to speaking freely to one another. Now, conversations will become more businesslike, respectful, and centered on child-focused topics (schedules, reminders, homework, clothing requirements, medical appointments, etc.) The question you should always consider is: "Would I say or share or ask this of a co-worker at a new job?"

#2: Co-Parenting CPR: Continuity, Protection, and Reassurance

Lois Gold, MSW, identifies an easy way to remember core co-parenting techniques. She calls them the CPR[1][14] of co-parenting, which stands for: **C**ontinuity, **P**rotection, and **R**eassurance. **Continuity** emphasizes a consistent and predictable experience for children. By maintaining regular routines, familiar surroundings, caregivers, and activities that existed prior to divorce, children feel secure and loved.

---

14 Gold, L. (1996). *The CPR of Helping Children: Continuity, Protection, Reassurance*. In *Between Love and Hate: A guide to Civilized Divorce* (pp. 87-91).

PART 17: HOW DO WE GO FROM PARTNERS TO CO-PARENTS?

With a cooperative co-parent, continuity can also extend to rules in both homes. Co-parents should work toward similar bedtimes, homework expectations, screen time rules, etc. Children need and crave boundaries, so try to find common ground. Remember that it is not about either parent *winning*. Rather, find a happy middle ground that you both can get behind. So, if bedtime is 15 minutes later than you want, it's okay. A consistent bedtime outweighs extra sleep. Finally, decide on a dependable parenting timeshare plan and then follow it. Always be on time and never be a no-show. This lets your child know that they can reliably depend on time with *both* parents.

Protection refers to **protection from conflict** and the **divorce** itself. Exposure to conflict correlates directly to increased adjustment problems in children. It follows that avoiding arguments in front of or within earshot of your child is key. Next, protect your children from divorce logistics and negotiations. Your child should not be a messenger delivering information back and forth. Similarly, do not involve children in divorce decision-making. Children need to know what you decide and how that will impact their lives. Unless they are older teenagers (who may be allowed to weigh in about living arrangements), keep the divorce discussions between the parents.

Practically speaking, this also means working through your emotional issues privately. It is not your child's job to be your friend or therapist. **It is your job to protect them from conflict and concern related to the divorce.** Think of yourself as a flight attendant on an airplane. No passenger ever wants to see the flight attendant freaking out. As parents, we are the flight attendants for our children during turbulent times!

Finally, **reassure** your children that they will continue to have a relationship with *both* of you. Because children are one half of each parent, a healthy self-identity develops from a relationship with *both* parents. So, as hard as it feels, nurture their relationship with your co-parent. Do not speak badly (or let your friends or relatives speak badly) about them. Be positive and upbeat when they spend time together. This gives children permission to enjoy their time with them, because they know you are okay with it. This is a crucial element of impeccable co-parenting, and it bolsters emotional well-being in children in every age group – even adult children of divorce.

Equally important, reassure children that the divorce **is not their fault**. Children are master storytellers. The younger they are, the more capable they are of stringing together random facts to create a story to explain their world. Sadly, children often cast themselves as the villain and wrongly conclude they are the cause of your divorce.

Finally, show children that you are **both** still in charge of managing the family's affairs. Remind children that their job is to live *their* life – not to worry about you or solve your problems.

#3: Nurture Emotional Expression

One of the worst aspects of divorce for children is feeling alone with their emotions; as such, emotional expression is a necessity.[15] Parents should help children recognize, label, and share their emotions – exploring how emotions impact them physically and mentally. Finally, it is essential for parents to validate children's feelings. Helping your children express emotions is not easy, and it requires more than just saying, "How do you feel?" Instead, consider the following:

1. Create a **calm and loving environment** where all subjects are welcome including what happens at the other parent's house. Now, this isn't a fact-finding mission. Instead, it is an open invitation for them to share – in the same way you might ask about a visit to a friend's house. The vibe is, "I'm okay with whatever you want to talk about."

2. Listen, and then take an **educated guess** about their emotions. Try to assume what they might be feeling. Say, "It sounds like you might feel _____." Generally, they will agree or disagree and start talking.

---

15 See L., B. A. J., & Fine, P. R. (2014). Chapter 3: Core Concepts of Positive Parenting. In *Co-parenting with a Toxic Ex: What to Do When Your Ex-Spouse Tries to Turn the Kids Against You* (pp. 47–58). chapter, New Harbinger Publications.

3. Again, **listen**. Don't kill the conversation. Your job is to create space for *them* to talk, not you.

4. Don't try to solve their feelings or make things better. Instead, follow up and get more information. Help them understand how their feelings look and feel in their body.[16] You are teaching them to be **mindful of their emotions**. Consider sharing how these emotions make *you* feel, and share techniques you use to process emotions such as controlled breathing techniques or focusing on your five senses.

5. Next, **validate and normalize** their feelings, reminding them that as human beings, we are hardwired to feel things like they are feeling. Explain that emotions are like the weather and do not last forever. In the meantime, remind them you will be there to help.

6. If the other parent said or did something upsetting, emphasize that **the situation is not their fault**. Without comment or blame, let your child know that the parents will figure it out.

I highly recommend *Helping your Kids Cope with Divorce: The Sandcastles Way* by M. Gary Neuman, LMHC.[17] This book provides targeted suggestions by age to mitigate the impact of divorce and encourage healthy emotional expression.

#4: Make Choices that Value Your Child's Well-Being

Your child's well-being must come first before proving you are right, getting the last word in, venting your frustrations, or satisfying your needs. Every action you take, every word you speak, every text you write should only happen if you answer "yes" to this question: *Am I doing right by my child?* This question keeps you honest and accountable because it encourages conduct that values your child's well-being above everything else.

---

16 Ask: Do you feel like crying? Does your chest feel tight? Does your face feel hot? Do your hands feel cold?

17 M. Gary Neuman, LMHC, *Helping Your Kids Cope with Divorce* (1998).

Co-parenting is not about getting what *you* deserve or want. Co-parenting is about building a support system around your child that lets them grow into the people they were meant to be. Whatever form that takes, good co-parents always consider the impact on the child above all other considerations.

Final Thoughts...

No one is suggesting that the process of moving from spouses to co-parents is simple. It takes discipline and requires you to be mindful of what you say and do. It demands that you prioritize your child's emotional well-being above all else, and that your conduct is not a byproduct of negative emotions. Simply put, co-parenting is selflessness in its highest form. But, if your guiding light and North Star is your child, then, as a parent, you can do this!

Dara L. Marias, JD, MSW
AV Preeminent Attorney
A.P.F.M. Certified Advanced Practitioner
Certified Amicable Divorce Professional
Las Vegas, Nevada

Chapter 71
Relationship Between Children and Parents
by Kathryn Harry

Parents Forever

Even an amicable divorce can be challenging for your minor children who are learning to navigate the new normal in two households. As a family law attorney, I have witnessed firsthand the impact that a positive relationship between both parents and their children can have on the overall well-being of the minor children. I often tell my divorcing clients, "It may have turned out that you were your spouse's life partner for only a short period of time, but you will be parents together forever."

As parents, you will see each other for many years at the exchange of children, for parenting time, and at graduations, marriages, funerals, and other family-related functions. Therefore, it is paramount to not only maintain a good relationship with your former spouse but also to promote the relationship between the other parent and your children. In fact, there are some practical, actionable steps you may implement to foster a healthy relationship between your children and your former spouse. By doing so, you not only support your children's emotional health, but also you pave the way for a more amicable divorce experience for both parties.

Fostering a positive relationship with your former spouse will result in a smoother co-parenting experience and less conflict, and create a more stable environment for your children. Promoting cooperation and mutual respect between parents is a win-win.

Why Does It Matter?

Do it for the children. Children who maintain strong relationships with both parents after a divorce tend to fare better emotionally, socially, and academically. It is well known that children who have regular, meaningful contact with both parents exhibit fewer behavioral problems and higher self-esteem compared to those who do not.

Children benefit from the stability and security that comes from knowing both parents are actively involved in their lives. This involvement helps mitigate the potential negative effects of divorce, such as anxiety, depression, and academic struggles.

Do it for yourself. Maintaining a low-conflict relationship with your ex-spouse is healthy for you. You will experience less anxiety and stress. Your children will see you happier, and in turn they will feel better about themselves.

Regardless of why you do it, your actions will reassure your children that both parents are there for them, or they will imply that the other parent is not worthy of the children's respect and love. Choose your actions carefully. Your children are watching…always.

Simple, Specific Actions to Promote the Relationship

Encourage regular communication: Facilitate regular phone calls, video chats, or in-person visits between your children and your former spouse.

Be flexible with schedules: Life is unpredictable, and sometimes plans change or the unexpected happens. Show flexibility with the visitation schedule to accommodate your former spouse's commitments and your children's needs.

Speak positively about your ex: Avoid negative talk about your former spouse in front of your children. Instead, highlight their positive qualities and the good times you shared as a family.

Support the parent-child relationship: Encourage your children to share their experiences and feelings about their time with your former spouse. Do not pump your children for information about your former spouse or a new partner. Let the children tell you as much as they are comfortable telling you. Instead, show genuine interest in their relationship, reinforcing that it's okay to love both parents.

Coordinate parenting approaches: Work with your former spouse to establish consistent parenting rules and routines across both households. You may create a shared document outlining bedtime routines, homework expectations, and disciplinary measures. This type of consistency can provide your children with a sense of stability and security, knowing that both parents are on the same page.

Share important information: Keep your former spouse informed about important events, school activities, and medical appointments, and any other items required in your Parenting Plan. This ensures they remain involved in your children's lives. Using an app like OurFamilyWizard does the trick.

Both of you attend events: Encourage your former spouse to attend school events, sports games, and other important activities in which your children are involved. Your children will benefit from you remaining respectful of the other party's space and those individuals who may be enjoying the event with them.

Make parental decisions together: Your parenting plan probably outlines when you must confer with the other parent on big issues like medical decisions. What about the other "stuff" that arises almost daily about which parents must make decisions? The simplest thing you can do is to parent the children, rather than expecting them to parent themselves.

Celebrate milestones together: Even after your divorce, you may choose to celebrate your children's birthdays, graduations, and other important milestones together. You might plan joint parties and make sure both sides of the family are included. This tradition may help your children feel loved and supported by both parents, despite being a two-household family.

Benefits for You as a Parent

Supporting a positive relationship between your children and your former spouse offers several benefits for you as well:

- Reduced conflict
- Improved emotional well-being
- Better co-parenting relationship

A Special Note About Gray Divorce

A gray divorce occurs when two middle-aged or older adults choose to get a divorce. Gray refers to the color of hair and implies that the parties are older and have different needs or goals than those individuals divorcing at a younger age. Often, the parties are parents to adult children. These types of divorces are occurring more and more frequently and create different challenges for adult children and their parents.

Although in gray divorces topics like child support or parenting time are less likely to be an issue, parents and adult children often provide each other with social, emotional, and financial support. It is recommended that you take care in how much you tell your adult children and how you speak about your former spouse in front of them. Negative talk and too much information can lead to adult children blaming one parent for the divorce and cutting off ties with that parent. Consider making a pact with your former spouse to never speak negatively about each other in front of your adult children. Focus on each other's positive qualities and the good times you shared as a family when interacting with adult children. This positive approach can help the children maintain a balanced, loving view of both parents, and strengthen family connections.

Making a Difference

Promoting a positive relationship between your children, whether young or old, and your former spouse is an investment in your futures. By taking simple, specific actions and avoiding negative behaviors, you can support your children's emotional well-being and create a smooth co-parenting environment. Remember, the goal is to ensure that your children feel loved, secure, and supported by both parents, even as you learn how to be a single-parent household.

Kathryn L. Harry, Esq.
Cumming, Georgia
Oak Brook, Illinois

Chapter 72
Dealing with a Challenging Co-Parent
by Dara L. Marias

The single biggest challenge a parent can face is working with a co-parent who undermines the best co-parenting practices outlined in the chapter "Co-parenting 101." So, what are you to do? As a co-parent, your main goal is to deepen and strengthen your bond with your child so they are less susceptible to the other parent's attempts to interfere with and undermine your relationship.[18]

In this chapter, we will focus on one common problem: the other parent says or does something that disparages you and causes a **loyalty conflict** for your child.[19] A loyalty conflict arises when a child feels they must choose between two parents because of the parents' antagonism toward one another.

When children are impacted by a loyalty conflict, they may develop: headaches, stomachaches, tension, lack of energy, anxiety, depression, behavioral problems such as becoming withdrawn or disobedient, or other physical and psychological symptoms. If they are young, they may regress developmentally (e.g., a six-year-old starts having potty accidents). When the pressure is too much, some children just *pick a parent* with whom to side in order to make the unpleasant feeling of having to choose between the two go away.

Below are concrete steps to take if your co-parent disparages you and sets a loyalty conflict in motion[20]:

1. Don't let your mind race. Take a moment to breathe and calm down.

2. Be mindful of what you are feeling, and do not let yourself become defensive. Table it for now.

3. Do not immediately try to correct the misunderstanding, lie, or misinformation. Instead, focus on your child's emotional state.

4. Remind yourself that what you say and do next must promote your child's well-being.

---

18 L., B. A. J., & Fine, P. R. (2014). Chapter 3: Core Concepts of Positive Parenting. In Co-parenting with a Toxic Ex: What to Do When Your Ex-Spouse Tries to Turn the Kids Against You (pp. 47-58). chapter, New Harbinger Publications.
19 L., B. A. J., & Fine, P. R. (2014). Chapter 1: Causes and Consequences of Loyalty Conflicts in Families of Divorce. In Co-parenting with a Toxic Ex: What to Do When Your Ex-Spouse Tries to Turn the Kids Against You (pp. 5-22). chapter, New Harbinger Publications.
20 L., B. A. J., & Fine, P. R. (2014). Chapter 5: When Your Ex Is Sending Poisonous Messages About You. In Co-parenting with a Toxic Ex: What to Do When Your Ex-Spouse Tries to Turn the Kids Against You (pp. 83-106). chapter, New Harbinger Publications.

5. Consider the emotion your child is probably experiencing.
6. If your child is disrespectful because of the poisonous information, here are things you can say to bring the child back:
   a. "I love you too much to let you talk to me that way."
   b. "It's hard for me to understand you when you talk in that tone. Can you say it again politely and calmly so I can really hear what you are saying?"
   c. "It's hard for me to understand what you are saying because you're yelling at me. Can you find a more respectful way to share? Maybe you need some time to cool off?"
7. If your child makes a specific accusation about you in an angry tone, consider this type of response:

   "You seem really upset right now. I'm wondering whether you are feeling angry and maybe hurt because you think I did [insert action]. Can you tell me more about your feelings? I really want to understand what is going on."

   This **cool and nonreactive response** acknowledges what was said but brings it back to the feelings.
8. If your child calls you names and accuses you of something…
   a. First, take a beat to acknowledge your own pain.
   b. Next, consider: If those things were true, how would your child feel? Focus on that.
   c. Example:

      Let's take an example where a child's father called her mother greedy and mean because she requested more financial support. The child tells Mom. Mom's response should be child-focused, validating what the child said and then taking a guess at how the child might feel:

      "So, you think I'm greedy and am doing things that hurt your daddy, and that makes you feel sad maybe? Or angry? Maybe at me? I wonder whether you feel as though I really don't love you, or else I wouldn't do these things that you think I did. Can you tell me whether that is what you are feeling? I want to understand what's going on with you."

Again, the focus is on *how the information is impacting the child emotionally*, not so much whether it is true or not.

If the child says to his mom, "Don't you love me?"

Mom can respond: "This isn't easy for you. You're hurting and need to know how much I love you. I love you very, very much. I can assure you that I didn't steal your money, and I want you to know that it's Mommy and Daddy's job to work this out."

9. Always aim to get to the underlying feeling and pivot away from the child's involvement in this situation.

Sometimes the other co-parent brings up a version of something that actually happened and twists it to make you look like a horrible person. Below is a true story that provides an extreme example of superlative management of challenging co-parent behavior. My client, Dad, had his own emotions under control, focused on the CPRs, and nurtured *emotional expression*.

Here is what happened according to Dad…

> While still married, Dad and Mom had an argument. In a fit of anger, Mom threw the TV remote at Dad, barely missing his head. In response, Dad slammed the table so hard a bowl shattered and sent glass flying. A small piece grazed Mom's leg, and she called the police. A Temporary Protective Order was issued that led to a criminal battery case against Dad. The parties separated, and four months later Dad was due in court. During her parenting time, Mom informed the kids that Dad is "violent" and is "going to jail." Their 11-year-old son tells this to Dad and is visibly shaken after a week with Mom.

Here is what Dad did…

Previously, Dad had done a lot of work learning emotion management and the co-parenting practices discussed in the chapter "Co-Parenting 101." Before this happened, Dad made a commitment to his children's well-being above everything. Because of this (as told by Dad), he did the following:

1. He recognized that he still felt very angry, and ashamed that he wasn't in control of his anger on that night.
2. Then, he paused and took a deep breath, committing to be mindful and in control. He fought the urge to prove that he wasn't violent and that it was Mom who had started things and threw the remote.
3. Instead, he focused on his son's anguish. He purposefully pivoted away from defending himself and leaned into guessing what his son was feeling. He told me he'd said:

    "Son, I'm guessing when Mom called me violent that might have made you confused and scared? I wonder whether you are worried that I might do something violent?" The child told him, "No."

4. Next Dad asked:

    "Are you worried that you aren't going to be able to see me?"

5. Then his son began to cry, saying he was very worried that Dad would go to prison and they wouldn't see each other, and that he was angry at Mom.
6. Instead of co-opting his son's anger to get back at Mom, Dad did not fuel a loyalty conflict. He focused on his son's fear and said:

    "I want you to know that spending time with you and your brother is my highest priority. I will always do everything I can to see you."

Dad could have brought up Mom's violent conduct on that fateful night. Instead, he stayed focused on his son's life experience and said:

> "I also want you to know that I would never do anything to hurt you or your mom."

7. Finally, in the greatest jujitsu move of all, he focused on preserving his son's relationship with his mother, and removed the burden of the situation from his son. He said:

> "Sometimes when moms and dads divorce, they get angry and say things that aren't accurate. Have you ever said something when you are angry that you didn't really mean? Sometimes moms and dads do that too. But you don't need to worry about this. Mom and I will get this worked out. In the meantime, we are going to work hard to be respectful and kind to each other."

My client's response was shaped by two things: (1) a knowledge of core co-parenting skills and (2) prioritizing his child's well-being. Even though the loyalty conflict was working in my client's favor, he knew how bad a loyalty conflict could be for his child. This is important. Instead of focusing on himself, Dad focused on the child. The child was able to express his feelings – Dad validated them and took the pressure off the child to solve the situation.

The takeaway? When confronted with challenging behavior from your co-parent, the goal is not to clarify what happened, defend yourself, or prove why you are in the right. The goal is to help your child identify and express their underlying feelings, validate them, and take the pressure off. Let your child know the adults are handling the grown-up things so they can get back to their life of school, friends, and activities.

Dara L. Marias, JD, MSW
AV Preeminent Attorney
A.P.F.M. Certified Advanced Practitioner
Certified Amicable Divorce Professional
Las Vegas, Nevada

PART 18

How Do I Move Forward After Divorce?

Chapter 73
The Post-Divorce Checklist
387

Chapter 74
Finding Yourself Again
388

Chapter 75
Estate Planning After Divorce
392

Chapter 76
Rebuilding Financially
398

Chapter 77
Prenuptial Agreements for Remarriage
403

Chapter 78
Cultivating Mindfulness
408

Chapter 79
Moving Forward
413

Chapter 80
Closure and Healing
418

Chapter 73
The Post-Divorce Checklist
by Tracy Ann Moore-Grant

Now that your divorce is final, you'll want to make sure that you take care of a few things to tie up loose ends:

- **Get a new last will and testament.** Laws vary greatly on whether your former spouse would continue to inherit from you. This is a good time to make sure all documents are up to date, now that the divorce is final.
- **Make sure you change the beneficiary on all life insurance** policies – unless you are required to maintain a policy as part of your divorce.
- **Change the beneficiary on all accounts.** The beneficiaries on such accounts do not automatically change upon divorce for your investments and banking accounts.
- **Be prepared to document.** If you and your spouse share children – or have any ongoing financial connections like real property, child support, or spousal support – it is important to keep good records. Text messages may not be admissible in court, and memories get hazy. Document any issues with payments or parenting – you may need good records if questions arise in the future.
- **If you have moved, make sure you do a change of address** with all institutions, and in particular with those who send you tax forms. With so much that's possible to do online, people often forget that sometimes snail mail is still important. You should also complete a change-of-address form for the Internal Revenue Service.
- **Make sure that your spouse does not have signature authority or a credit card** on any of your accounts. When in doubt, just call the number on the back of your card to check.

- **Make sure all utilities are in the proper person's name** for each residence. Even if parties have moved, utility accounts can still linger in the other's name. Check on all accounts, including the trash service!
- **Double-check your recurring expenses.** If you have subscriptions, like a monthly gym bill or streaming account, make sure the person paying for them is the one getting the benefit.
- **Change your passwords.** Your spouse knows you well and can probably easily guess your passwords for social media, banking, and so forth. Go with totally new passwords, moving forward!
- **Consult with a CPA or tax professional.** The year of divorce can be confusing regarding deductions, filing status, and determining who is claiming what.

The immediate post-divorce period can be overwhelming. Take some time to plug away at this list and get everything separated and handled properly. Also, be aware that mistakes happen. If you get the other party's tax form, or a charge that you didn't make hits your account, cooperation is key. Remember, something like that could happen to either of you. Be prompt about sending proof of any charges, or about forwarding any important documents or mailings.

Chapter 74
Finding Yourself Again
by Stephanie Robins

Going through a divorce can feel like losing a part of yourself. It's not just about ending a relationship, but also about navigating a new world where you might no longer recognize who you are. The good news? This time can also be a powerful opportunity to reconnect with yourself and shape a future that truly reflects who you are. Here's a friendly, step-by-step guide to help you rediscover yourself during and after divorce.

Step 1: Embrace Your Emotions

First things first – let yourself feel. Divorce stirs up a whirlwind of emotions, from sadness and anger to relief and even guilt. These feelings are normal, and bottling them up won't help. It's okay to cry, vent, or take time to reflect. Grieving the loss of your marriage is a crucial part of moving forward.

If you feel overwhelmed, don't hesitate to seek professional help. A therapist or counselor can offer a safe space to unpack your emotions and provide tools to help you cope. Remember, asking for help is a sign of strength, not weakness.

Step 2: Revisit Your Passions

When was the last time you did something just for you? In the hustle of married life, personal hobbies and interests often take a back seat. Now is your chance to bring them back into focus. Did you love painting, hiking, cooking, or dancing? Dust off those old passions or try something entirely new.

Start small. Pick one activity that excites you, and carve out time each week for it. These moments of joy will help you reconnect with yourself and remind you of who you were before your marriage.

Step 3: Reflect on Your Values and Goals

Divorce offers a unique opportunity to redefine your life. Take some time to think about what truly matters to you. What are your core values? What kind of life do you want to build for yourself?

Write down your goals – big and small. Maybe you want to advance your career, travel more, or create a peaceful home environment. A clear vision of your priorities will give you a sense of purpose and direction as you move forward.

Step 4: Lean on Your Support System

Divorce can feel lonely, but you don't have to go through it alone. Surround yourself with people who uplift and support you. Whether it's friends, family, or a support group, having a network of people to lean on can make all the difference.

Be open about what you need. Sometimes, that might mean a shoulder to cry on; other times, it could mean a fun distraction. Letting others be there for you is not a burden – it's a way to build connection and strength.

Step 5: Establish New Routines

Divorce can turn your daily life upside down. One way to regain a sense of stability is to create new routines and rituals. They don't have to be complicated; even small habits can help you feel more grounded.

Maybe it's a morning walk, journaling before bed, or dedicating Sundays to self-care. These routines will not only give your day structure, but also serve as acts of self-nurturing.

Step 6: Set Healthy Boundaries

Now is the time to protect your peace. Setting boundaries – especially with your ex – is essential. Whether it's limiting communication to specific topics (like co-parenting) or defining personal space, boundaries will help you maintain emotional distance and focus on your healing.

Don't be afraid to enforce these limits. Boundaries are a way of respecting yourself and your journey toward growth.

Step 7: Reconnect with Yourself

One of the most important relationships you will ever have is with yourself. Divorce can be a chance to nurture that relationship. Start by practicing self-compassion. You've been through a lot, and having days you don't feel your best is okay.

Spend time reflecting on what makes you happy, what challenges you, and what fulfills you. Try meditation, take yourself out, or journal about your hopes and dreams. Rediscovering who you are is a process, but each step will bring you closer to feeling whole again.

Step 8: Embrace the Unknown

The future may seem uncertain right now, and that's perfectly okay. Try to see this as an adventure rather than a source of fear. Without the constraints of your past relationship, you can explore new opportunities and experiences.

Think of one thing you've always wanted to do but never had the chance. Whether it's learning a new language, switching careers, or traveling solo, now is your time to go for it.

Step 9: Celebrate Your Growth

Every challenge you face is an opportunity to grow. Instead of viewing divorce as a failure, see it as a stepping stone to becoming a stronger, more authentic version of yourself. Take pride in the small victories, whether successfully setting a boundary, trying something new, or simply getting through a tough day.

Growth doesn't happen overnight; but with each step forward, you build a life that aligns with your true self.

Moving Forward

Divorce is undoubtedly a life-altering experience, but it's also a chance to rediscover your inner strength and create a future that excites you. Take it one day at a time, and remember: You're not just surviving – you're reinventing yourself.

Be patient and kind to yourself. Healing isn't linear, and that's okay. Most importantly, you're taking steps forward, and shaping a life filled with purpose, joy, and authenticity.

Stephanie Robins, LCSW, CADP
Alpharetta Family Therapy
Certified Amicable Divorce Professional
Alpharetta, Georgia

Chapter 75
Estate Planning After Divorce
by Misty Ralston

Divorce involves not only the dissolution of a relationship, but also the reshaping of one's financial life. While the last thing you may want is to see another attorney, seeing an attorney to do estate planning should be the first step in your journey of a new life.

So what is estate planning? Estate planning is the process of arranging for the distribution of your assets and determining who will make critical decisions on your behalf if you become incapacitated or die. It includes key legal documents such as wills, trusts, powers of attorney, and healthcare directives. Estate planning after divorce is essential because it ensures that your assets are distributed according to your wishes, your loved ones are protected, and your intentions are clear regarding end-of-life decisions. Additionally, estate planning helps mitigate the potential conflicts and legal issues that may arise between your ex-spouse, future spouse or partner, children, and other beneficiaries.

1. Ensure Proper Asset Distribution

One of the primary reasons estate planning after a divorce is so important is to ensure that your assets are distributed in accordance with your current wishes. In many divorces, especially those involving significant wealth, marital assets such as property, retirement accounts, and life insurance policies are divided between the spouses. However, this division may not suffice to cover your post-divorce financial needs, and you may want to make further adjustments in your estate plan.

After a divorce, your existing will or trust may no longer reflect your current preferences. For example, your former spouse may be named as a beneficiary, or you may have designated them as the person responsible for managing your estate in the event of your death. Continuing to leave assets to an ex-spouse, or naming them as an executor, could lead to confusion and unnecessary legal battles. If your estate plan is not updated, it could cause tension between your ex-spouse, children, and other family members.

Many states allow a spouse to be considered disinherited after a divorce, or they no longer can make decisions on your behalf. On the other hand, some divorced couples are still friendly and close and do still want to take care of their ex spouse after they are no longer living. Therefore, not having clear instructions in your documents could lead to unnecessary legal battles after you are gone.

To avoid complications, you need to review and potentially revise your will, trust, or any other estate planning documents to reflect your new reality. You may want to designate your children, other relatives, or trusted friends as your beneficiaries. Additionally, consider appointing someone other than your ex as the executor or trustee of your estate – someone you trust to carry out your wishes impartially and can be neutral – even when there is a trust for the benefit of your children.

2. Protect Your Children

If you have children from your marriage, they become an important focus of your estate planning after divorce. Depending on your custody arrangement, you may have concerns about your ex-spouse's ability or willingness to manage your children's inheritance or make important decisions regarding their care and well-being.

In the event of your death, a well-drafted estate plan will ensure that your children's inheritance is protected, and that someone you trust will be appointed as their guardian or conservator. It is especially crucial if your ex-spouse will not be raising the children, or if you are concerned about their ability to provide for them.

You might consider the following actions in your post-divorce estate planning:

- **Guardianship:** If your children are still minors, you can name a guardian for them in the event of your death. This person would step in and care for your children instead of leaving the decision to a court. While this would not, of course, take away the right of the other parent to be guardian, it would allow a court to know your preferences – especially if something happens to your ex after you are gone – and your children are still minors.
- **Trusts:** A revocable or irrevocable trust can help you designate specific assets for your children's benefit and ensure that they are protected from mismanagement, particularly if they are young. You can set terms in the trust for how and when your children will receive assets (for example, in stages as they reach certain milestones, like age 25.) You can name someone from your family to act as trustee so that your family still has a tie to the younger children and can, hopefully, still enjoy some relationship with them.
- **Healthcare and financial decisions:** If your ex-spouse was once the person on whom you would rely for healthcare or financial decisions, it may be time to update your healthcare proxy or financial power of attorney to designate someone else.
- **Updates:** When a couple divorces and the children are young, situations may occur after the divorce that create a need for any initial estate plan to be updated; so it's important to develop a trusted relationship with your attorney. Maybe your child gets hurt in some way and needs lifetime care – maybe they are diagnosed with a mental health issue – or turns to drugs, alcohol or gambling to cope with their own emotions after the divorce. You may want to update your estate plan to account for these circumstances. Finally, you will want to revisit your plan if you start thinking of remarriage – a blended family can make things even more complex when it comes to protecting your family.

3. Review Beneficiary Designations

One of the most overlooked aspects of estate planning after a divorce is reviewing and updating beneficiary designations on retirement accounts, insurance policies, and other financial accounts. Beneficiary designations supersede any instructions in a will or trust, meaning that your ex-spouse may still be entitled to assets from your 401k, life insurance, or other accounts if you do not change these designations.

- **Retirement accounts:** Many people designate their spouse as the primary beneficiary of their retirement accounts, such as a 401k or IRA. If these accounts are not updated post-divorce, your ex-spouse could inherit these funds upon your death, even if your will states otherwise. It's critical to update beneficiary designations on these accounts to reflect your current wishes.
- **Life insurance policies:** Similar to retirement accounts, life insurance policies often require you to designate beneficiaries. If you fail to remove your ex-spouse as the beneficiary of your life insurance policy, they could receive the payout upon your death. Depending on the terms of the divorce, this could cause confusion or disputes among your children, other beneficiaries, or even your ex-spouse.
- **Other accounts:** In addition to retirement and life insurance policies, be sure to review other financial accounts that may have beneficiary designations, such as bank accounts, brokerage accounts, and payable-on-death (POD) accounts.

Keep in mind that naming a relative as your beneficiary and assuming they will "do the right thing" and use the funds to care for your children may not be the best option. Once it is in their name, there is no legal requirement that the money be used for your children. The funds are also vulnerable to creditors or their own marital or family issues. If you want to benefit the minor children, a trust should be created and the children should be named as the beneficiaries of the account.

Changing these designations ensures that your assets will go to the people you intend, and will reduce the likelihood of future legal disputes or confusion.

4. Appoint a New Power of Attorney

Another critical aspect of estate planning that requires attention after divorce is appointing a new power of attorney. A power of attorney gives someone the authority to make decisions on your behalf in the event that you become incapacitated. If your ex-spouse was previously named as your agent under a power of attorney, you should update this designation immediately.

This change is particularly important if your ex-spouse was involved in making healthcare or financial decisions for you. If you become incapacitated and your ex-spouse is still listed as your agent, they may have the legal right to make decisions on your behalf, even though you may no longer want them to.

Consider choosing a trusted friend, family member, or advisor to serve as your new agent for both healthcare and financial decisions. You should also name one or two successor agents to ensure a backup if needed. Consider whether naming young adult children as a healthcare power of attorney is the best decision. Do you want to put your young adult child – 18, 19, 20 years of age – in the position of having to tell the doctor to take you off life support? Knowing what you want is one thing; having to say it and being the one responsible to do so is another.

5. Plan for Taxes

Divorce often results in significant changes to your financial situation, including changes to your tax obligations. Estate planning after divorce can help minimize your tax burden and maximize the value of your estate for your beneficiaries. For example, if you have significant assets, you may need to adjust your estate planning strategy to take advantage of tax exemptions, charitable deductions, or other tax-saving measures.

One key consideration in this area is the use of estate tax exemptions. Each individual can exempt a certain amount of their estate from taxes upon death. Following a divorce, your estate may be worth less than before, which may change your estate tax obligations. You may want to consult with an estate planning attorney or tax professional to ensure that your estate plan reflects your new financial circumstances and minimizes any potential tax liability.

6. Avoid Future Disputes

After a divorce, it's not uncommon for family members, including your ex-spouse, children, or extended family, to dispute your estate plan. By taking the time to carefully review and revise your estate plan, you can help prevent misunderstandings or disagreements down the road.

Proactively updating your estate plan and making your intentions clear reduces the risk of future disputes. It ensures that your loved ones respect your wishes and prevents unnecessary emotional and financial turmoil after you pass.

Conclusion

Estate planning after divorce is not just an important step – it's a crucial one. It allows you to regain control over your assets, protect your children, and ensure that your wishes are honored, even after the dissolution of your marriage. Revising your estate plan will help you avoid complications, conflicts, and confusion and will provide peace of mind knowing that your affairs are in order. As life continues to change, your estate plan should evolve with it, reflecting your new reality, desires, and priorities. By making estate planning a priority after divorce, you take a significant step toward securing your future and protecting the interests of those you care about most.

Misty L. Ralston, Esq.
Woodbury, New Jersey

Chapter 76
Rebuilding Financially
by Andrew Hatherley

You're divorced. Now what? You may be feeling a sense of relief. But now there are some things you need to do to ensure that the terms of your marital settlement are put into effect. There are also ongoing tasks that can support your financial and personal growth after divorce. If you need help, you might consider hiring a divorce CFO[21], if you have not already.

Key Tasks to Do Now

It's crucially important that you put the terms required in the divorce decree into effect as soon as possible. Delays can be costly.

Organize Everything

- The first step is to consult with your attorney and your financial advisor. Ask them what you should do next.
- Have copies of the divorce decree and marital settlement agreement handy to share with financial institutions for upcoming property transfers.
- Close joint credit cards and bank accounts, and in each case cancel *authorized user status* for your ex.
- Open new credit card accounts in your individual name if you have not done so already.
- Retitle real estate and automobile assets.
- Check your credit about two months after the divorce is final to verify no joint accounts remain.

---

21 https://www.transcendretirement.net/podcast/gray-divorce-podcast-episode-56-why-you-need-divorce-cfo

- Change passwords on all accounts.
- If your decree addresses changing your legal name, contact the financial institutions with whom you work – the Social Security Administration, the DMV, etc.

Meet with Your Divorce Financial Advisor

- Follow up with your attorney or drafter of the QDRO to ensure that the retirement plan administrator has accepted the order and it has been filed with the court.
- Speak to your financial advisor about setting up your own IRA as a destination for these assets. (Transferring the assets from the 401k to your IRA is not a taxable event.)
- Determine if you need any money from the 401k. Speak with the plan administrator before the divorce decree is finalized to review the plan's withdrawal rules. (If you're under 59.5 years of age, the IRS allows you to withdraw 401k funds pursuant to a QDRO without paying the 10 percent early withdrawal penalty. Once you roll the funds into an IRA, the early withdrawal penalty applies. Of course, ordinary income taxes need to be paid on withdrawals, whether a 401k or an IRA.)
- For bank accounts, investment accounts, and IRAs, you will need to call the specific institution holding the assets. They all seem to have slightly different procedures to transfer assets from joint accounts to new individual accounts, or from one spouse's IRA to the others.
- Once assets are transferred, review your overall investment portfolio to make sure it's in line with your individual needs and objectives. If your ex handled the investments, you may find that his/her level of risk is not suitable for your situation.

Taxes

Meet with your tax professional to determine your new tax status and any new tax strategies you might want to begin. If you are using a new tax preparer, be sure to have a copy of the previous year's joint tax return. And be sure to share a copy of the decree with your tax person as it likely contains language that will affect your next filing.

Insurance

- Obtain life insurance if required by the divorce decree. If you are receiving spousal support, you'll want to protect those payments by ensuring you are the beneficiary of insurance on your spouse.
- Make sure you change life insurance beneficiaries unless otherwise stipulated in the divorce decree. Revise health insurance as directed in the divorce decree. If insurance is not available through an employer, begin COBRA coverage or get a new individual policy. You should have determined your future health insurance coverage before the divorce settlement.
- Consider long-term care or disability income coverage if you don't have it already. Review and/or obtain new auto and homeowners insurance policies.

Estate Planning

Create a new will. Better yet, establish a trust and review your powers of attorney, both financial and health.

Social Security: Contact the Social Security Administration to review your eligibility. If you were married for 10 years or more, inquire about the Social Security benefit of your divorced spouse. You may find it advantageous to claim based on your ex's Social Security earnings record. Review your benefits if you're currently receiving Social Security.

Real Estate

If you keep possession of the marital residence, you may need to refinance it. Hopefully, you are working with a certified divorce lending professional and have reviewed the timeline for any refinancing or new financing on a new property before the divorce decree is signed.

Ongoing Tasks

Prepare a budget and a net worth statement to see your financial well-being, particularly if you are approaching retirement. The budget lists all sources of monthly income minus all your monthly expenses. The net worth statement lists your assets (the things you own) minus your liabilities (debts). The bottom line is your net worth.[22]

The Budget: Your Income and Expenses

Now that you are divorced, you live in a separate household and have your own set of unique expenses. Your budget should be based on *monthly* income and expenses. Your income includes: your job, spousal support, pensions, and income from investments. If you are receiving spousal support, stay aware of the day that support ends. For non-monthly income or expenses, such as travel or Christmas gifts, divide the cost by 12 to enter them as a monthly expense.

A new car, a new house, or all the expenses of the mortgage if you keep the house should all be assumed as potential expenses. These are all priorities, along with essentials like food, transportation, and insurance.

Are there expenses you can live without, or perhaps reduce? These are discretionary expenses, or items you want but don't necessarily need. I've experienced the $150 per month gym, and I've experienced the $20 per month gym. You don't get seven times the value in the expensive gym! You may not need to eliminate luxuries like restaurant outings entirely, but you may want to reduce their frequency.

If there's any money left over, you probably want to pay down any high-interest rate debt first.

If your budget shows a debit and expenses cannot be cut, you're going to need to find more sources of income. Everyone is different. Some people might be willing to work a couple extra hours a week to maintain their

---

[22] https://www.kiplinger.com/retirement/gray-divorce-keys-to-financial-planning

entertainment budget. Others may be resistant or unable to work. For older divorcees, finding a job may be more of a challenge due to health issues and ageism.

A budget isn't a static thing; it can change and *should* change over time. Experiences may become more important than things in your new life.

You may find that you don't miss driving a leased Audi, and that you would much prefer to put the money toward a trip to Machu Picchu.

> If you are using dtour.life, you can ask the account holder to turn it over to you after your case is over. You can continue to use the features to track balances and budgets.

Your Net Worth Statement

Tracking your net worth as you rebuild your finances can help both financially and psychologically. It can be disheartening to see your net worth cut in half as you approach retirement. After my divorce, I found that tracking my net worth quarterly showed me I was on the right track and built momentum to regain the wealth that I had lost.

The beauty of the net worth arithmetic is that your net worth can go up even if your bank account or your retirement account are flat or even drop. If your debts are decreasing faster on a dollar basis than your assets, your net worth is still improving.

It might be better to pay off any credit cards more promptly using any extra cash sitting in a bank or brokerage account. Just be careful about taking any money from retirement accounts where penalties and taxes might come into play. Speak to your financial advisor.

In Conclusion

There is a lot you can do to take control of your finances in divorce. Now you have a financial checklist of the things you need to act upon as soon as the ink is dry on the divorce agreement. You also have two key financial yardsticks, the budget and the net worth statement. Ideally you should be tracking those for the rest of your life. It has been my experience and the experience of my divorcing clients that those who commit to educating themselves about the financial aspects of divorce will emerge from the process in better shape both financially and emotionally.

Andrew Hatherley, CDFA®, CRPC®
Host, The Gray Divorce Podcast
Certified Amicable Divorce Professional
Las Vegas, Nevada
Greenville, South Carolina

Chapter 77
Prenuptial Agreements for Remarriage
by Alexandra Geczi

Don't Forget Your Prenup for Next Time

There's a saying that money is the last thing that people talk about before marriage and the first thing they fight about after marriage. For those who have experienced divorce, the idea of remarriage may come as a mixed bag of hope and precaution. And while prenups have a long history of being one-sided, the successful negotiation of a fair and balanced prenup can provide great value to a marriage.

Lessons from Divorce

Divorce, while challenging, provides valuable lessons about relationships, finances, and personal resilience. These insights can guide you as you plan for the future. Reflect on the complexities of your previous divorce – whether it was dividing assets, addressing debt, or navigating emotional challenges. Understanding what was most stressful or contentious can help you identify how a prenup could provide security in the future. Clarify your financial goals and boundaries and view the prenup as a tool to align those goals with the vision you and your partner share for the future.

Understanding What a Prenup Can Offer

So often, divorces are caused by misaligned expectations for the relationship. Prenuptial agreements offer a variety of ways that couples can clarify expectations and start things on a better footing. Couples can use prenups to ensure that assets they bring into the marriage – such as savings, real estate, or business interests – are protected. It can also shield you from your partner's debts and clarify financial responsibilities. A prenup can outline how expenses will be shared, how savings will be managed, and how investments will be handled. This is especially important if you are blending families and households that may have different needs.

Prenuptial agreements can also minimize the conflict that often arises in the event of divorce. A prenup can set clear terms for spousal support and division of community property. By using a prenup to preemptively minimize conflict, you ensure fairness and save time, money, and emotional distress in the event of divorce.

If you have children from a previous marriage, prenuptial agreements can safeguard assets or inheritance meant for them. This protection provides peace of mind and prevents conflicts over family resources.

Common Myths and Misunderstandings About Prenups

Despite their benefits, prenuptial agreements are often misunderstood. One common myth is that prenups signify a lack of trust or an expectation of failure. How unromantic! On the contrary, discussing and creating a prenup is an act of responsible planning – very sexy stuff. It shows that you value the relationship enough to approach it with transparency and foresight.

Many also believe prenups are only for the wealthy. However, prenups are equally valuable for individuals with more modest assets, significant debts, or specific financial goals. While prenups are not for every marriage, aside from the wealthy, prenups are also appropriate for older couples, people with children from previous relationships, and those with significant premarital or separate assets.

While premarital agreements can be one-sided, they don't have to be. People believe that the monied spouse holds all the power, but the less monied spouse also holds the cards. There is no better time to speak up than now in order to ensure that you are treated fairly in the relationship – when the two of you are committing to love and respect each other for the rest of your lives. And, from a legal perspective, you won't find much sympathy from most courts later, in the event of divorce, when you had this opportunity to "speak now or forever hold your peace."

Broaching the "P" Word

Discussing a prenuptial agreement with your partner can feel daunting, but it's an opportunity to build a stronger, more transparent relationship.

Broach the topic early in the relationship, before wedding plans begin. If you discussed it while dating, bring it up again to gauge if your partner still feels the same. You might use the experience of a friend, or the news of a celebrity couple, as a springboard and then segue into the conversation. Frame things positively, focusing on how a prenup can protect and benefit both of you. Create the right atmosphere, in a neutral location that feels safe, warm, and loving.

The process of creating a prenup requires open and honest discussions about financial goals, values, and concerns. As such, begin the conversation with the same open and honest approach. Raise your concerns as to why you want a prenup and invite discussion about the underlying issues. Avoid reaching conclusions or making decisions at this point. And absolutely avoid threats and ultimatums, which can have a chilling effect on the entire process. Consider bringing a counselor or therapist into the discussion to help with clarity and communication.

If your partner is not receptive to the idea of a prenup, give them some time to think about the reasons you've set forth. Provide them with resources or information that can help them consider the options. If they respond with seemingly harmless but passive-aggressive remarks like "whatever you want" or "I'll sign whatever you draft," don't dismiss those statements at face value. If you proceed without your partner's engagement in the process, you're starting your marriage off on a foundation of resentment. You should both be satisfied with the agreement, and you should both get something you want from it.

Ultimately, a successful marriage requires open and honest communication about often uncomfortable topics. If you and your partner can't communicate about these things now, then you may need to set aside the idea of a prenup and consider whether you are ready for marriage at this time.

Sample Opening Scripts

"I went through a nasty divorce. I love you and recognize that our relationship is not like that one. But I'm scared of going through something like that again."

"My children want me to be happy, but they are concerned about what the marriage might mean for their inheritance/college expenses/etc. I'm worried about this, too. Let's do some estate planning and include a prenuptial agreement so that we can have peace of mind."

"I believe marriage is a 50-50 partnership, and I'm worried about giving up my career to become a homemaker. I want to make sure that my contributions are valued, and that my financial future is secure, no matter what happens to us."

"I'm worried about how [my/your] debts will affect our assets. I think it would benefit us both to keep our property separate."

"I worked hard to acquire a nest egg, and I want to be sure that it will stay intact in the unlikely event that we break up or you pass away before me."

Red Flags

If you or your partner do any of the following, then it signals a red flag. If your partner does any of the following, you should seriously consider whether signing the prenup (or even getting married) is a good idea:
- Presenting the prenup for the first time just before the wedding.
- Asking you to stop at his or her lawyer's office to sign a simple document (i.e., the prenup) without you thoughtfully reviewing it with your own attorney.
- Telling you that you don't need a lawyer, and their lawyer will handle everything.
- Promising that the prenup will be destroyed after the wedding, or once you've reached a certain milestone in your marriage.
- Hiding assets or debts and avoiding a full financial disclosure of all property or liabilities.

Working with Legal Professionals

To ensure equity, both parties should have separate legal representation. This not only protects individual interests but also reduces the risk of future disputes over the agreement's validity. Work with a family law or estate planning attorney who specializes in prenuptial agreements. Their expertise ensures that your interests are protected and that the agreement is enforceable. Customize the agreement to address your specific financial situation, goals, and preferences, whether that includes protecting a business or setting terms for spousal support.

Conclusion

A prenuptial agreement is not about anticipating failure but about preparing responsibly for the future. It can be a catalyst for open and transparent communication that builds a foundation of mutual respect and trust. It is a tool for protecting yourself, your partner, and your shared goals, ensuring that your new marriage starts on a solid ground.

Embrace the idea of a prenup as an empowering step in building a life together. By taking the time to create a thoughtful, fair agreement, you're prioritizing clarity, fairness, and the long-term health of your relationship – essential elements for a successful and fulfilling partnership.

Alexandra Geczi, Esq.
Founder of Alexandra Geczi PLLC
Certified Mediator
Certified Collaborative Law Attorney
Certified Amicable Divorce Professional
Dallas, Texas

Chapter 78
Cultivating Mindfulness
by Dara L. Marias

Have you ever looked around and felt like everyone else has it all figured out? When times are tough, it's easy to feel like you are on the outside watching the rest of the world leading their best lives. Meanwhile, there you are just doing your best to get through the day. Of course, the truth is that *no one* goes through life unscathed. Loss, disappointment, sorrow, anguish, and fear are part of everyone's experience. They just come in different forms and at different times for all of us. Health issues, financial setbacks, deaths, family challenges, relationship problems, job losses, divorces, unlucky breaks, and global crises can and do touch all of us. If you are going through a divorce right now, this will count as one of your life's challenges.

Going through a time like this is bound to stir profound emotions – right when you need to be at the top of your game making big financial decisions and perhaps adjusting to a new co-parent role. For this reason, I have always prioritized helping my divorce clients cultivate *mindfulness* and develop *emotional agility* skills. Emotional agility is awareness of our emotions in a spacious and balanced way so we can relate to our feelings with balance, clarity, and wisdom.[23] Emotional agility contributes to good choices and smart decision-making in divorce and life.

Why Bother with Emotions?

Emotions cannot be ignored. They are part and parcel of being a human in this world. People are hardwired to feel things; if you do not acknowledge and process those feelings, they can control your conduct and impact your mood without your knowledge. It is therefore essential that you not only become mindful of your emotions, but also understand how they present in your body and what you can do to relate to them with balance and equanimity.

Meditation

The information in this chapter originates from a course by Oren Jay Sofer on the Happier Meditation app called "Emotions." [1] Wait! Don't flip to the next chapter. You don't have to run because I mentioned the word *meditation*! This app is designed for the average person who has perhaps 10 minutes a day to spare, can't sit still, and isn't into that type of thing. Honestly, you can listen while taking a walk or driving in the car. All that matters is that you start the process of training your brain to pay attention to what's going on in your head. That is all mindfulness is. With that said, this chapter draws from that course. Engaging with the meditation sessions will help reinforce this information.

What Are the Key Characteristics of Emotions?

Emotions are a byproduct of engaging with the world. Just as your skin burns when it touches something hot, you will feel emotions when

---

23 Sofer, O. J., Harris, D., & Happier Inc. (2022). *Happier Inc.* (6.9.2) [Meditation Courses on Emotions]. Happier Inc. Readers are encouraged to purchase a subscription to the *Happier Mediation* app to access the "Emotions" course.

you interact with people and the environment. Your interactions lead to *thoughts* in your mind, your brain gives *meaning* to what happened, and an *emotion* arises. Keep in mind that emotions are separate from us even though they impact us physically and mentally. **You and the emotion are not one and the same.** Creating space between *you*, the thinking being, and the *emotional experience* is key to maintaining control of what you do and say.

Emotions are like the weather. Just like it doesn't rain indefinitely, emotions, too, do not last forever (even though they trick you into believing you will always feel that way). In reality, emotions are constantly changing. They increase, decrease, morph into another feeling, or disappear. This is great to keep in mind especially when dealing with hard emotions. If you do absolutely nothing, the feelings will pass.

People lose emotional agility when they fall out of balance either by **avoiding** their feelings (e.g., pull away, ignore, suppress, distract, or numbing behavior) or by becoming **entangled** with them. When the emotion controls everything and the person is just along for the ride, that is hallmark entanglement. Examples include: speaking without thinking, banging the table, yelling, wallowing in a deep sadness, sending a nasty text, and feeling out of control.

Identifying Emotions in Real Time

Awareness is the first step in developing emotional agility. You become a scientific observer, turning your microscope inward. Once you notice an emotion, *name what you are feeling*. Give it a label: happiness, sadness, anger, frustration, impatience, relaxation, contentment, anxiousness, ease, calm, etc. The act of labeling emotions can zap their power. Labeling creates distance between you and the emotion.

Physical and Mental Impact of Emotions

Next, consider where and how you feel the emotion in your body. Turn your mindfulness to your head, neck, jaw, shoulders, eyes, eyebrows, forehead, throat, feet, hands, stomach, and back. Are you feeling any of these **physical sensations?** If so, mindfully identify them: tightness or constriction, tension, heaviness, lightness, pain, openness in chest, tingling, vibration, goosebumps, cold extremities, flushed, heat, nausea, rushing current, exhilaration, rapid or slow heart rate, shaking, fast or slow breathing, sinking or lifting, a rising feeling, paralysis, rigidity, or difficulty seeing or hearing?

Just like we have physical responses, there are changes that happen in our minds when we experience emotions. Ask yourself if you are experiencing any of these **mental sensations**: tunnel thought, clarity, being pulled, no control, entangled, lost in feelings, weighted down, pushing against, avoiding feelings, overwhelmed, confusion, no space to think, clouded, separate, balanced.

Ironically, just by identifying these physical and mental responses you turn your attention away from the circumstances that led to your emotion. **By focusing on something else, you can cause the response to the emotion to change**. You might notice in real time that these sensations dissipate the more you try to notice them!

Staying Balanced

Balance is finding the middle between the two extremes. Balance helps us find space to feel emotions without becoming overwhelmed by them, which generates emotional agility.

Quick Fixes for Entanglement

It is not a question of *if*, but *when*, you will feel strong emotions in the divorce process. Because of this, it is essential to plan for this ahead of time. You want to stay in control of yourself so that what you say and do is what you *intend* to say and do, not what feels good in a fit of anger. If you feel like you are suddenly overwhelmed by a feeling, **depersonalize it**. Remind yourself that you are not the emotion. For example, say, "This is anger," or "I am experiencing anxiety." Alternatively, **zoom out to your senses**. What are you seeing, smelling, hearing, touching, or tasting? Or, **zoom in** and focus on one **particular physical sensation**. Are you breathing short, rapid breaths? If yes, try breathing in for four counts, hold for four counts, and out for four counts.

Consider **feeling the weight of your feet** on the floor, or if you are seated, sit up straight and **notice your spine** – gently rock back and forth until you feel settled and balanced. Or stand up and get some ice water. If you aren't alone, don't be afraid to **exit a situation**. Use the statement "I'm sorry I can't discuss this anymore right now, but I will definitely get back with you as soon as I have had time to digest it." Better to say and do nothing than to say or do something you will regret later.

Quick Fixes for Avoidance

Alternatively, if you find you are judging yourself, or pulling away from an emotion, bring your mind back to what you are feeling. Say, "I am experiencing a lot of anger right now." When you bring the emotion to the forefront of your mind, you can and should think about the circumstances that triggered your emotion. Then you can consider: *Did something objectively bad take place?* Or: *Were the circumstances themselves not objectively bad, but your interpretation of them made you pull away?* Either way, this helps you stop avoiding the emotion and gets you back in balance. Emotional agility happens when we are balanced.

You Are in Control!

In many divorces, the default *root cause* for negative emotions is thought to be the other person. "They did X, which makes me angry. They did Y, which makes me sad. They want Z, which makes me furious. They don't deserve Z after doing X and Y!"

I hate them.
I want them out of my life.
If only I didn't have to deal with them, I'd be happy.

PART 18: HOW DO I MOVE FORWARD AFTER DIVORCE?

The truth is the person who controls your emotional experience is you. You cannot control what other people do, but you can control how you respond to the situation. No other person can *make* you happy. They might do things you like that satisfy your needs; but they themselves do not make you happy. On the flip side, no other person can *make* you sad, angry, etc. Yes, they may do things that cause negative emotions and unpleasant feelings to arise in you, but how *you* handle those emotions will ultimately determine your emotional experience. When you have emotional agility, you are in control!

Dara L. Marias, JD, MSW
AV Preeminent Attorney
A.P.F.M. Certified Advanced Practitioner
Certified Amicable Divorce Professional
Las Vegas, Nevada

Chapter 79
Moving Forward
by Stephanie Robins

The end of a marriage does not always mean the end of your emotional connection. For many, letting go after a divorce is challenging, especially when the emotional ties are still strong. Whether it's lingering attachment, unresolved feelings, or the constant presence of your ex, learning to let go is crucial for your emotional health and ability to move forward.

This chapter will help you understand why letting go is so tricky; how to recognize if you're struggling to move on; what to do if your ex can't let go; and how to begin the process of moving forward in a healthy way.

Why It's So Hard to Let Go After Divorce

Divorce doesn't just signify the end of a relationship – it also brings about the loss of a shared future, familiar routines, and a part of your identity. Some common reasons people find it hard to let go include:

1. **Emotional attachment** – Emotional bonds don't disappear the moment the marriage is over legally. Even if the relationship was unhealthy, you may still care for or feel deeply connected to your ex. The longer you were together, the harder it can be to disentangle your emotions from your shared experiences.

2. **Fear of the unknown** – The future after divorce can seem daunting. You may worry about how you'll rebuild your life, whether you can form new relationships, or how your children will adapt. This fear of the unknown can keep you clinging to the past, even if that past was painful or unsustainable.

3. **Unresolved grief or anger** – If you are still holding onto unresolved feelings of grief, anger, or resentment, these emotions can keep you tethered to your ex and prevent closure. Whether it's anger over how the marriage ended, or sadness over the dreams that didn't come true, these unresolved emotions can make it difficult to move forward.

4. **Sense of failure or guilt** – Many people view divorce as a personal failure, even though the end of a marriage is rarely one person's fault. This sense of failure can make it hard to accept the reality of the situation and move forward. You might also feel guilty – about your children, about your inability to *save* the marriage, or about the pain you feel you caused.

How to Know if You Are Unable to Let Go

Recognizing that you're stuck is the first step toward healing. Here are some signs that you may be struggling to let go:

- **Constantly replaying the past:** You frequently replay conversations or scenarios, wondering if you could have done things differently or tried to understand what happened.
- **Continuing to feel strong emotions about your ex:** Whether it's anger, sadness, or even longing, strong emotions about your ex that persist long after the divorce might signal that you're still emotionally attached.
- **Struggling to form new relationships:** If you're unable or unwilling to open yourself up to new relationships, it could be a sign that you're still holding on to the emotional connection with your ex.
- **Difficulty moving forward with life plans:** You might find yourself avoiding big decisions or changes because part of you is still clinging to the life you envisioned with your ex.

How to Deal with Your Ex's Inability to Let Go

Sometimes, it's not just you who is having trouble letting go – it could also be your ex. This can make the process even more difficult, especially if they are clinging to the past or engaging in behaviors that keep you emotionally connected, such as reaching out unnecessarily or stirring up conflict. Here's how to handle it:

1. **Set clear boundaries** – Establish clear boundaries around communication and interaction. If you're co-parenting, limit conversations to logistical issues regarding the children. If you do not have children, it may be best to limit or cut contact entirely for some time to give both of you the space to heal.

2. **Avoid engaging in drama** – If your ex is stirring up conflict, try not to get pulled into it. Engaging in arguments or emotional exchanges will only prolong your emotional connection. Stay calm, focus on facts, and avoid personal attacks.

3. **Seek legal or professional support** – If your ex refuses to let go in more problematic ways – such as violating agreements or misbehaving – consider seeking legal guidance. You might also find it helpful to

seek support from a therapist to navigate the emotional dynamics of responding to an ex who won't move on.

What to Do if You Are Stuck and Unable to Let Go

If you've recognized that you're stuck in the process of letting go, there are practical steps you can take to help yourself move forward:

1. **Acknowledge your emotions** – Acknowledging your emotions fully – no matter how uncomfortable – is key. Grieving the loss of your marriage, feeling anger toward your ex, or even recognizing the lingering love you have for them is normal. Instead of pushing those emotions down, permit yourself to feel them.

2. **Consider professional support** – Sometimes, it's hard to work through these feelings alone. A therapist who specializes in divorce recovery can help you untangle your emotions and offer strategies to let go healthily. Therapy can also help you deal with unresolved grief, anger, or fear.

3. **Focus on your own life** – Shift your focus away from your ex and your past life. Consider engaging in activities that bring you joy, invest in supportive relationships, and start exploring new interests or hobbies. Reclaiming your life will help you rebuild your sense of self outside the context of the marriage.

4. **Journal or meditate** – Writing down your thoughts or practicing mindfulness can help you process your emotions. Journaling is a way to release the emotional weight of what you're experiencing, while the practice of mindfulness helps you stay grounded in the present rather than being stuck in the past.

How to Move Forward – and Healthy Ways to Manage Your Feelings

Letting go is not something that happens overnight, but you can begin the process of moving forward with some practical steps:

1. **Create new routines** – After divorce, the life you once knew is gone; but creating new routines can help establish a sense of stability. Whether it's a new exercise routine, hobbies, or daily rituals, building new habits can help you feel more in control of your life.
2. **Find a support system** – Lean on trusted friends or family members who support you through the transition. Having people who listen without judgment and offer encouragement can make moving forward easier.
3. **Limit contact with your ex** – Even if you share children, limiting nonessential contact with your ex can help create emotional space. Communicate only when necessary, and try to keep conversations focused and neutral.
4. **Forgive yourself and your ex** – Forgiveness does not mean forgetting or condoning the past, but it does involve letting go of the anger, guilt, or resentment that might still linger. This can free you from the emotional ties that keep you stuck. Forgiving yourself is just as important – you did the best you could with the knowledge and tools you had at the time.

Moving Forward

Divorce is undeniably challenging, and letting go can feel like a mountain that's too steep to climb. However, you can confidently move forward when you recognize your emotions, set boundaries, and find healthy ways to manage your feelings. Remember, letting go is a process, not a one-time event. Be patient with yourself, and trust that with time and self-care, you'll begin to heal and open up to new possibilities.

Stephanie Robins, LCSW
Alpharetta Family Therapy
Certified Amicable Divorce Professional
Alpharetta, Georgia

Chapter 80
Closure and Healing
by Suzanne Winlove-Smith

When a romantic relationship ends, individuals often experience myriad emotions, including grief, anger, sadness, and confusion. Some folks describe it as like a car crash, where everything is in chaos, thoughts go haywire, and life turns inside out. Others say that it's like time slows down. Most people in the situation feel completely devastated.

A relationship breakdown is one of the most stressful things you can face in your life. It is a shock that can be likened to post-traumatic stress disorder (PTSD). Science has even discovered that emotional pain triggers the same area of the brain as physical pain. In such an emotional state, you are not able to see the bigger picture or to make good decisions. You would be acting on emotion, and emotion clouds our thinking and reasoning.

If you are the one being left, your partner's sudden shift away from you can evoke feelings of betrayal, anger, and inadequacy. Individuals find it very difficult to grapple with the abrupt disconnection from their partner. It is no wonder that domestic violence incidents go up more than 80 percent when there is a relationship breakdown.

But in the middle of all the mess, there's a common process. Both partners – no matter who did what – go through a tough time. Both must deal with the loss and both face many unknowns. Questions pop up, like: "Is it really over?" "Why didn't you say something earlier?" "Can we give it another shot?" Questions like those are normal; asking them is part of being human.

Dealing with the ending of your relationship – especially when it's someone you thought you'd be with forever – is really hard. Dealing with the loss is not unlike grieving for someone who passed away. Adding to the challenge is separating your feelings about your relationship as a couple from those about being a parent. No parent can ever feel good about losing time with their kids. It can be tricky for the parent who doesn't live with the kids to maintain a strong relationship with them.

Your identity changes – from being part of a couple to being single, and from being parents together to being one parent with the kids and the other figuring out a new way. There are still more questions during the transition, such as: "Do we have to sell our home?" "I haven't worked since we had kids; how will we manage money?" "What will our friends and family think?" "How much will getting divorced cost?"

Divorce is a time when you will experience many different emotions, and they can change in an instant. It can feel as though you are riding a roller coaster. How can you find your footing in all of the turmoil and upheaval?

When a relationship ends, you can feel like a piece of you is missing. Well, it likely *is* missing – a part of it is with your ex. But you can learn how to get that piece back, and even find the life you were destined for. Divorce actually can be an opportunity to find your true calling in life.

Often, individuals experience distress during divorce because they have developed deeply ingrained patterns over time. However, when you break the unhealthy pattern, you shift the energy, and take your power back. There are some simple techniques that can save you months – even years – of unnecessary suffering.

Most people think it takes years to get over a broken heart. But in fact, you can use the emotion from the breakup to move yourself forward at lightning speed. You are stronger than you realize, and this is the beginning of *you* coming back to *you*. A strong person asks for help, and doing so is an act of courage. Develop a plan; it's a crazy, messed-up ride otherwise.

A plan is like a map that can steer you in the right direction. Without a plan, you'll still end up somewhere – but not necessarily where you want to be. Given the emotional complexities during the divorce process, it is crucial to get proper support.

No matter how hard it feels, there's always a way through – and there are people who have been where you are. They can help you find your strength and peace again. My journey, starting out of the challenges of my parents' divorce, led me to become a family mediator. Later, after navigating my own difficult divorce, I became a relationship and divorce coach. You too can turn challenges into stepping stones toward a brighter future.

So, channel your emotions into positive momentum. Doing that will make it easier to grow and heal through life's challenges. Here are some practical tips for managing your emotions and even using them as a catalyst for positive change:

- **Pause and breathe** – When emotions feel overwhelming, pause and take a few deep breaths. A small moment of mindfulness helps calm the nervous system, giving you space to respond thoughtfully instead of reacting impulsively. When we react, we lose our power.
- **Identify the root cause** – Take time to understand what's triggering your emotions. Most people are unaware how past experiences can negatively influence present circumstances. Journaling, or talking with a trusted friend or coach or therapist, can help uncover deeper feelings. Recognizing them will allow you to address them constructively.
- **Transform energy into action** – Strong emotions like anger or frustration can carry powerful energy. Energy = emotions. Energy cannot be destroyed; however, it can be channeled. Channel your energy into a productive activity such as exercise, a creative project, or setting new goals. Turn those emotions into fuel for positive action.
- **Practice self-compassion** – Remember that pain, struggle, and difficult emotions are natural and part of being human. Instead of judging yourself, practice self-compassion, allowing yourself to process feelings without guilt or shame.
- **Set small, positive goals** – Use your emotions as motivation to make positive changes. Set small, achievable goals that align with your values. Having those goals will bring you a sense of purpose, helping you move forward in a constructive and fulfilling way.
- **Create healthy outlets** – Establish regular activities that help you release emotions, like writing, painting, exercising, or meditating. Healthy outlets can give you clarity and a sense of relief, and can help

keep emotions from building up. You get to choose how you direct your life!
- **Let your children inspire you** – As a mom of three amazing kids, I find constant inspiration in their energy and curiosity. They keep me adventurous and grounded all at once, reminding me daily to be the best version of myself.

Remember, your divorce is not the end – it's the beginning of a new life. Taking action is what's most important. This is one of the biggest challenges you will ever face; get the proper guidance that you need. You can navigate your journey with resilience, emerging on the other side with hope and a renewed sense of self.

Suzanne Winlove-Smith
CEO & Founder, The Clean Divorce
Accredited Family Mediator, Relationship & Divorce Coach
Ontario, Canada

About the Author

Tracy Ann Moore-Grant has practiced exclusively in the area of family law since 2002 and is a founding partner of the firm Patterson Moore Butler in Georgia. She focuses on non-litigation law, helping parties resolve issues outside of the court system as an uncontested and amicable divorce attorney, mediator, arbitrator, and parent coordinator.

Tracy founded the Amicable Divorce Network in 2019 as a way to transition her own practice away from the destructive family law system. The Amicable Divorce Network has now grown into an international association of vetted professionals who are dedicated to helping people navigate the process of divorce in an efficient and low-conflict manner utilizing the network's unique process and technology platform.

Tracy is the host of the Amicable Divorce Network Podcast, has been the guest on many podcasts, and has authored many articles on issues relating to low-conflict divorce. She is the recipient of both a Georgia Legal Award (2020) and a Southeastern Legal Award (2023) for the positive impact the Amicable Divorce Network has had on the legal process for divorce. She resides in Georgia and is a wife, stepmother, and schnauzer lover.

www.ingramcontent.com/pod-product-compliance
Lightning Source LLC
Chambersburg PA
CBHW070124080526
44586CB00015B/1548